POST-
COMMUNIST
STORIES

POST-COMMUNIST STORIES

On the 25th Anniversary of the Fall of the Berlin Wall

ABOUT CITIES, POLITICS, DESIRES

STAN PERSKY

Cormorant Books

Canada Council for the Arts **Conseil des Arts du Canada**  ONTARIO ARTS COUNCIL CONSEIL DES ARTS DE L'ONTARIO an Ontario government agency un organisme du gouvernement de l'Ontario

 Canadian Heritage Patrimoine canadien  Canadä

The publisher gratefully acknowledges the support of the Canada Council for the Arts and the Ontario Arts Council for its publishing program. We acknowledge the financial support of the Government of Canada through the Canada Book Fund (CBF) for our publishing activities, and the Government of Ontario through the Ontario Media Development Corporation, an agency of the Ontario Ministry of Culture, and the Ontario Book Publishing Tax Credit Program.

LIBRARY AND ARCHIVES CANADA CATALOGUING IN PUBLICATION

Persky, Stan, 1941–, author
Post-communist stories : about cities, politics, desires / Stan Persky.
Issued in print and electronic formats.

ISBN 978-1-77086-446-7 (pbk.). — ISBN 978-1-77086-447-4 (html)

1. Europe, Eastern — Politics and government — 1989–. 2. Europe, Central —
Politics and government — 1989–. 3. Europe, Eastern—Social conditions — 1989–.
4. Europe, Central — Social conditions — 1989–.
5. Europe, Eastern--Intellectual life—1989–.
6. Europe, Central — Intellectual life — 1989–. I. Title.

DJK51.P47 2014   943.0009'049   C2014-906020-3
C2014-906021-1

Cover design: Angel Guerra / Archetype
Interior text design: Tannice Goddard, Soul Oasis Networking
Printer: Marquis

Printed and bound in Canada.
The interior of this book is printed on 30% post-consumer waste recycled paper.

CORMORANT BOOKS INC.
10 ST. MARY STREET, SUITE 615, TORONTO, ONTARIO, M4Y 1P9
www.cormorantbooks.com

for Tom Sandborn

in memory of my father,
Morris Persky

Neither was it as it first seemed
Nor as you now make it into a story.

CZESŁAW MIŁOSZ

Contents

Preface

Post-Communist Stories is a reflection of my long-standing interest in central European politics, life, and culture (especially literary culture) that began in 1980, the year of the emergence of the Solidarity trade union movement in the shipyards of Gdańsk, Poland. The next spring, as soon as I had finished the teaching semester at Malaspina College on the west coast of Canada, I travelled to Poland, interviewed shipyard workers about their movement, and wrote *At the Lenin Shipyard*, which was published later that year. After the fall of Communism in 1989 occurred, I returned to Central and Eastern Europe, touring its post-Communist capitals just months after the governmental changes and interviewing a broad spectrum of people. Again I wrote a book about what I had seen and heard, *Then We Take Berlin*. Since 1990, I've lived part-time in Berlin, and have continued to write about political events and cultural developments.

The present text includes new writing along with significant revisions of pieces of literary non-fiction that I had published in various earlier books. I begin with the story of "A Walk in Prague" in May 2014, followed by an autobiographical account of my experiences growing up in a world whose emblematic image was the Iron Curtain. What follows are stories that took shape as I travelled in such places as Tirana, Warsaw, Budapest, Zagreb, Sofia, and Vilnius.

These stories include an essay about my sense of Berlin and its history, as well as its place in post-Communist Europe. How the stories took shape is itself a subtheme of the narratives. I conclude with an essay that reflects on the meaning of the end of Communism, and offers some conjectures on how recent events in Ukraine in 2013–2014 represent a continuation of the hopes that motivated the revolutions that occurred twenty-five years ago. If this writing helps readers, even in a small way, to resist the forgetting of history and what philosopher Martin Heidegger called the "forgetting of Being," I will consider that the work has achieved its purpose.

S.P.
Berlin
August 2014

A Walk in Prague (2014)

On a Saturday morning in Prague, I walked down toward the city's main square from the hotel where some friends and I were staying. We were on spring holiday, and our ten-day trip included stops in Venice, Trieste, Vienna, and Prague. Prague was the last stop on the tour because, well, it's a beautiful city — "the sleeping beauty of Central Europe," writer Timothy Garton Ash called it — and it was just a five-hour drive home to Berlin. I'd been to Prague a couple of times in the early 1990s, but I didn't have any special reason to be there now — at least not until I took this walk.

Our hotel, located on the winding, gently sloping Štěpánská street, had been built within the last decade, and was a Best Western affiliate; but, with its cladding of what resembled dark-stained wooden beams, it had the architectural look of a four-storey postmodernist log cabin. Its odd facing seemed of a piece with my idea of Czech culture in general — quirkily experimental and armed with a barbed sense of humour. The hotel services pamphlet in my room boasted that Jaroslav Hašek (1883–1923), one of the three great Czech writers of the first half of the twentieth century (the other two are Franz Kafka and Karel Čapek) and the author of the satirical post-World War I anti-war classic, *The Good Soldier Schweik*, had been born in the building originally located on the site.

It was the unseasonably chill and damp long weekend of May Day 2014, the year of the twenty-fifth anniversary of the fall of Communism in Central and Eastern Europe. From the hotel, I walked for a couple of blocks, past the restaurants, banks, shops, and other more posh hotels that line the street, pausing for a second at the entrance to the landmark Lucerna Palace building, and then continued down to the Czech capital's main square, *Václavské náměstí*, or Wenceslas Square, as it's known in English. The tourists were out in force on this holiday weekend, bundled up against the ten to twelve degree Celsius cold and mist, except for a few leftover partygoers, mostly youthful foreigners travelling in groups, who seemed impervious to the frigid weather, some of them wearing only T-shirts and jeans, having come to Prague on cheap flights for weekend drinking parties.

Wenceslas Square — named for the tenth-century patron saint of Bohemia, whose equestrian statue sits on a rise at the southern end of the square — isn't really square; it's an almost kilometre-long narrow rectangle. The square is more of a boulevard that is partially open to traffic, although much of the thoroughfare that morning was under renovation, blocked off by street-work sidings; the few cars were being detoured into side streets. Wenceslas Square is a mix of formidable buildings and monuments, and the usual degree of big-city downtown seediness that began to appear as early as the end of Communism in 1989. The square is now lined with expensive hotels next to fast food joints and old-fashioned cafés adjoining currency exchange booths; the guidebooks assure visitors that city officials are dismayed by the strip clubs and sex workers.

In 1989, hundreds of thousands of Czechs, led by the dissident playwright and philosopher Václav Havel, demonstrated in the square against what turned out to be a tottering, exhausted Communist regime that would soon fall. The Soviet tanks that had brutally ensured the regime's existence after the Prague Spring of 1968 were long gone, and four decades of tenaciously held power ended in the Velvet Revolution.

The square tilts down in a northerly direction, and at its far lower end gives way to the labyrinth of pedestrian streets that lead into the sixteenth- and seventeenth-century version of Old Town. The *Staré Město*, as the Old Town is known in Czech, in fact dates back to the fourteenth century and beyond, when Wenceslas Square was known by its medieval designation, the Horse Market. The splendours of the Old Town's architecture and the charms of its tangled streets, plus its good fortune in escaping bombings and damage during World War II, are the basis of Prague's justified reputation as one of Europe's most beautiful cities.

I had trekked through these lanes of the older city with my travelling companions and a crush of other tourists the day before, shivering and huddled beneath an umbrella. Eventually, we emerged into the vast main square of Old Town, which, in addition to the imposing public buildings of that era, features the monumental statue of one of the Czech national heroes, Jan Hus, the proto-Protestant religious reformer who was burned at the stake in 1415 at the Catholic Church's Council of Constance. It was one of those wet, nasty spring days that made me glad to get back to familiar Štěpánská street and its sheltering hotels.

The next morning, I stopped first at the news kiosk at the top of the square, a few steps from one of the several McDonald's in the area. Across the street, beyond the statue of Wenceslas on his horse, is the neoclassical Czech National Museum, a dark nineteenth-century repository of the nation's history. I picked up a copy of the *International New York Times* to check the latest on the political crisis in Ukraine. In the *Maidan Nezalezhnosti*, the main square of Kiev, Ukraine, hundreds of thousands of protesters, after months of occupying the heart of the capital, toppled the country's deeply corrupt, Russian-controlled president and his henchmen. The Euromaidan movement, as it styled itself, sought to move the country closer to European democracy, genuine rule of law, and a market system less dominated by capitalist oligarchs and kleptocrats, and thus away from the ideas and influence of the authoritarian regime of Vladimir Putin in neighbouring Russia. Although the conditions are different, what happened in Prague in 1989 and in Kiev in 2014 bear striking similarities, certainly of political intention if not the configuration of contending forces.

From the newspaper stand, I ambled down the square toward a bookstore on the other side of the boulevard, the Luxor Palace of Books, a multi-storey old-fashioned emporium, whose main floor takes the form of an open shopping arcade, with an entranceway that brought in a windy draft from the square outside, as well as a stream of customers. After I bought a couple of books that I wanted — English translations of Czech writers — I'd had enough of the square, the crowds, and the weather, and headed back up Štěpánská street.

About a half block up from the square, I ducked out of the cold into the entrance passageway of the Lucerna building to have a late-morning coffee in the upstairs café next to the movie theatre. Shopping arcades run through the ground floor of the art-nouveau Lucerna (Lantern in English), an early twentieth-century building. The developer of the Lucerna was the grandfather of Václav Havel, the leader of the Velvet Revolution who went on to become the first post-Communist Czech president.

The entrance from Štěpánská street leads to a marbled two-storey atrium covered by a well-maintained glass cupola that illuminates the passageway. Suspended on wires from the top of the atrium is a sculpture of an upside-down dead horse, and mounted on its belly is the familiar figure of Wenceslas, an obvious if gruesome satirical reference to the sober equestrian statue of the saint in nearby Wenceslas Square. David Černý's sculpture *Horse* (*Kun* in Czech) was made in the late 1990s for the main hall of a Czech post office, but the satire proved a bit much for the postal service bureaucrats, and the sculpture found a more congenial home in the artsy Lucerna complex.

I climbed the marble staircase to the second-floor coffeehouse, mercifully free of tourist hordes, where I found a window table overlooking the entrance gallery of the Lucerna. Beyond the hanging upside-down dead horse, in the centre of the passageway down below, was a photographic exhibit commemorating the centenary of the birth of the Czech writer Bohumil Hrabal (1914–1997), author of *Closely Watched Trains* (1965), *I Served the King of England* (1971), and *Too Loud A Solitude* (1977), among many others — books respected throughout Europe. Photos of the elderly writer, carousing at a pub table, feeding his cats at a country cottage, sitting at his writing desk, filled the exhibit space.

The centennial for Hrabal seemed quite fitting. All the European lands where Communism ended a quarter century ago had been noted for their literary cultures; there is a long roster of honoured novelists, poets, and essayists, from Nobel Prize-winning poet Czesław Miłosz and Tadeusz Konwicki in Poland, to Ismail Kadare in remote Albania, György Konrád and Nobel laureate Imre Kertész in Hungary, Serbian novelists Danilo Kiš and Aleksandar Tišma, Bulgaria's Blaga Dimitrova, and Christa Wolf in East Germany, to name a few. But of all the literary cultures that resisted their respective Communist regimes through the maintenance of a cosmopolitan intelligence, none was more remarkable than that of the ten million Czechs, both in terms of the quality of their writing and the quantity of good writers per capita.

In the spring of 1990, a few months after the Velvet Revolution, and just before the initial post-Communist elections that summer, I was getting ready to go to Prague. I planned to travel with my friend Tom Sandborn on a vaguely defined journalistic and academic mission, and I turned to Czech writing to prepare for the interviews I would conduct, as well as to understand the conditions of life under Communism that had motivated the upheaval of 1989.

The number and quality of writers is one of the features of Czech culture almost impossible to miss, even if you weren't, as I was, a writer and university professor. Yet it is apparently possible to remain ignorant of it. I recently read an interesting autobiographical novel, Caleb Crain's *Necessary Errors* (2013), about a group of young Anglophone expatriates living and working in Prague in late 1990 and the first half of 1991, shortly after I'd been there. The book's protagonist is a recent Harvard grad, an aspiring writer, and a somewhat prudish gay man in the process of coming out as well as coming of age, who is exploring the city and attempting to understand the recent Czech political revolution. The book's one curious omission is that there's no mention of Czech writing whatsoever, even though the book's central character is certainly bookish enough — he's read-ing Stendhal in French. I put the anomaly down to the author's intention of portraying his younger self as a callow youth. But maybe it wasn't so obvious to Crain's autobiographical hero and to his fictional contemporaries that indigenous literary culture might be the most reliable guide to a place you don't know.

By 1990, a good deal of Czech literary work had been translated into English. Havel's essay collection *The Power of the Powerless* explained the moral aspiration "to live in truth" as poignantly as any single document from dissident Europe; his plays, in the "theatre of the absurd" mode, showed why it was so difficult to do so. The work of Milan Kundera, author of the international bestseller *The Unbearable Lightness of Being* and a half-dozen other memorable books, was widely available to readers everywhere. Ivan Klíma, with whom I would later become acquainted, had written several volumes of stories and a novel, *Love and Garbage*. There were many more.

And then there was Hrabal.

Bohumil Hrabal was the literary descendant of Jaroslav Hašek and his novel *The Good Soldier Schweik*. Hašek's novel is the recurring tale of a kind of simpleton or holy fool caught, like the rest of us, in the bitter, often brutal absurdities of a world that he hadn't made. In a letter to an American scholar, Hrabal praises the way that *The Good Soldier Schweik* is "written, as though he had tossed it off with his left hand, after a hangover, it's pure joy in writing." Hrabal's own writing has much of that tone.

In Hrabal's *Too Loud A Solitude*, the voluble protagonist, Hanta, operates a strange paper-compacting machine for decades, working for shadowy employers, and rescuing from the heaps of trash unloaded upon him books destined for the dump. The "apparent idiocy" of each of Hrabel's many anti-heroes, notes the critic James Wood, "hides an intelligence bent on thwarting the authorities" with whom the anti-hero only appears to comply; Hanta, "the man who rescues books from the compacting machine ... is not only a uselessly learned auto-didact, but a little rebel against a large book-censoring regime." (James Wood, "Bohumil Hrabal," *London Review of Books*, January 4, 2001.)

I don't know if there's yet a consensus on the great Czech writers of the *second* half of the twentieth century (I've already mentioned the great Czech writers of the first half), but Hrabal, I'm pretty sure, would be among them. Maybe Kundera and Klíma would also be candidates for the other slots in this imaginary Czech pantheon, assuming there are still readers in our future (an assumption I no longer automatically make).

In the cozy café in the Lucerna building, I was perfectly happy in a solitude buffered by the conversational buzz of other customers. I sipped my cappuccino, kept the upside-down horse in the corner of my vision, and checked my purchases from the bookstore. I'd picked up a novel by one of the younger generation of Czech writers, Jáchym Topol, whom I hadn't yet read, and I'd found a volume of journalism by Karel Čapek (1890–1938). I wanted to read Čapek because of Ivan Klíma.

Just before going on holiday with my friends, I'd been reading *My Crazy Century* (2014), the latest book by Klíma, now in his early eighties. The book is a memoir, interleaved with essays, and I'd been thinking about writing a review of it as a way of marking the twenty-fifth anniversary of the fall of Communism. Klíma tells the story of growing up in the concentration camp at Terezín during World War II, improbably surviving, and later becoming a writer and a member of the Communist Party — as were many of his colleagues, including Kundera. Although he was safely in the United States as a visiting professor, Klíma returned to his homeland after the summer of 1968, when the Russians invaded Prague to crush the reform movement within the Communist Party of Czechoslovakia. At the time, he was dangerously out of favour with the Communist authorities and their Russian minders. Yet he chose to return to his birthplace, to live as a dissident writer whose works were banned in Czechoslovakia, but published in the West.

On my earlier trip to Prague in 1990, I had also read a book by Klíma. His novel *Love and Garbage* is about his experience working as a street cleaner in Prague during the period when the Communist regime banned his books, meditating on Kafka — something every

Czech writer does sooner or later — and having a bumpy love affair with a sculptress. You could say I'd gotten into the habit of reading a book by Klíma before I went to Prague.

I met Klíma later in Vancouver, where he was appearing at a writers' festival, a few years after the Velvet Revolution. I was introduced by friends who knew of my interest in European — and particularly Czech — literature, and I invited Klíma to give a talk to my students. He consented, and before we entered the classroom, I warned him that the students might not know much about the events of 1989, and that it would probably be best to keep it simple. "I should make sure they know I'm talking about Czechoslovakia, not Yugoslavia," he said. "Exactly," I laughed.

In Klíma's recent memoir, there's a chapter about his education where he mentions that he wrote a dissertation on Karel Čapek. Reading that, shortly before the May Day weekend in Prague, I realized that I knew almost nothing about Čapek. These periodic realizations are tinged with a sense of catastrophe: How is it possible not to know anything about Čapek — to say nothing of the "et al." that belongs here? I don't know if there's an answer to that rhetorical question, but if there is, the good part of the answer is that the world's too big, too full of things worth knowing, and another part of it is that we just don't pay sufficient attention, or practise what the Buddhists more politely call "mindfulness." I also notice that my astonishment at my ignorance, constantly rediscovered, produces a little frisson of pleasure because I'm cheered to be reminded that there's more to read, to know, to do.

Well, I knew that Čapek's play *R.U.R.* (Rossum's Universal Robots), first published in 1920, introduced the word "robot" into languages around the world. His science fiction novel *War with the Newts* was Čapek's response to the rise of Nazi Germany in Europe, whose end, unfortunately, he didn't live to see. But I knew nothing about his journalism; he was apparently a master of a newspaper column form known as the "feuilleton," an often witty, but always sharply pointed piece about some topical issue. The form was a Czech tradition, and after Čapek's time it was continued, even during the repression subsequent to the Soviet invasion in 1968, principally by Ludvík Vaculík, the underground author of *A Cup of Coffee with My Interrogator* (1986). So now, at long last, I had a volume of Čapek's feuilletons that I started to read in the Lucerna and would continue in my postmodernist log cabin hotel room, protected from the cold and damp, until it was time to join my friends for dinner at the top of Štěpánská street that evening, in the restaurant of a small brewery.

IF THE COFFEE HOUSE in the Lucerna was a good place to contemplate Czech writing, it was also the right place to commemorate the anniversary of the Velvet Revolution that unfolded in the *annus mirabilis* of 1989.

For those whose memories have faded, in June of 1989 there were free elections in Poland, which brought the independent Solidarity movement into office and spelled doom for the Communist, Soviet-allied Polish United Workers' Party that had run the country for four decades. A similar process was unfolding in Hungary.

On the evening of November 9, 1989, the Berlin Wall, which had separated Communist-controlled East Berlin and the rest of East Germany from the Western-oriented enclave of West Berlin, was breached as a result of months of non-violent political demonstrations in East Germany, and hundreds of thousands of Germans on both sides of the divide freely crossed the boundary for the first time in nearly thirty years. Within a year, the Wall was largely dismantled, East Germany and its ruling Communist party — as well as its pervasive Stasi secret police — were gone, and Germany was reunited.

Ten days after the fall of the Berlin Wall, the Velvet Revolution began in Prague in the very streets and squares I was strolling through that Saturday morning a quarter century later. Indeed, in the Magic Lantern theatre in the basement of the Lucerna building, the civic opposition, led by Václav Havel, had daily met, improvised, and decided what to do to maximize the power of the heretofore powerless who gathered in their tens of thousands in the square a half block away.

Now, sipping my coffee, paging through Čapek's book, I also had the poignant feeling of being in the place, the exact building, where the course of a particular history had been changed by human intelligence. The best English-language account of the events in the Lucerna, I should mention — since I think reality, to put it as grandiosely as possible, is inseparable from the narratives we make of it — is Timothy Garton Ash's *The Magic Lantern: The Revolution of '89 Witnessed in Warsaw, Budapest, Berlin, and Prague* (1990; 1999). It's an eyewitness report by a British historian-cum-journalist whose judgments about the Czech revolution, I think, hold up remarkably well a quarter century later.

Before the year was out, the Czechoslovak opponents of the weakened Communist government overthrew the regime. Havel became the country's president. And, as his election posters had urged — "Havel to the Castle!" — the new head of state was soon established in the Prague Castle, where he remained in office for the next decade and a half, until his retirement from politics in 2003.

That's where my friends had gone that day — to the castle, the monumental thousand-year-old building and church complex that broods majestically over the city from the far side of the Vltava River, and serves as the seat of the Czech Republic head of state.

I'd wanted to be alone that morning to wander and reminisce. Through it all — the walk, the ordinary encounters with newspaper vendors and café waiters, the imposing and absurdist sights, including a reminder that we should pay some attention to the horses as well as the kings and saints who ride them — I was suffused with nostalgia for what had happened here, but with an edge, an odd anticipatory fear. The nostalgia consisted of memory traces — finding myself in a vaguely familiar street at the bottom of Wenceslas Square, unsure whether this was the route to a cellar restaurant we'd eaten in years ago, or the way to an interview that Tom and I had conducted in the days shortly after the events of 1989. At the same time, the nostalgia also caused a sharp pang of mourning for those who had changed the world and were now no longer present, including Václav Havel, who died at age seventy-five in 2011.

This year, 2014, is a year of multiple anniversaries: the centennial of the beginning of World War I, the seventy-fifth anniversary of the attack on Poland by Nazi Germany and Soviet Russia that initiated World War II, the twenty-fifth anniversary of the fall of the Berlin Wall and the end of Communism throughout much of Europe, and even the twenty-fifth anniversary of the birth of the World Wide Web, and its accompanying mixed blessings, in that same year.

The following month I would see the televised ceremonies marking the seventieth anniversary of the D-Day landings on the beaches of Normandy; there was eighty-eight-year-old Queen Elizabeth II, one of the few heads of state present who, as then-Princess Elizabeth, had served in World War II, now greeting military survivors of the invasion.

In early June, the *New York Times* recalled the massacre of students by the Chinese Communist Party and its army in Beijing's Tiananmen Square in 1989, an event that most young Chinese know almost nothing about a quarter century later — the still-surviving regime having demonstrated its ability to erase history, the Internet notwithstanding.

The *Times* also noted the twenty-fifth anniversary of the first post-Communist election in Poland, although the contemporary crisis in Ukraine tended to crowd out historical commemorations. There would be more such columns and commemorative articles in the coming months throughout 2014.

In this year of remembering, what I feared above all was forgetting. For the young Chinese generation, the historical past had been suppressed by the regime. Any inclination was diverted by the Chinese state's enticements for consumption and enrichment — a successful massive cultural campaign encouraging young people to acquire more goods and higher-paying jobs.

In Western cultures, especially in North America, we had access to all the devices and information that the digital manufacturers could supply, as well as a great deal of state and corporate surveillance that apparently came with using those machines to which we had become habituated. Despite the enthusiasm and bromides of the technophiles, the general amnesia, pretty much as Aldous Huxley anticipated in *Brave New World*, is as great as in formally repressed societies, particularly among the young, whose memories don't extend twenty-five years back.

This is the generation with whom I was in daily contact in classrooms. They didn't seem hostile to knowing about human history, just oddly indifferent. Their indifference extended to much of the political present. On bad days, it seemed to me that everybody had forgotten everything, or never knew anything and, what's more, didn't want to. On more reasonable days, I knew that some people did know something, and wanted to know more. But they were an educated elite, five or ten per cent at best — far from the ideal of a democratic citizenry. Many of the students, born after the dissolution of the Soviet Union, had never heard of it. The epochal events of 1989 were unknown to them, and so was much that had followed.

Sitting in the coffeehouse of the Lucerna, having a cappuccino after taking a walk down Štěpánská street and through Wenceslas Square, I now had an idea, an inkling, of why I was in Prague. I'd been aware of the twenty-fifth anniversary of the fall of the Berlin Wall, and all the other events of 1989, including the ones that had unfolded in the very building in which I was sitting. The reminiscences evoked by my walk, the memories, the mourning, began to take purposeful shape.

In the midst of the sweep of history, it's easy to anticipate that the events of twenty-five years ago might soon be lost to memory. We might forget why any of it mattered. In such conditions, it's the responsibility of those of us who, among other things, write for the record, to use the occasion of a significant anniversary to ensure there are accounts of what happened, what we saw, and what we think it meant.

"When experience is not retained … infancy is perpetual," the philosopher George Santayana remarked more than a century ago. His more famous aphorism, "Those who cannot remember the past are condemned to repeat it," is inscribed on every historian's banner, although perhaps it is not repetition that threatens us so much as the condemnation to ignorance. I was in Prague at the beginning of May 2014 to remind myself to say something.

The Iron Curtain

One day in June 1991, I was riding the S-Bahn, Berlin's urban railway, from west to east Berlin. I was on my way to a museum or to some office on a bureaucratic errand, I can't remember which. The elevated train passed over the old boundary where the Berlin Wall had been a year and a half before. Now all that was left was the rubble and bare ground of a sort of no man's land below the tracks. Beyond the ruins, a twist of the Spree River lay ahead. The train would cross over the water just before it pulled into Friedrichstrasse station, which had previously been a border checkpoint. The year before, visiting what was then still East Berlin, rather than simply the east side of Berlin, I had been herded through its cattle-pen of holding areas, passport-stamping guards, and the clanging doors of the checkpoint building known as the Palace of Tears (or *Tränenpalast* in German), so named for all the painful separations of people that had occurred there.

Gazing absently out the window at the place that had divided two worlds for some three decades, I looked up to find myself exchanging a glance with a woman seated across the aisle. We were approximately the same age — old enough to have lived most of our lives within that fixation of history whose remains were now scattered beneath us.

As though we were being watched, our eyes cautiously met,

glanced away for an instant at the barren landscape below, and then locked again. I had the unmistakable and unsettling intuition that she and I were thinking almost precisely the same thoughts. The entire exchange lasted two or three seconds at most. We didn't know each other, most likely we didn't speak the same language, yet there passed between us — I'm fairly certain it wasn't merely my projection — an intimate recognition of the shared and forbidding world that once had been. The train slowed into Friedrichstrasse station, the S-Bahn doors opened onto the busy platform of commuters, and we both, going our separate ways, disappeared into the moving crowd. In no more than the blink of an eye I crossed from the shore of memory to the rippling waves of the present.

IN 1946, WINSTON CHURCHILL gave a speech at Fulton, Missouri — the home state of the then-American president Harry Truman — in which for the first time he used the image of the Iron Curtain to describe the new post-World War II division of the world. I was five years old then, and wouldn't learn of the former British prime minister's speech until years later. In fact, by the time I discovered the oratorical origins of Churchill's catchphrase, the Iron Curtain was a fact of life for me and everybody I knew.

The Iron Curtain represented a division of land as compelling as the division that occurred in the sixteenth century, in which the Pope split the non-European world between the Spanish and the Portuguese. On one side of the modern divide were the Communists, on the other the Free World. But what intrigued me as a child was the image itself. Indeed, I didn't understand it as a metaphor at all, but imagined it with a certain literalness. For whatever reason, I didn't conceive of it as a "curtain" — like the drapes in our apartment — but as a steel wall the thickness of a bank-vault door.

In a sense, the Iron Curtain was my initiating encounter with history — the idea, however crude, that there was a flow of events *out there* that affected our lives *here*. With that image I acquired a notion of both the existence of the world — that is, a world larger than the working-class Chicago neighbourhood of Jewish and Irish boys who played baseball on factory sandlots and "war" in the milk-weed-infested empty yard adjacent to our apartment building — and the even more abstract concept of time.

Through the window of our kitchen, I could see past the empty lot, across the street, and beyond the baseball field provided by the Calumet Baking Powder Company, to the train viaduct, a raised concrete structure that cut through the neighbourhood. Most days the tracks carried long strings of freight and tanker cars, but one afternoon I saw a khaki-brown passenger train, its windows filled with men in uniform, troops returning from the war in Europe or the Pacific. That same afternoon with Johnny Tallone, the boy who lived in the basement apartment below us, I stuffed lead soldiers his father had made for us (from scraps in the fabricating plant where he worked) into the windows of my Lionel model train, attempting to replicate the troop train.

There were men in uniform in the family: Herb Alpert, at whose grocery store and meat market my father worked, and my cousin Herbie. It was the stuff of out-of-the-mouths-of-babes precociousness that one Friday night when we were having dinner at Aunt Dora's and Uncle Docky's — actually, since they were my mother's aunt and uncle, they were my great-aunt Dora and great-uncle Nathan Kane, M.D. — the doorbell rang unexpectedly. Since the late-arriving men — my father and Cousin Harry, who was married to Dora's daughter, Marge — had already come from their respective store and insurance office, who could it be? "It's Herbie," I declared (at age five or six). Or, more accurately, I heard it repeatedly told at subsequent family gatherings that that's what I declared. It *was* Herbie.

I remember — or better yet, I can *see* — my aunt Dora taking off her glasses and wiping her eyes with the hem of her apron as she excitedly came from the kitchen through the dining room to the glass-paned door, which separated that part of their flat from the entrance hallway, to greet her son home from the war. For a moment I completely forget what I'm writing — post-Communist stories, pre-Utopian essays — to see the folds of skin, the pouches beneath her eyes, with tears of joy trembling in them; I forget my subject to see a world that's gone.

I first heard of Communists, or "Reds," at the Friday night dinners at Aunt Dora's, where furious political arguments sometimes broke out. It was usually after we listened to the evening news on the radio, which always began with the sonorous bass of newscaster H. V. Kaltenborn intoning, "There's good news tonight," or alternatively, in the event of crisis or tragedy, "There's ba-ad news tonight." This verbal brawl was focused on my Uncle Docky. He was a lean, stern, rather forbidding figure who had delivered me into the world. I knew he was fond of me (perhaps a reflection of his fondness for my mother), so I wasn't frightened by his austere manner. In the waiting room of his office was a reproduction of a painting, "The Boyhood of Raleigh," by John Everett Millais, a popular nineteenth-century English painter. In it, an older man and two boys are on a beach. One boy is in knickers and hose, knees drawn up, while the man is bare-calved, barefooted. The man, a sort of ancient mariner, is sitting on a log and enthusiastically pointing out to sea, as if urging the boys to adventure.

The arguments were about Communism and, since the establishment of Israel was in the offing, about Zionism as well. These people — the older ones on my mother's side of the family — were originally Russian and Polish Jews. My father's people, also Russian Jews, came to America via Vilnius in Lithuania, where my father was born early in the twentieth century. Voices were raised. Uncle Docky must have been defending the Soviet Union and the Reds. I didn't understand it at all, of course. Nor can I remember who was Uncle Docky's antagonist.

It was certainly not my father, who wouldn't have held anti-Communist views and, anyway, was far too courteous to engage in shouting matches. Perhaps it was Harry, who worked at Prudential Life Insurance. But no, he also was too well-mannered, and something of a milquetoast (to use a word from that era). It must have been Herbie, who had a fearsome temper. And who else but a son would end up yelling at his father? All I remember is his punchline, followed by someone stalking out of the living room, leaving behind a host of simmering emotions. The punchline was, "Well, if you like the Communists so much, go back to Russia, then!"

Seldom, though, was the family drama of such a high political order. After dinner, the men would retire to the living room to drink coffee and listen to the radio while the women washed up. Then everyone would return to the dining room for a friendly game of cards.

There was a recurrent bit of byplay from those card games. Aunt Dora would refrain, for reasons (as near as I can recall) of frugality, from enjoying a cigarette during the game. Everyone was aware of what they regarded as her spurious reluctance. Was it because of her memory of the necessary economies practised during the Depression of the 1930s?

"Mom, have one of mine," Marge insisted. To which Aunt Dora, shrugging and holding up her hands as if to fend off something, would reply, "No I don't feel like smoking." (She pronounced it "schmoking," with a Yiddish-Germanic accent that the others sometimes mocked.) Finally she'd be persuaded to accept one of Marge's Pall Malls, which were longer than Aunt Dora's own Lucky Strikes. The climax of the routine — which so touches me at this remove and reawakens my love for her — came when Aunt Dora cut the long cigarette in half with scissors, declaring, against a chorus of protests, that the unsmoked half would be "saved for later."

In the midst of the family tumult — cards slapped down, general kibbitzing, impatient cries of "Play, play already!" — I crawled between the chairs, under the table, and, amid its claw-shaped legs, calmly drifted off to sleep. Later I would half waken for a moment as my father lifted me into the back seat of the car for the ride home.

IT WAS MY FATHER, Morrie, who taught me to read at an early age, before I went to school. His method was quite simple. He bought a blackboard on an easel, which had inscribed across the top of it the letters of the alphabet. I would ask him to draw something for me — a cowboy, say — and along with the drawing he would write the word, pointing out how it was derived from the alphabet at the top of the board. Soon he was recommending books for me to read. Since I trusted him completely, I was an eager student.

My father was then in his forties, vigorous, bald, resembling a photo that I'd seen of his father, Jacob (by then dead), which had been taken by my Uncle Lew. (That gruff grandfather, according to family lore, had taken me as a child of two or three for long walks in Garfield Park, where he uncharacteristically indulged me with ice cream cones. I was credited with Grandfather Jacob's autumnal mellowing.) My father wore a white T-shirt and, on the side of his right biceps, bore a blue tattoo of a five-pointed, three-dimensional star, which he could move by wiggling the muscle — a magical feat of will since he didn't clench his fist or otherwise move his hand.

A great many of the books he gave me were about the sea — Jack London's *The Sea-Wolf*, Jules Verne's *Twenty Thousand Leagues Under the Sea*, Richard Henry Dana's *Two Years Before the Mast*, and novels by Herman Melville. I liked *Omoo* and *Typee* better than *Moby Dick*, which at first I found too formidable.

There was a goal to my father's pedagogy. It became clear near the end of the "course," when I was about nine or ten and could go off to the library and choose my own reading, or select volumes from the Book-of-the-Month Club — say, Martin Russ's *The Last Parallel: A Marine's War Journal* (the Korean War was on then). One day, my father said, "I've been saving this one for you until you got a little older." He handed me Jack London's *The Iron Heel*, a socialist novel set in the future, in which, to my delight, there were scenes of civil war in the streets of Chicago — the very streets in which I now wandered.

The Iron Heel, I came to understand, was a book connected with my father's sense of politics. As was Upton Sinclair's *The Jungle*, a proletarian novel set in the stockyards and slaughterhouses of Chicago, whose odours we could sometimes smell wafting across the city on hot summer nights. I was impressed by the notion that it was possible to set both imaginary and historical events in a landscape that I actually knew, and that the present and visible were not the full extent of our reality.

These books also reflected the political sympathies of people in my life. My father's first vote in a presidential election had been cast, he told me, for the socialist candidate, Eugene Debs, who at the time of the election had been jailed for sedition. Later, during the Depression, my father had ridden the rails and been a hobo. The railways may have been owned by the great corporations, but the yards and hobo jungles were informally controlled, for a time, by the Industrial Workers of the World (the IWW, or "Wobblies," as its adherents were known). The railway of the hobos was called the Silver Dollar Line, because for a dollar you were issued a red card that secured your entree to boxcars across America.

Gradually, I acquired a repertoire of such stories from my father. By then, I was following the front-page map of the Korean War in the *Chicago Sun-Times*, which depicted a scrimmage line that oscillated wildly from Pusan in the south, where American G.I.s were in danger of being driven into the sea, to the Yalu River in the north, which they dared not cross for fear of plunging the United States into war with China and, ultimately, the Soviet Union. Now Communists were portrayed in the pages of the bulky morning tabloid as "gooks," the Chinese and the Koreans indistinguishable to crude, racist eyes.

General Douglas MacArthur wanted to take his troops across the Yalu River into "Red China," but President Truman forbade it. A great public debate ensued. Truman fired MacArthur, and white plaster busts of the rebellious hawk-nosed general went on sale for $1.49 at Walgreens drugstores. (The nose on mine quickly chipped.) I watched MacArthur, relieved of his command, on television, testifying before Congress in 1951. "Old soldiers never die, they just fade away," he said, announcing his retirement.

The drama of MacArthur's retirement was the beginning of my initial, brief, passionate interest in politics, a time when I monitored congressional activities with the same avidity with which my mother listened to the soap operas on the radio. The first of those marathon televised legislative hearings was Senator Estes Kefauver's investigations into organized crime. I got into the habit of dashing home from school and watching the hearings on television each afternoon, as alleged leaders of the Mafia were brought to the witness table, where, in a mumble, they invoked the Fifth Amendment, which permitted witnesses to refuse to answer questions that might incriminate them.

But it was a subsequent congressional spectacle — the hearings of Senator Joseph McCarthy on the question of Communist "subversion" in 1954 — that first moved me to go beyond being a mere spectator of public affairs. Day after day on television, the puffy-faced, jowl-shaking senator from Wisconsin pursued his hunt for Communists throughout America, demanding from hapless witnesses, "Are you now, or have you ever been, a member of the Communist Party?"

In addition to Communists, the senator was also seeking to expose homosexuals. In McCarthy's mind, Communist subversives and "sexual deviants" were inextricably linked. This idea had been inspired by a spy scandal of the time, in which a pair of British nationals, spying for the Soviets and on the verge of being exposed, fled to Moscow. Subsequently, it was learned that the men were also homosexuals, which was more than enough evidence for the senator to conclude that Communists and homosexuals were invariably connected.

At the time of McCarthy's rants, I'm not sure if I had any idea of what homosexuals were, though my own fantasy life (I was now thirteen or fourteen) was focused on a group of my schoolmates and baseball-playing neighbourhood friends. Little did I realize that the adolescent scenes I was imagining were among the very acts that the senator was seeking to extirpate. Not until at least a year later, in my first year of high school — when I became enamoured of a classmate with whom I hung out in the locker room after gym class — did I recognize that such desires were "homosexual," and thus forbidden. And even then I made little connection between the pleasures of the imaginary world I had invented and the lives of witnesses destroyed by Senator McCarthy's suggestions, often unsubstantiated, that they were homosexual.

How ironic to learn years afterwards that McCarthy's closest asso-
ciate — the feral Roy Cohn, who was the committee's chief counsel
and who often conducted the preliminary questioning of witnesses
— was a closeted homosexual, and may have been having an affair
with a special assistant to the committee, a private in the army. And
that McCarthy himself was not above such suspicions. (Decades
later, Cohn — closeted to the end — died of AIDS.)

The highlight of the hearings, to my ears, was the abrasive dia-
logues between McCarthy, perched on the senatorial dais, and
Joseph Welch, a shrewd elderly lawyer from Boston and counsel to
the US Army, seated at the witness table below, next to a beribboned
general. McCarthy's attack on Fred Fisher, a young lawyer from
Welch's own law firm, elicited an impassioned response from Welch.
"Have you no sense of decency, sir? At long last, have you left no
sense of decency?" asked the elegant Welch.

These daily encounters between two protagonists battling for the
soul of the country inspired me to join the chorus of public commen-
tators. Perhaps I didn't realize that the tide of opinion was already
turning against McCarthy. The notion of government offices rife with
Communist agents was being exposed as his paranoid delusion; he
would soon be formally censured by the US Senate, and shortly there-
after would die in an alcoholic haze. I still feared that his outrageous
claims might be taken at face value before there was an opportunity
to refute them.

The vehicle I chose for my political and literary debut was the
Chicago Sun-Times, whose tabloid format I thought more modish than
the sombre broadsheet of the *Chicago Tribune,* the city's paper of record.
As far as I can recall, it was entirely my own inspiration to write a
letter to the editor. Apparently, all by myself, I invented liberalism.

In my letter, I urged that the public not jump to conclusions about
the dispute, but rather view the matter with impartiality and fair-
ness. Instead of denying McCarthy's extremist charges in the manner
of lawyer Welch's suave reminder of the need for decency, I seemed
to think that a full airing of views would be sufficient to arrive at
the truth. If this was a form of homemade liberalism, it was a rather

mealy-mouthed version of it. To make matters worse, I was not above calculated disingenuousness. Among other things, I had figured out how to improve my prospects for publication. Appended to my signature were the words "8th grade," designed to catch the eye of editors and readers, dazzling them with my precociousness. The letter was printed.

Despite the doting admiration of my family upon seeing my first published work, there were those who saw through my ambitions and shaky convictions. One day, walking home from school, I met one of the older teenagers in the neighbourhood, a heavyset, non-athletic intellectual named Ben Rubin. "Did you write that letter?" he asked. "Yes," I proudly acknowledged, awaiting his plaudits. Instead, he coolly gazed at me, nodded, and passed on without a word.

A FEW YEARS LATER, at the end of the 1950s, I joined the US Navy and went to sea. Although this occasioned something of a familial scandal (the children of the aspiring classes were intended for the University of Chicago, not common seamanship), my father resolutely defended my right to freedom, adventure, and desire. Jack London, Herman Melville, Millais' painting in Uncle Docky's office won out over middle-class respectability.

One night at sea when I had midnight watch, I walked out onto the fantail of the ship for a smoke. The North Atlantic heaved like a sighing sleeper, its great blocks of purple marble shifting, rising, falling under the moon's light. The sea, I knew then (I was eighteen), was not *of* the world, with its affairs of men, its division into east and west, Free World and Communist. And yet the ocean bound me to language and art, fulfilling as it did the promise of wonder that had begun in Homer's "wine-dark sea," and in all those other books my father had given me. Like my father, I acquired a blue tattoo — not of a five-pointed star but an unfouled anchor, which I had admired on the forearm of a shipmate.

During those years my interest in politics was mostly replaced by art and desire, though I read, with admiration, Senator Jack

Kennedy's patriotic *Profiles in Courage*. I was of so unsuspecting a temperament that it never occurred to me that the book might have been ghostwritten, or that its primary purpose was to advance the senator's presidential ambitions. I favoured Kennedy for the presidency over Dwight Eisenhower's vice-president, Richard Nixon, though I was too young to vote. And when I was stationed at a naval air base outside Naples, Italy, I was a member — however unwittingly — of the NATO forces in the "European theatre," defending the Free World against the powers lodged behind the Iron Curtain.

In August 1961, as I neared the end of my tour of duty, the Communist government in East Germany gave concrete visibility to the image of the Iron Curtain by building the Berlin Wall, cutting off the enclave of West Berlin. Did I think about any of that? Well, a little, because if war broke out in Europe as a result of the Berlin Wall, my tour would be extended indefinitely, "for the duration" (of the war), as the official military jargon put it. But the threat of war receded, and my attention turned to my impending honourable discharge, shipping out, and the journey homeward.

My father picked me up at the airport in Chicago when I returned from Europe. He paused a moment before we got out of the car and went into the house to greet my mother.

"I suppose by now you've experienced pretty much everything in the way of sex," he said.

"Yes," I acknowledged.

"Both with girls and ...?" he asked.

"Yes," I said.

He inquired delicately — I can't remember the exact words — if my desires were by now firmly determined. Nor can I remember my reply, precisely; it may have been slightly ambiguous. What was apparent to me was the non-judgmental nature of his questions. It was also perfectly clear to me that he too, while riding the rails and in those hobo jungles, had had similar experiences.

"Well, old salt," he said rather jovially, and heaved my duffel bag onto his shoulder, leading me home as he had led me into the world.

In all that followed over the next several decades — I became a writer; moved to San Francisco, where I served a sort of literary apprenticeship under the tutelage of the poet Jack Spicer; settled in Vancouver, Canada; and eventually became a philosophy teacher at a university — I lived in a world permanently divided by the Iron Curtain.

As an adult, I developed a more serious interest in the theory and history of the great Communist experiment of the twentieth century. I read the pro-socialist classics by Marx and Engels, and the polemical texts of the leader of the 1917 Russian Revolution, Vladimir Lenin, as well as scholarly and dissident histories of the Soviet Union. I studied the Soviet Union's descent under the dictator Joseph Stalin into a totalitarianism that was evident by the late 1930s and depicted in such novels as Arthur Koestler's *Darkness at Noon* and George Orwell's *Nineteen Eighty-Four*, and whose horrors were more fully revealed in Aleksandr Solzhenitsyn's narrative documentary of Soviet concentration camps, *The Gulag Archipelago* (1973). Still, long after I'd acquired a more nuanced understanding of the politics the Iron Curtain represented, on both sides of the divide (I was also a critic of the "Free World"), I continued — as did we all — to live in a binary political configuration.

The Canadian painter Michael Morris, who had grown up in the midst of the bombing blitz of London during World War II, and who was living in Berlin when I first arrived there, once remarked to me, "We're shaped by it," — by "it" he meant the world or life itself — "even before we're able to come to terms with any of it." He was explaining why, as a middle-aged man, he still occasionally slept with a pillow pressed over his head.

My imagination had been frozen by the Cold War. I couldn't conceive of a world in which the Iron Curtain didn't demarcate its unalterable boundaries. Numerous spy novels, the rhetoric of countless political speeches and campaigns, movies that reproduced the chilling nighttime lights at Checkpoint Charlie in divided Berlin, fuelled my imagination of the unknown world behind it.

Today, though the Berlin Wall and the image of the Iron Curtain have been gone for only twenty-five years, there are those who cannot imagine that a wall was once built around half a city not by its inhabitants to protect it, but by its adversaries to prevent their own citizens from enjoying the allures of the enclosed city. In a time when memory, history, and imagination are degraded, whose task is it to remind us of those ideas and events that offer human and earthly continuity? It's mine, which explains why I've written this autobiographical vignette. But I'm not the only one to whom this responsibility belongs.

On television one night in early November 1989, long after my beloved father was gone, I witnessed the breaching of the Berlin Wall — that embodiment of the Iron Curtain whose history was part of my personal experience. German youths partied atop the graffiti-covered façade of the wall, crowds poured through the Brandenburg Gate, and the world changed. It was, as Michael Morris told me in Berlin some months after the great event — he had been there, in the streets — the *Stunde Null*, zero hour, the moment of beginning again.

Oddly enough, the decisive instant appeared to me not in that celebrated event but several months before, in May 1989. In Poland — where I had been almost a decade earlier — they were about to elect a non-Communist government. The Hungarians would soon do likewise, and gentle rumblings emanated from Czechoslovakia. Even the young people of China had gathered in Beijing's Tiananmen Square, only to face a brutal, bloody response. "Openness" and "restructuring" marked the Soviet Union of Mikhail Gorbachev, who would refrain from committing Soviet troops to the forcible maintenance of Central and Eastern European Communist regimes, instead permitting the nations of the Warsaw Pact to pursue their own fates.

Thousands of East German citizens were attempting that year to flee their country by a circuitous route. They were legally permitted to visit Czechoslovakia and Hungary, but from there they faced the difficult problem of crossing the heavily guarded Hungarian border into Austria. Should they manage that, they would have passage to West Germany.

On the six o'clock TV news one evening in May, it was announced that the Hungarian government, in violation of Warsaw Pact provisions, was dismantling its border with Austria. Within months the East Germans would be permitted to cross freely into the West. And on the screen, most unspectacularly — simply to provide visuals for the voice-over — there was incidental footage of Hungarian soldiers snipping strands of the barbed wire that separated their nation from Austria.

It was at that moment that I realized, even as the barbed wire was being cut — snip, snip, with ordinary metal-cutting shears — that after all those years of picturing it in my mind, I was at last looking at the Iron Curtain, its bank-vault-door thickness reduced to strands of rusted wire punctuated with snags.

The Translators' Tale
(Tirana, Albania, 1991)

The Globe and Mail (Toronto) reported that the two men, translators in Tirana, Albania, had shared "a tiny, Spartan office" in the state publishing house for most of the previous twenty-two years. "Behind battered typewriters," the article said, a bit melodramatically, "they have battled to keep fragments of literature alive in the darkness of Stalinist orthodoxy." (Paul Koring, "Awakening from the Nightmare," *The Globe and Mail*, April 10, 1991.)

The story had been published a few months ago, in April. Reading the brief account of the two now middle-aged men, one wondered the simplest things: How had they spent their time? What did they talk about? Keep necessarily silent about? What loyalties had caused them to persevere? How had they maintained their sanity? It seemed an ultimate test of sanity, something like those stories one occasionally ran into about World War II, in which a pair of Japanese soldiers emerged from a jungle in Burma or Java twenty years after the end of the war, never having heard that it was over.

In the case of Mr. Simoni and Mr. Qesku — those were their names — the endurance had been similar, but the cause was more recognizable. The convulsions that swept away Communist regimes across Europe, from Warsaw to Bucharest, in the late 1980s had at last, by 1991, reached the hills of what was once ancient Illyria. And blinking into the uncertain sunlight — for it was hardly clear that our vaunted free markets would provide a panacea for their woes — there appeared the translators of Tirana, having, you could say, kept the faith. Albania was not a Burmese jungle nor an island in the Indies, but a southern European nation wedged between Greece and what was then Yugoslavia. It was a mere eighty kilometres across the Adriatic from Bari or Brindisi in Italy. Yet for all that, it might have been as distant as the moon, so successfully and for so long had its self-proclaimed "Glorious Leader," Enver Hoxha, sealed it off as the last and purest bastion of Communism.

THAT SPRING AND SUMMER I was in Berlin, thinking about the fall of Communism (it was more than a year since the opening of the Berlin Wall), reading a little philosophy (the subject I teach at university) and some fiction (Joseph Conrad), and pursuing the amorous adventures that leisurely evenings in bars and cafés sometimes yielded — in about that order.

I was often to be found at a table in the Café Einstein in the late afternoon, engrossed, like many of the other patrons, in a book or newspaper (this was in the time before everyone's attention was absorbed and fragmented by the screens of cellphones and other electronic devices). Though it was something of a reading-list staple when I went to school, somehow I had never got around to Joseph Conrad's *Heart of Darkness*. Or perhaps I had and had merely read it carelessly as a student — since, upon taking it up now, it seemed both fresh and yet strangely familiar to me.

As I began Conrad's tale of a journey to what had once seemed like the ends of the earth, it called up the ideas I had about Albania. My interest in Albania had been inspired by the brief newspaper story about the translators I'd read earlier that spring. In fact, I'd clipped the article and tucked it into the back of my notebook.

I never really admitted to my friends in Berlin that I intended to go to Albania. At most, I'd say something casual and indirect like, "I wonder if it's possible to fly to Tirana from here." But I made the necessary phone calls, inquired at a travel agency, and checked the airline office. One day I got a friend to accompany me to the Albanian consulate in east Berlin, only to find the dilapidated building locked and to be informed by a caretaker that I needed to contact the office in Bonn, the then-capital of Germany.

My method — to use a word that appears prominently in Conrad's tale — was circuitous at best. Indeed, it was a sort of game that I called "Following the Story," in which one set certain events in motion by some ordinary but deliberate act — reading a book, walking a certain route, going to a particular place. If something happened as a consequence, the challenge then — the whole point of the exercise, really — was to attend to the ensuing possibilities in such a way that the pattern of meanings we call a story resulted.

Reading the opening pages of Conrad's story, I found it easy to identify with its narrator, Marlow, the veteran sailor, as he made his way around Brussels to secure a posting on a Congo riverboat of the Belgian trading company that, for all practical purposes, ruled that distant African land. I too had been to sea. As I read — while at the same time arranging my own curious journey — Albania seemed as distant as Marlow's Congo destination, and Comrade Enver Hoxha, who had ruled Albania, was a figure as bizarre as Kurtz, the god-man who gradually becomes Marlow's obsession.

I was aware of the cliché of reading Conrad in this way. The "heart of darkness" was anybody's metaphor, and virtually anyone who travelled to what might be regarded as an obscure corner of the earth invoked it. But there was nothing I could do about it. If you're a reader, sooner or later you read Conrad and, by happenstance, I was reading *Heart of Darkness* at exactly that moment. Although most academic readers appear to think that the "heart of darkness" is a psychological location in the human soul, I read it as a constantly moving physical location, and Albania seemed to me an accurate contemporary instance of what Conrad meant by his famous phrase.

In the end, I found myself filling out a visa application for Albania at my table in the Café Einstein. I was in the high-ceilinged room of the villa that overlooked the café garden, which was almost empty that afternoon. Even the garden's tame sparrows, who hopped up on tables to filch stray crumbs of *Apfelkuchen*, had flown off. Wettest, coldest June in memory, the German tabloids moaned, along with the requisite references to global warming and other weather disturbances. And still chilly, even into July. The black-vested waiters moved among the huddled-up patrons at a glacial pace, carrying hot drinks on sterling trays.

When I said to my friends, in the studiedly casual voice I'd adopted, "I wonder if it's possible to fly to Tirana from here," they invariably replied, with barely restrained politeness, "But why would you want to go there?" Or else they would fail to hear me correctly, thinking perhaps, since I was a Canadian, that I had said, "Toronto," and they would make me repeat the name of the Albanian capital. Then they, who had been almost everywhere, would quizzically repeat it themselves — "Tirana?" — in the slightly bemused tones reserved for impossibly distant places or vanished cities of the past.

Occasionally someone would attempt to dissuade me by pointing out the difficulties of acquiring a visa. "I phoned," I'd report. "To Bonn, of course," one of them assumed. "To Tirana," I said. "You can phone Tirana?" I was asked, warily. "Easier than east Berlin," I replied, drawing a wan smile from my friends for all the times we'd tried to make appointments across the once-divided city with its still-divided communication lines.

The Albanian attaché in Bonn suggested that I needed an invitation from someone in Tirana in order to complete my visa application. When I asked him if he happened to have the number of the state publishing house there, he supplied it, and soon after I attempted to phone Simoni, one of the men mentioned in the newspaper story. After bursts of static on the line and a babble of languages (Albanian, English, German, Italian), then a long pause (he had been walking down a flight or two of stairs), I was speaking to Mr. Simoni. He promised to send me a note of invitation.

And thus I "followed the story," even as I was following other stories. If the invitation from Tirana arrives, if mail service from Tirana even exists, I told myself, then I guess I'll get some photos from the machine at the train station to attach to the application form. And indeed, one by one, each of the items appeared, until at last I signed my name in the Café Einstein and sent the papers off.

A few nights later, while I was in the bath, the phone rang. Annoyed and dripping down the hallway, I picked up the phone to be told by the Albanian attaché in Bonn — unusual that he should be working on a Saturday evening, I marvelled — that my visa had been approved.

In the post, along with the appropriately stamped papers, he sent me a signed postcard wishing me a good journey. I didn't know what to make of such an unbureaucratic gesture. On the postcard was a picture of an ancient adolescent boy's head — marble — from Apollonia, one of the places down the Adriatic coast that the Greeks had built in the fifth century BCE. "Best wishes," the postcard said.

I WAS ON THE Swissair Berlin–Zurich–Tirana flight, with a date to meet the two translators at 7 p.m. at the base of the Skanderbeg statue in the town square. I'd acquired the necessary historical background from a guidebook, *Eastern Europe on a Shoestring*. Skanderbeg, the terse potted history informed me, fifteenth-century warlord; castle in the hills at a place called Krujë, a bit north of Tirana; fought the Turks twenty times, never beaten. National hero. Once Skanderbeg was out of the way, it was the Ottoman Turks for the next five hundred years. Succeeded by King Zog, then the Fascists, and finally by the Glorious Leader, Comrade Hoxha.

I didn't know what I was after. Oh, to find Simoni and Qesku, certainly. And to find out how a country in the middle of Europe could more or less disappear from the face of the earth for half a century. But I also wanted to know what was there now. The "West" had ignored Albania, even though it was located well within Western civilization. Sure, Albania had been sealed off for God knows how long, but was that a sufficient excuse for our failure to consider it? Marlow's celebrated utterance (I'd tossed my copy of *Heart of Darkness* into my bag) echoed in my mind: "And this, also, has been one of the dark places of the earth."

So I had a rendezvous. But first there were the "pilgrims," to use Conrad's term. I mean, if I could think of it, then surely the business pilgrims would already be figuring out how to turn a dollar in post-Communist Albania. He was a Swiss engineer named Weber who boarded at Zurich. Some Texans were seated in front of us. As soon as we were in the air, Weber had a powerful thirst. By the descent, he had persuaded the flight attendant to sell him some cans of beer in a paper bag. But he knew the country, I had to give him that.

When Weber wasn't courting the woman in the window seat, I asked him the usual traveller's questions. I'd heard of the Hotel Tirana. No, the Dajti, he recommended firmly. Reservations? No problem, he'd fix it up if it came to that. And was there a bus into town from the airport? *Kein Problem*, I could ride in with him. Hail fellow, well met. Well lubricated too, by the time we were on the ground in Albania.

The airport was a patch of cement in the countryside, halfway between Tirana and the town of Durrës on the Adriatic coast. It was thirty degrees Celsius at 4 p.m. By the time I was walking down the double row of palm trees into the terminal, I was poached in my own juices. Lads in green with machine guns. The usual madhouse — babies, relatives, heaps of baggage. "Fixers" everywhere.

Weber had several thousand dollars in trading goods, by my estimate. Cigarette lighters, Swiss Army knives, textiles, camcorders, the whole store; vast quantities of personal belongings, bottles of Johnnie Walker, cigars, suitcases for an expedition. We showed our papers, then lugged the whole caboodle past the boys with guns, and we were in the courtyard of the terminal. I'd barely a moment to get my bearings. It was sheer confusion — the crush of relatives, officials, much weeping and kissing on the cheek, the yard crammed with taxicabs, children begging for coins, the swelter. A whole family was there to greet Weber with hugs, kisses on both cheeks, bouquets of flowers already wilted in the heat. I was introduced, of course, and our party divided into two cabs, Weber's trading goods stuffed in the trunk. He was already passing out cigarette lighters to everyone within reach. And then we were off.

I experienced that moment of pure exaltation at being in a strange place, and never mind whether or not my project would bear fruit. Soon enough there would be the practicalities, interviews, putting together bits and pieces of history. But for now we were barrelling down a country road, the driver honking as we passed peasants on horse carts, bicycles, sheep on the road, men without shirts in a field, squinting at us through the sunlight.

The countryside was dotted with concrete mushroom-cap shapes, overgrown now, which were apparently defence outposts, gun emplacements and the like, pointed in all directions. The Glorious Leader was ready to fight the Turks, the Western imperialists, Titoists from Yugoslavia, Russian revisionists, the Chinese renegades who came after Mao Tse-tung, everyone that Hoxha had broken with in the name of Marxism-Leninism, in the name of Comrade Stalin, of the Truth. I had the unnerving sense, for the briefest moment, that I was peering into Hoxha's besieged mind.

At the fork in the road from the airport, one way leading to Durrës and the other to the capital inland, we took the turn for Tirana. And all the time Weber, sitting in back between a pale girl in a white blouse and her father, lectured the lot of us. I missed most of it, I confess. Words lost in the wind, while the driver was running peasants on bicycles off the road with his terrible honking. Of course the pilgrim had a plan to set the country right, something about playing Beethoven on the radio, and the phrase, "They're really children, you know."

Finally we entered the city. All the main roads of Tirana converged on Skanderbeg Square. It was a large open space. I marked the equestrian statue as we passed; that was where my rendezvous would be. Around the edges of the big traffic circle in the square there were various official buildings — "people's palaces," according to the old terminology — with windows bashed in and boarded up after the recent rioting. I was informed right off that the towering statue of the Glorious Leader, set in the middle of the traffic circle, had been pulled down some three months ago by the people, the same "people" whose name the regime attached to the palaces and the "people's republic."

We dropped off the girl and her father and some of the engineer's booty. Weber ordered them about genially, drank his beer, handed out gifts. He was a lean, nervous pilgrim, but no fool. Then we headed back to the square, this time south, past yellow and red stucco buildings — government ministries, Weber said — and down Martyrs' Boulevard a block or so to the Dajti Hotel. The hotel was a four-storey job built by the Italians before World War II, big Mediterranean pines all around, shading it, and facing a spacious public park.

Crowds of fixers, drivers, cadging children, and arriving pilgrims jostled in the hotel driveway. Predictably, there were no rooms available. But the engineer was jovial, offered the extra bed in his suite, no problem for the night, would fix me up with a room in the morning. He'd enjoy a bit of company — more like an audience for his elaborate unpacking. I barely had time to splash a few drops of water on the dusty wraith I'd become, and the engineer was off, for business in Durrës, I think it was.

An hour later, just before the onset of dusk, I made my way over to the square. I sat beneath the fearsome Skanderbeg, perched on his mount. Presently two men arrived, as ordained. The younger one, Pavli Qesku, struck me as quite elegant — mid-forties, lean, prematurely grey hair, tinted glasses. The other man was older and had one good ear, so he had to position himself to a person's left to catch the conversation. That was Zef Simoni.

I'd brought books for them — I suppose in my way, I was a pilgrim, too — but rather than examine them at once, they suggested we take a stroll down Martyrs' Boulevard. They pointed out where the statues of Lenin and Stalin had flanked the thoroughfare; now only the pedestals remained. Everything had come down in the last six months, more than a year after the wave that swept the rest of central Europe, and more than five years after Hoxha's death. The Albanian Communist Party had attempted to make the transition smoothly, had assumed that everything would continue forever — simply parade the image of the old Glorious Leader, gradually insert that of his successor, a man named Ramiz Alia. They figured they would carry on into eternity. But now everything was breaking up. Statues toppled, street names altered.

I'd noticed on a map that the continuation of the boulevard north of Skanderbeg Square had been named for Stalin. I wondered if it still was.

"Oh, we never called it that anyway," Zef said, dismissing the issue in an understated, slightly ironic way I would quickly get used to.

"But this is still the Boulevard of National Martyrs?" I inquired, just to check.

"Well, after all, this is true," Pavli said. "We are still a nation and, indeed, there have been martyrs."

"So there is no need to change it," Zef added. They had been in each other's company for so many years that they'd acquired the habit of completing each other's sentences, as old couples do.

I was impatient to get to the heart of it, to the only question I really had for them — namely, how had they survived? As we passed the Hotel Dajti on the left, and twilight came down on the big park facing it, they represented themselves as timid men, unheroic, cautious creatures, never members of the Communist Party, though they had worked in the state publishing house translating the Glorious Leader's works and speeches all those years, Zef into German, Pavli into English. Another translator, Jusuf Vrioni, had put Hoxha into French. I'd seen Vrioni's name, about a month before, in an article in an American magazine. He'd been cited as the French translator of the great Albanian novelist Ismail Kadare, who was now living in Paris. I'd glanced at *The General of the Dead Army*, one of Kadare's novels.

But the immediate answer to my question was relatively simple. They had translated literature — Dickens, Conrad, Lawrence, Orwell even — I knew that already from the newspaper piece. But there was a new bit, a bit that hadn't been in the newspaper, and that was the key: they made dictionaries. It was an obvious thing for translators to do, now that they mentioned it, but it hadn't occurred to me. "So," I said, "in a sense, words saved you."

We crossed a little trickle of water, the Lana River, just beyond the hotel. It flowed in a ditch below us, beneath the boulevard overpass — grass slopes, a paving-stone embankment. To the right, from the west, the last of the day's light hit it.

"Working with words saved us from the situation in which we lived, sort of," Pavli replied. Then he added, almost more to himself than me, "Yes, to a certain extent, it is true."

"A justification," Zef explained. "In our work as translators, we used words to express other people's thoughts — and we were not in agreement with those thoughts. So we wanted to use the same words to express, not our thoughts, but something neutral at least." It was put with perfect modesty. My curiosity was at once satisfied. Strange how quickly it went. Now we were simply evening strollers, casually conversing.

The boulevard, a broad four-lane thoroughfare, came to an abrupt dead end at the university, a cluster of buildings set at the base of a hill. The students had demonstrated here the previous December, and then again in February. That, apparently, was what had started the overthrow of the regime. Beyond the boulevard, we took a footpath that wound around and up a wooded rise. Saint Procopius Hill, Zef informed me.

At the top of the hill we came out of the pines onto an outdoor café, which was our destination. It was well attended, mostly by couples of men and women, and some uniformed guardsmen, also in pairs. On our way up the hill, as the darkness settled in, Zev had pointed out the lighted windows of some barracks in the woods. The barracks of the National Guard, Zef noted, making it clear by the tone of his voice that the institution wasn't exactly loved. At the café, a table was found for us, and the waiter came to take our order for drinks.

"Raki," Pavli said to me. "Perhaps you won't like it."

It was acrid stuff, perfectly drinkable. And there was bread, soup, and some roasted chicken. My hosts half-apologized for the poor quality of everything, but in fact it was fine — a perfectly good café on a summer evening, and a bit cooler up here on the hill. After the food, we enjoyed more raki and smoked cigarettes.

Oddly enough, we didn't talk about politics at all that evening. Zef mentioned that he had learned to read Greek and had read Plato's *Phaedo* in the original. It was a work with which I was familiar; I often taught it in philosophy classes. Indeed, I had opinions about the death of Socrates, the principal figure of that dialogue.

I confess I did most of the talking. The part about Socrates' last day in jail, his weeping friends, the hemlock poison he drank, all that was true, in my opinion. But the part about the immortality of the soul, I insisted to Zev and Pavli, that was added by Plato himself. I don't think Socrates believed any of that. Socrates simply thought you died and consciousness ceased, or — well, it doesn't matter about my views. But it was all so wonderfully odd. I'd come all this way, to the moon, to the last outpost, to inquire about the fall of Communism, and instead we were talking about Plato, just as educated people anywhere might have done. Of course, I had to acknowledge that the places where civilized people could talk of such things were much diminished in our time, even in my own part of the world.

It had grown late, the café had emptied, the guardsmen were back in their barracks. Zev and Pavli walked me down the hill, back into the heat of the town, now in darkness. Behind the hotel there was a sleek building that bore the only electric sign I'd seen. It alternately flashed the temperature and the time, lighting up the night. The Institute of Strategic Studies, Pavli informed me. They came into the Dajti with me for a minute so I could give them the box of books I'd brought, and arrangements were made to collect me in the morning.

The engineer soon returned from Durrës. He produced a bottle of Johnnie Walker and we sat on the balcony outside the room, overlooking Martyrs' Boulevard — little traffic at that hour, only the gear grinding of the occasional truck, a late-night bus.

IN THE MORNING, THE engineer and I took breakfast together. The other pilgrims were there, impatient with the service, anxious to get on with business, to make the world go. Weber was soon off, the brooding Swiss of last night — he too read some philosophy — giving way to the nervous energy of deal making.

Across the corridor from the breakfast room was the bar. The engineer left me there with one of the fixers he knew, in case I needed anything. Instead, I drifted out to the cement front veranda of the Dajti. Even though the blinking sign, forever reminding us of time and heat, reported nearly thirty degrees before nine o'clock, a pleasant breeze wafted in from the park across the boulevard. Below me, in the driveway, taxi operators were taking the pilgrims off. There were all sorts of kids hanging around. Small boys, and teenagers too.

One in particular attracted my attention. He was in his mid-to-late teens, blue-eyed, with pale sandy hair and a quick smile. He was with a couple of his friends, and at first all I noticed was the kids' friendliness among themselves, the way they leaned against each other, casually draping an arm over the other's shoulders. Then the one with blue eyes and I exchanged glances and there was a brief, wordless encounter, the sort of meeting I might have forgotten if nothing else had happened. But as he passed behind me on the veranda, he ran a feathery hand across my shoulders, just as he did with his friends. And as quickly as he'd appeared, he was gone.

Just then, Zev and Pavli turned up to show me around. I tried to make apologies for chattering on about the *Phaedo*.

"No doubt you like the part about the soul," I said to Zef. He had told me he was a Catholic, or from a Catholic family, and I feared that I may have offended him. But apparently there was no harm done.

"It was very good conversation," Zef assured me.

"Yes, nice to talk," Pavli seconded.

We crossed Skanderbeg Square and were soon in a maze of side streets and then back lanes. There were some market stalls set up on the walks. Little potatoes, green onions, dark fresh figs, all in small quantities. Housewives spent hours gathering the day's provisions.

"Looking for things that don't exist," Pavli said.

We came to a five-storey building, made of oddly spaced bricks — a hand-done job, it seemed. "Zef's flat is on the top. He built it himself," Pavli told me.

Looking up, you could see from the fresh colour of the brick that the top floor had been added recently. One could imagine the difficulties of a man in his fifties hauling the bricks up those stairs, mixing the cement, mortaring them in himself.

By the time we climbed to the top, my shirt was soaked through. Zef's wife met us, and while we settled in she brought us bottled water, raki, some Turkish delight sweets, and then coffee. I reminded myself that I was in one of those southern European cultures where the protocols of hospitality mean that they give you everything they have, even if they have very little.

There were shelves of books along the back wall. With a very slight ceremonial gesture, Zef presented me with a copy of the German–Albanian dictionary he had compiled, which had been published the year before. He quoted Milton on justifying God's ways to man. "I had to justify myself to myself," he said. "To do something useful."

About noon, we went down and made the short walk over to the publishing house where they worked. First there had to be a formal meeting with the director in his suite of offices. Pavli translated. I had been through this sort of thing, in Poland, years before. Formalities to be observed, cups of strong coffee served. I intimated that I had access to paper supplies, something the director — who, of course, was a Communist Party member — could note in his report if necessary. Even though it was all breaking up and the Party was in the midst of a chameleon-like effort to appear in more acceptable colours, much of the old organizational infrastructure was still in place. And all the old habits. Although the director was the only Party member I would actually meet, I was little inclined to question him about his view of the recent political changes. I knew I'd only get the current official line, and, in any case, the shadow of "the last Communist," Hoxha himself, still lurked everywhere.

On the stairway, going up to their office, Zef said, "Very good," appraising my performance, and the three of us laughed about it.

Then we were in the "tiny, Spartan office" that I'd read about in the newspaper piece. Well, a small quibble here, a detail. It was Spartan in the sense of equipment, and the absence of reference books. But it

wasn't tiny. It was noticeably larger than the cubbyholes most journalists and instructors had in the newsrooms and faculty offices I was
familiar with back home. Spacious enough for facing desks, walls a
glossy, pale green, and a big window, with a breeze coming in, and a
view from the second floor looking west to the hills, in the direction
of Durrës on the coast.

We talked about making dictionaries; there was a large old one
on a revolving stand on Pavli's desk. I'd never thought about them in
precisely this way before.

"Where do you start?" I wanted to know.

"You begin from anything you like," Pavli said. "Just collecting
words, finding phrases, putting them on cards, keeping files. But that
is only preparatory work. The real work begins when you touch a
typewriter and put a white sheet in and write 'A.' What shall we write
about 'A'?" he asked.

I wanted to know how they had survived all those years, and here
was a clue under my nose. You know how you're so familiar with an
object that you barely notice it? You're looking for a big answer —
something about the spirit of history — but the answer is right in front
of you in some simple, material thing. It was in the German–Albanian
dictionary Zef had given me, in the old definitional dictionaries in
their Spartan but not tiny office. It's a matter of seeing it, of resisting
your own familiarity.

Zef said, "We wanted to use the same words to express, not our
thoughts, but something neutral at least." Harmless things. Words.
And in the pages of his dictionary were thousands of words — "tree,"
"sky," "beach," "sea" — each one a possible expression of thought
uncontaminated by the regime.

"Something neutral," Pavli repeated, adding, "despite the fact that
sometimes other people, outside us, put in words that expressed the
reality that existed at that time. As they did with Zef's dictionary.
They put in expressions like 'the dictatorship of the proletariat' and
'scientific socialism' and so on."

"Not very scientific," Zef commented wryly.

"But also the definitions," Pavli said. "Here, look." He turned to the word "liberal" in the dictionary on his desk. "'One who makes concessions toward shortcomings and mistakes,'" Pavli read, "'who is not exacting toward others, who allows irregularities which harm the work of society.' This dictionary is full of such stupidities."

Over the years, they had compiled words, usually at night, while at work they translated documents, position papers, the "works" of Comrade Hoxha. On the far wall, facing the open window that looked out toward Durrës, there was a bookcase containing the books of the Glorious Leader. Zef went to it and pulled out a couple of paperback volumes to give me. He made a show of banging them against the side of the case to shake the dust from these translated but seldom-read memoirs. On the cover of one, called *With Stalin*, was a photograph of the two leaders, shot from below, standing on a rampart. Later, in my hotel room, I skimmed its hagiographic, childishly humble accounts of Hoxha's reception in Moscow, hosted by "Comrade Stalin."

PAVLI WALKED ME BACK through the mid-afternoon heat to the Dajti, and we arranged to meet again that evening. The desk clerk at the hotel had a room for me. Weber was still out when I moved my things to the new room. It was small but sufficient — a bed, a writing table, lace curtains, a shower, a little balcony, and a roll-down metal shade to keep out the heat. The room faced east, looking directly onto the blinking electric sign with the time and temperature. By the time I came up from the hotel bar, bringing back a litre of mineral water, I was soaked from the exertion. I showered, made my notes, drank some water, read a page or two of Conrad, and then napped.

Pavli returned to fetch me in the early evening and took me to his apartment, where Zef was waiting for us. Pavli's wife brought us raki and then went into the kitchen while we watched television. There was an interview with a visiting Albanian political leader from Kosovo, the southernmost, so-called autonomous province of Yugoslavia, but actually under the thumb of the Serbs. Two million Albanians lived there, and now, with the hostilities in Yugoslavia, the old dream of Greater Albania was again in the air. I learned a little more about it when I read a translation of a novella by Kadare set in Pristina, the Kosovan capital, about a failed uprising there a decade or more ago. Zev and Pavli watched the interview intently; such open discussion was still something of a novelty on Albanian television.

Then Pavli's wife brought in food and they switched channels to an Italian game show. It was announced as a "light supper," but in fact it was a full plate, carefully laid out. Mussels, olives, tomatoes, onions, hard-boiled eggs, and a fruit compote for desert. All the time we were watching the politician from Kosovo, Pavli's wife had been working in the kitchen. I thought of a feminist friend back home and knew exactly what she would make of it.

After Mrs. Qesku cleared the table, I turned on the tape recorder for our formal interview. Now I was at work, as I had been a hundred times before, in many places. And later, no doubt far away from where this encounter was occurring, I might hear these voices again, or they would be transcribed into a sheaf of notes that would find a place in a manila folder or in the depths of the maroon-coloured gym bag I lugged around with me, a homely object I sometimes described as "my office."

Zev Simoni was born in 1933 in the northern town of Shkodër, to a well-to-do Catholic family. As in neighbouring Yugoslavia and Greece, the ending of World War II inaugurated civil war in Albania. While Greece was allotted to the western Allies, in both Yugoslavia and Albania the partisan triumph was not impeded.

"Immediately when the partisans came into Shkodër," he recalled, "they started shooting people in batches. Behind the town graveyard. And after having a batch of people shot, they put up a proclamation with the names and crimes they were supposed to have committed." Zef was eleven.

"So they came in 1944?" I calculated.

"Yes. And they were my first exercises in literacy."

I was momentarily puzzled.

"To read the names," Pavli explained.

"It was just reading matter for me," Zef said. I had a glimpse, no more, of a child peering up at a freshly pasted sheet on a brick wall, absorbing the litany of the newly dead and their alleged crimes. Outside, in the night, we could hear the shouts of children at play.

Pavli's wife offered us brandy. "It's a very fine brandy, made at home," Pavli recommended. "Wild cherry." We each accepted a glass.

"They were people of a conservative mind," Zef said, recalling his family. "Right wing, I would say now. My father was first an import-export merchant, then he had a printing shop, then a magazine, and he made some translations. He was the first Esperantist in Albania."

"He translated *Pinocchio*," Pavli noted.

"Into Esperanto?" I wondered, slightly amused. But no, he had put the Italian tale into Albanian.

"He translated the biography of Skanderbeg into Esperanto," Zef said.

"So you're a second-generation translator," I observed.

"Second generation," Zef nodded, laughing.

Once again, it was a matter of words. Words for civilization, words in self-defence. But wasn't the ruling party's concern also the use of language?

"Propaganda is made of words, of course," Pavli agreed.

"But everything is distorted," Zef replied. "You are told you have freedom, which others, you are told, have not. And you have not freedom. You are told you have free speech — it is written in the constitution — and you land in jail for saying the wrong things. You are told you are free to move about, and you must have documents to move from one city to another. Everything is told it exists, and it doesn't exist, or exists its counterpart." Zef spoke rapidly, losing his grip on English grammar in his excitement.

"My own family," Pavli said, "was a little more exposed to such propaganda. My father was a partisan, then a Communist, and fought in the brigades of the national liberation army. After the war, he began to realize that there was something amiss. But he couldn't grasp what it was. He was a tailor. In a small town in central Albania. Slowly but surely he began to realize that the cause of the situation was the Party itself, and he began to dislike it, until in 1949, after five years in the Party, he refused to be a member." Pavli had been five then. "But in my family there are still some people who believe that the Party is good, just that something went wrong somewhere. There are some people who are still Utopians, who have the hope that socialism is something good for humankind."

I was curious to know how they had become friends.

"We worked together," Pavli said.

"They just put us in the same room," Zef added, "and they said, 'Work together.'" The two of them laughed at the simple absurdity of it.

"And this has gone on for over twenty years," I said, laughing also.

"Yes, twenty-two years," Pavli confirmed, "except for a period of three years when I was in Peshkopia, a small town in the mountains."

They had escaped the terror of executions and prison, but not entirely. They had spent their years together carefully.

"Very careful," Pavli reiterated. "What we said in the streets, what we said in the café."

"We expressed our more delicate thoughts in English, just in case," said Zef. "We were very careful about where we talked, how we talked."

"Or we had code names for things."

The way their voices alternated reminded me of the strophe and antistrophe of a Greek chorus. "Code names?" I repeated.

"For the government, the Party, the leaders, our Party secretary." Like a children's game, I suggested. "It was very childish," Zef said, "and very horrible."

"But it was not Newspeak," Pavli added.

Yet their caution hadn't protected them completely. Pavli had been shipped off for three years, in 1975, a decade and a half ago, to a sort of internal exile.

"The reason they gave Pavli for sending him to Peshkopia," Zef began, then changed tack. "Well, the true reason was that he didn't accept to become a member of the Party, but the specious reason they gave him was that you keep too much Zef's company. They kept me in Tirana."

"But Zef was frightened then."

"Because in their sick mind, I was infected, hopelessly. There was some hope for saving Pavli."

So Pavli was shipped off to work as a schoolteacher in a mountain village. "Did you think you would ever return?" I asked.

"It was a closed chapter," Pavli replied. "I just took my bag, my typewriter, and my books."

"Were you married?" I asked.

"Yes, but happily we had no children then. My wife was allowed to go on working here. The government needed her work because she was chief engineer of the porcelain factory. She kept working in Tirana, and I went to Peshkopia."

Pavli's wife was sitting in an armchair, away from the table the three of us were gathered around. For all her fulfillment of the traditional duties, she was an educated woman, professionally skilled, and able to follow our conversation in English, occasionally supplying a correction to their account. I saw her then as if for the first time. I had only a moment to imagine their three years of separation, caused by an ideological whim, which they treated, in retrospect, as a minor inconvenience. Compared to the fates of so many others, I suppose it was.

Pavli went on about Peshkopia. "The headmaster of the school was a very nice chap, very understanding. He gave me a whole room to myself, a bare room of course, but it was a room. There was a round stove which the schoolboys were careful to supply with firewood. It is fifteen or twenty degrees below zero in the winter there. I was all by myself. The dictionaries were there, and whenever those people, security, came from time to time, unannounced, to search my room, they saw they were harmless books. I never gave them cause to suspect."

"And in the place of Pavli," Zef said, picking up the other end of the story, "into the office stepped a chap who had been Pavli's schoolmate. He had some connections with the minister of internal affairs, and I am sure he informed on me, but he informed only on the good side." Zef laughed at this small irony, then added, "I was very careful, of course."

"My former schoolmate didn't do anything while he was there," Pavli said. "He was supposed to be a translator, but he couldn't do the job. When Zef was away, he just sat there, doing nothing."

Sitting there, comforted by cherry brandy, I had to remind myself that I was listening to an account of political terror. Not executions, torture, jailings — though there was that, of course — but quiet terror, everyday terror.

"When we translated that book which I gave you, *With Stalin*," Zef began again, "we worked day and night."

"Three months of hard work in the midst of summer," Pavli said.

"Then they gave us four or five days to recover," Zef continued. "On one of those days, the chief of the enterprise came to me and said, 'You are invited to the Tirana branch of the Ministry of Internal Affairs. I don't know what they want from you, but you must go.' I went there. Certainly, I was very afraid. But I tried to keep control of myself. I told myself that maybe they had some translations for me to do. I was ushered into a room and there were two armchairs, and they smelled of sweat, a heavy stink of sweat. Because the people who went there sweated profusely under interrogation."

They asked Zef about various people he knew, and he offered bland replies. The verbal fencing went on for some time. Then the interrogators asked about a certain person. "I said, Yes, I know him. I couldn't say I didn't. And what are his opinions? they asked. I said, The generally current opinions. And what are his literary tastes? I mentioned the most conventional tastes I knew of. Then they told me, He has been slandering the Party, and you must know. I know nothing, I have not seen him for six months. After that, they gave me a cigarette. They did not make direct threats to me. They told me, Look, we are going to arrest this man. If you warn him, first, it will be useless, and second, you will be arrested too. So I went home. On my way home, I wanted to have a double portion of cognac, just to steady my spirits." He laughed, recollecting his fear. "Then I thought that I might be followed. If they saw me drinking, they might think I had something to fear. So instead I went straight home and lay in my bed for about half an hour. Only then did I come out and go to the café, where I had my double portion of cognac. In about six months' time, Pavli, who knew nothing about these things —"

"Zef didn't whisper a word," Pavli interjected.

"Had I told Pavli, he would think, first, that I was a hero, and second, that I must have blurted out something. So I said nothing. And six months later, it was Pavli who mentioned to me that so-and-so had been arrested. And still I said nothing."

"You didn't tell Pavli about the interrogation?" I asked Zef.

"I learned of it only last year," Pavli said.

"When did this incident happen?" I asked.

"In 1980," Zef said.

"You only told him ten years later?" I said, astonished.

"Ten years," Zef said, and we all broke out laughing, but for different reasons. They laughed at the mixture of absurdity and horror, and because it was now possible to laugh at it, and because it was a small thing compared to what others had endured. And I laughed nervously, half embarrassed to be made a party to this terrible intimacy.

"After six months, Pavli told me, you know, this chap so-and-so has been arrested," Zef repeated. I turned off the recorder, stuffed the tapes into my gym bag.

It was a story no different from those I had heard countless times in recent years. But that was the point of it: there was nothing "Albanian" about the anecdote. The insidious method was ubiquitous throughout the Communist regimes. And it was not absent from our own "democracies." But here in Albania, anyone, even the most intimate of your friends, might inform on you. A remark you made in the sanctity of your home, thoughtlessly parroted by your child at school, might bring the authorities to your door. No letters unread by the censors, no movement without approved documents, and no passports. Your fate was decided in rooms, by committees — none of which you had access to — while you waited in their anterooms. And though the blinking clock at the Institute of Strategic Studies registered the passing minutes, the Glorious Leader had made time stand still.

Yet from the outside, to a visitor, the place appeared but a small, dusty, inconsequential town of a quarter million inhabitants, baking in the sun, poor, but with people going about their business. There was now little visible sign of the oppression, only recently relaxed, or of the methods that made it possible. It was as if I had travelled the length of a river — like the Congo River in Conrad's story — to reach, as Marlow did, the kingdom of a madman.

The parallels were eerie. Like Kurtz, Hoxha had not always been mad. He had begun with the intention of improving the lot of humankind, the great dream of most Communists. And those of us on the left had even sometimes grudgingly admired Hoxha as the ruler of a tiny, mostly agricultural country who had rather heroically broken with first the Soviets, for deviating from Stalinism, and then from the Chinese, when China abandoned Maoism. There was even a far left political organization where I lived in Canada, one of those Marxist-Leninist groupuscules that developed in the 1970s and '80s, almost a cult, who trumpeted the virtues of Communist Albania and venerated Hoxha. But in Kurtz's, or Hoxha's, obsessive effort to perfect human beings, to create, like a god, "the new man, the new woman," he had gradually turned the inhabitants into slaves.

"You translated Conrad," I said to Zef, after citing the similarities between Conrad's story and life in Albania.

"And perhaps you think you are a bit like Marlow?" Zef joked, intuiting my pretension.

But there was no Kurtz *left* at the heart of this darkness, no self-critical last cry of horror to ponder. There was only the rubble of Hoxha's rule. And its survivors. Just as Conrad had learned, despite how the imperium viewed the distant peoples of a different colour a century ago, I too had discovered that the seemingly benighted, seldom thought of, almost invisible Albanians were the same as us.

I didn't think all this at that moment. It came later, when the voices recorded in my little machine had become words on pages. But there was something more, something that did occur to me as we spoke, though I didn't mention it to Zef and Pavli. It was that I had yet to free myself from the human dream of a better world, a project that had been defeated here because of the dictator's inhuman methods. I wasn't tempted to abandon that dream. But the cautionary tale of Albania was a reminder that even in our dreams, we bear responsibilities, as one poet put it.

It had gotten well on into the evening. There was more to ask them, but they had arranged for me to do interviews with some other people beginning early the next morning, a Saturday, and the following day we would hire a driver and car and go to Durrës, so there would be time to talk then. I couldn't resist asking about the present, now that the nightmare was over, or almost over.

"The change can be seen if you follow a couple of people walking in the streets," Pavli said. "They have stopped turning their heads back to see if we're following them. We no longer turn our heads back."

ZEV WALKED ME BACK to the Dajti through the silent streets of Tirana. From the balcony of my room I faced the electric sign flashing in the night. It was almost midnight. Just under thirty degrees. The sign blinked on and off. In bed, I turned away from the wall and fell asleep.

Six hours later, I woke. Beyond the Institute for Strategic Studies, beyond where the town ended, there were pale brown mountains, with Mount Dajti to the east. A haze lay between it and the edges of town. I stood on the balcony, drinking coffee. Directly below me, three floors down, was the raggedy, semi-abandoned hotel garden. Palm trees, an empty fountain, untended bushes. A skinny yellow cat prowled through the brush.

The opposition Democratic Party was headquartered in a villa, set back from a busy street, with a wide gate at the front to admit vehicles. Inside, even at 8 a.m., clusters of men were gathered in the driveway-courtyard — petitioners, perhaps, or local functionaries. An outside staircase led to a warren of offices. We were ushered into a large room with a long rectangular table. At the head of it, talking on the telephone, was a stocky young man in his late twenties with unkempt curly black hair. There was a window behind him, covered with shutters through which slivers of sunshine played through the gauze curtains.

He put the phone down, and we were introduced. His name was Azem Hajdari. He was a graduate student at the university and came from a small mountain village, Tropojë, in the north. He was married and had two children.

"If you want," Hajdari said, via Zef's translation, "I will tell you about the democratic movement in Albania, the Democratic Party, the political life, and the Parliament."

As a result of the elections in the spring, I learned, he now sat as a member of that body. We had about an hour's interview, variously interrupted by the telephone and by people poking their heads through the double doors with brief messages. It was a standard interview; he spoke as a man with responsibilities. But I saw that both Zef and Pavli admired him. They liked his vigour and, apparently, the colourful mountain villager's way of speaking — he didn't mince words. When he was on the phone, I could get a hint of a more animated, indigenous style that no doubt had popular appeal. But with me he was diplomatic, speaking without irony.

Here was the person, as much as anyone, who had loosened the grip of Hoxha's successors. "The dictatorship was so savage there was no possibility of even thinking of establishing another form of government, because the mere thought of it put your life in jeopardy," Hajdari said. But the explosions in eastern Europe had their echoes even in Albania. Hoxha's successor, Ramiz Alia, had seen, like everyone else, the events in Romania in December 1989 that had resulted in the swift execution of Nicolae Ceaușescu, the long-time Communist dictator there.

"Mr. Alia, recalling the fate of Ceaușescu, saw that he had to do something for democratization. But his speeches, his manoeuvres, were only for export," Hajdari said dismissively. "They were intended to give the impression that something was being done, whereas nothing was being done." It was that impasse that led Hajdari to take political action, organizing the students. The way he put it made it seem innocent — it was the language of the nineteenth century's "Springtime of Nations," of the European revolutions of 1848 — and yet it had the self-deprecating awareness of a man standing before a mirror, giving an account that would later be read as history.

"When I was a student, I always recalled President Kennedy's words, 'Ask not what your country can do for you, ask what you can do for your country.' So I decided to give my all for Albania, even my life. At first, the possibility of emerging alive from the first demonstrations after forty years of Communist rule was very slim indeed. Nevertheless, against all these odds, we succeeded in carrying out our peaceful demonstrations. The moment came to do something for Albania, and I am very happy this offer of sacrifice was accepted." The demonstrations provided the impetus to, if not topple the regime, at least to shake its foundations.

Later, toward the end of the hour, the mountain man declared, "I love life, but I have the opinion that life should be loved for as long as it lasts, and we should not think to prolong it more than its course. You can't escape your fate." It was not the first time I'd heard young men fearlessly proclaim such things, and I've seldom doubted them. Yet it was always eerie to hear someone say it.

Just at that moment, the phone rang. Hajdari picked up the receiver and soon was speaking more animatedly. I saw alarm in Zef and Pavli's eyes.

"There's been a shootout," Pavli said, following the progress of the conversation. "One of his cousins, a young cousin of his, has been shot."

"Where?" I asked.

"In Tropojë."

"How did it happen?"

"The situation is stable," Pavli reported.

"But who was shooting?" I wondered aloud. Hajdari's voice subsided.

"He made a speech in Parliament about Kosovo," Pavli explained. I put it together in bits and pieces. The arrival of the visiting politician from Kosovo we'd seen on television had heated the political atmosphere. Then there was Hajdari's speech on the suppression of the Kosovan Albanians by the Serbs — no mincing of words, apparently — and somehow the news of the speech (was it heard as a call to arms?) had triggered the flare-up in his home village in northern Albania, not far from the border with Kosovo.

On the outside staircase going down, Zef said, "In six months Hajdari could be dead." Then we were back in the streets, in the unforgiving heat. In the mid-thirties before noon. As we walked, Pavli recalled that the former student leader had accurately predicted that the newly elected government would be forced to form a coalition with the opposition "by the time the cherries were ripe."

"And when do they ripen?" I asked.

"In May and June," Pavli said. "And it happened. Now he says the present government will fall by the time the watermelons are ripe at the end of summer. By the time the watermelons ripen." Pavli seemed taken with Hajdari's agricultural turn of phrase.

Many years later, my brief encounter with the young Albanian politician suddenly returned to mind. In September 1998, I read in the newspaper that Hajdari, then thirty-six, and still a Member of Parliament, had been assassinated by gunmen in front of the party headquarters from where we had taken our leave that morning. Most often, reportage of the kind I did in Tirana is simply the news of the day; occasionally, it is a mirror held up to the future.

OUR NEXT INTERVIEW WAS with a writer named Kasëm Trebeshina. It was held at the apartment of a young colleague of his, also a writer. Trebeshina was in his mid-sixties, but you could see he had been badly used. He spoke in a hoarse whisper through yellowed and broken teeth. His was a tale of jailings and neglect. He had been imprisoned twice by the Fascists, against whom he had fought in World War II, and then three times by the Communists. The first time the Communist regime jailed him, in the 1950s, it was a literary jailing. "I was always against the socialist realism," he said. "I was of the opinion that if there is realism, there is no need for socialist- or

Fascist- or so on." He wrote an open letter to Hoxha and got three years for it.

I didn't quite catch the reason for the next incarceration, but the third one, in 1980, came about when he publicly declared his refusal to vote. For that he got a longer stretch. He'd only been released three years ago, in 1988. And though he'd written much after the open letter, none of it had been published. He had been ignored, neglected, always at odds with the party-controlled Writers' League. He didn't share the conventional estimate of the internationally best-known Albanian writer, Ismail Kadare. "A collaborator," Trebeshina rasped. When I asked him about hearing of Hoxha's death while he was in prison, he replied, "He's not dead." At the end of his fragmented recital, Trebeshina said, "I always wanted to ring the bell for the others, but I did not. During all my life, I was a Don Quixote."

Recently, thanks to the sometimes dubious wonders of modern digital information, when I googled "Trebeshina," there he was, duly listed in *Wikipedia*. He had been able to publish his writings in the 1990s — and though none of his work was available in English, one novel had been translated into German — and at last sighting, he was still alive, in his late eighties, living in Istanbul, Turkey, where he had moved after further major political upheavals in Albania in the late 1990s, around the time of Hajdari's assassination.

Pavli walked me back to the hotel. We went along the Lana River, where a peasant sat on the grassy embankment, tethered to a couple of grazing sheep. The electric sign now registered thirty-six degrees. Pavli left me in the driveway of the Dajti. He and Zef had arranged a meeting with Kadare's French translator, Jusuf Vrioni, for that evening.

I had worn my lightest short-sleeved shirt, but I was soaked through and slightly dazed from the heat, grateful to get to the shade of my little hotel room, clutching the bottles of water I'd acquired in the bar on the way upstairs. Before I showered and napped, I made my notes, the paper practically melting under my hand. It was as if all substance was dissolving into primordial ooze — the water I drank greedily, the perspiration pouring out of me, smearing the ink, dampening the pages. The interviews with Hajdari and Trebeshina had been ordinary enough, the sort of tales of courage and suffering in an almost unknown place, which are then inadequately condensed into the columns of the dailies. I had conducted such interviews before, in many places, though I only practised journalism sporadically. But this time I had been affected. I could feel the ends of my nerves. Perhaps I too, like Trebeshina, was a Don Quixote, or maybe a Sancho Panza. It seemed to me, at that moment, that your entire life as a writer leads to the one street you are walking down, to the miserable pile of dark figs you are unthinkingly looking at, to the rasping, bitter voice you are listening to. Everything had led to this moment, and its possible description was infinite. And yet you do not know the story, except as it unfolds before you. *You do not know the story*, I repeated to myself as I fell asleep.

I WENT DOWN TO the veranda of the hotel early to await Zef and Pavli. The teenager I had seen the first morning was there. We shook hands and introduced ourselves. I learned that his name was Ilir, as in ancient Illyria. It was impossible not to think of the head of the boy from Apollonia on the postcard that the Albanian consul in Bonn had sent me.

Ilir was with a friend his own age, to whom he introduced me. They both had a little English, although I had some difficulty following the anecdote they were trying to tell me. His friend was a music student, as was Ilir, or perhaps a dancer. I couldn't quite get it.

They knew all about current music. "Michael Jackson," Ilir said, "he is a great man. And MC Hammer, very beautiful."

I was surprised by their knowledge, though also appalled that, of all things, this was what had penetrated the ideological defences of their shrouded land. "But how do you know all this?" I asked Ilir. They had seen it on television from Belgrade, which apparently transmitted the European version of the American music channel MTV. Score one for the global village.

There was a complicated story about a man named Hussein —

"not Saddam Hussein of Iraq," Ilir laughed, referring to the Middle Eastern strongman who had been much in the news recently for his attempts to invade Kuwait, a neighbouring oil-rich kingdom.

This Hussein had promised them something, but I couldn't make it out. "Rap," Ilir said, "for the rap." There was something about video-tapes, but I got it mixed up.

Zev and Pavli turned up to take me to meet Vrioni. The farewell with Ilir and his friend was elaborate — handshakes, kisses on the cheek, assurances that we must get together soon, as if we were old friends.

Walking to Vrioni's, I must have babbled, telling Zef and Pavli about my new young Albanian acquaintances. They seemed amused that I was so taken with them, the way you are amused when someone comes to your town and enthuses about something you haven't really thought about, but that leaves you pleased for both your guest and yourself.

On the way, they reminded me that Vrioni had for a time worked in the publishing house as a translator. In fact, at the time of Pavli's exile, Vrioni's name had also appeared on the list of those to be sent off to get "closer to the people."

"He was sent away, too?" I asked.

"He was meant to be sent," Pavli said, "but on special instructions from His Highness —"

"— who knew some French," Zef interjected.

"— who read his own books in French," Pavli continued, "and liked the way they had been rendered in French —"

"— because Vrioni had translated his own works," Zef put in.

"There was no one who could translate his works as well as Vrioni did," Pavli added.

"So Hoxha was not going to saw off the branch he was sitting on," Zef concluded.

Vrioni lived in a detached two-storey house with a small front garden. His wife greeted us at the door and led us into the living room, where Vrioni was waiting for us. He was a tall, elegant man. I was told later he was seventy-eight years old, but I wouldn't have guessed it from his looks or his manner. He was the son of a wealthy land-owner and had been raised and educated in France before the war. When he returned to Albania after the partisan triumph, Hoxha had him jailed for thirteen years. Then he became a translator — of Hoxha's books as well as those of Kadare.

His wife brought in a bottle of Johnnie Walker whisky, with glasses on a tray, and after placing them on the low, glass-topped table before us, she retired upstairs, explaining that she was feeling poorly. Our conversation was in French. Vrioni could speak English, but he made it clear that to discuss certain concepts, only French was adequate. Zev and Pavli filled in for my deficiencies.

We hit it off right away. I mentioned that I liked jazz and uttered the name of the legendary French jazz guitarist Django Reinhardt. Immediately Vrioni lit up. He rummaged around beneath the music sound system at the side of the room until he produced a tape cassette. The room filled with the instantly recognizable riffs of the three-fingered jazz guitarist, joined by a violinist. It was Reinhardt's jazz version of "La Marseillaise," accompanied by Stéphane Grappelli, recorded just after the Allied victory in 1945, Vrioni told us. For a few minutes we simply listened with pleasure and sipped our whisky.

Vrioni was dubious about Albania's prospects. He began to tick off on his aristocratic fingers the reasons for his doubts in the precise manner of French intellectuals. First, the level of Albanian culture was abysmally backward. I interjected that I had met a teenager in Tirana who was extraordinarily well versed in contemporary music, having watched television from Yugoslavia. Vrioni was unimpressed, and continued his dissection of the country's gloomy future.

I mentioned to Vrioni that I had seen his name in an American magazine article about Kadare. It was clear that he had more than a proprietary interest in the Albanian writer. His translations into French had been crucial in making Kadare's reputation outside Albania. Without the translations, which had so pleased the French public, the great novelist might be unknown today. There was even a hint that something more than translation was involved. It was almost as if he regarded himself as Kadare's co-author. And he had also translated the Glorious Leader. Vrioni went to the bookshelves on the far wall and returned with a couple of volumes, opening one to the title page. On it was Hoxha's inscription, in his own hand, to his "Comrade" for his "tireless work" in rendering the leader's writing into "perfect" French. Vrioni translated Hoxha's praise of himself with considerable drollery, assuming our appreciation of the implicit ironies.

I noticed that, on the low table before us, there was also a copy of the French translation of Milan Kundera's latest novel, *Immortality* (1990), which I had recently read. That led to Vrioni inquiring about a Mexican novelist he had only heard of on his last trip to Paris. Did I know of Carlos Fuentes? I remarked to him that the conversation we were having might take place in any capital of Europe. Yes, people were always surprised to encounter a cultivated Albanian, Vrioni said. "Of course, you know Montesquieu's *Persian Letters*?" he asked.

In that eighteenth century work, the imaginary Persian through whom Montesquieu provides his portrait of the ills of France appears in a Paris salon and is asked, with near disbelief, How is it possible for a Persian to be in Paris?

"I, too," Vrioni said, "have been at a salon in Paris, and upon identifying myself as an Albanian, I was asked, by a man who knew his Montesquieu, 'But how is it possible for an Albanian to be in Paris?'"

For all his civility, even the charm of his vanity, there was something unsettling about Vrioni. I remembered the rasping voice of the much-abused Trebeshina, the Don Quixote; at the mention of Kadare's name, he had spat the words "a collaborator." To be able to write, and to use his fame as a platform from which to criticize the regime, even indirectly, had Kadare not also had to lend that renown to a tacit justification of the regime? Had Kadare not faced the moral dilemma of the person who sustains the culture, which he imagines as belonging to posterity, but at the cost of a partial endorsement of the totalitarian power, which he must persuade himself is only temporary? I hadn't read much of Kadare at that point, but I'd read enough to know that the authenticity of his writing had not been undercut by the moral dilemma of his relations with the regime. That dilemma, albeit to a lesser degree, confronted other prominent Albanian intellectuals, like Vrioni, who had survived the regime. Here we were in this comfortable home, with whisky on the table, the latest books, and amid all these elements necessary to the maintenance of a civilization was the hand of the Glorious Leader, the madman, thanking his "tireless Comrade."

Vrioni's ailing wife appeared at our departure to say goodbye. It was already night as Zef and Pavli walked me back toward the hotel. Martyrs' Boulevard was jammed with people on that Saturday night, walking in family groups, sitting on the low wall along the park, milling about in conversation in the hot darkness. I was struck by the sheer physicality of bodies. When the ideological shroud is pulled away, what you're left with is warm, breathing, perspiring, human beings.

WE WANTED TO ARRANGE for a car for the following day. Ilir was again hanging around with some friends in the congested driveway beneath the veranda of the Dajti. He dashed off into the shadows to secure a driver, soon reappearing with a man who seemed trustworthy enough. We agreed to meet in the morning, and Zef and Pavli melted into the throng of strollers on the boulevard.

I told Ilir that we were going to Durrës the next day. "I also," he said, "for the swimming." But perhaps we could meet later in the afternoon, around five, for a soft drink. "Yes, yes," he agreed.

In the morning, as the sun came in through the chinks of the half-pulled metal shade, I could hear the birds below in the otherwise empty garden. The driver proved to be reliable, and we were promptly on the road for our little holiday. We passed busses jammed with like-minded weekenders heading for the sea.

At Durrës we inspected the ancient Roman amphitheatre. First century CE, I was told. It had been but semi-excavated, located as it was right in the middle of a residential neighbourhood. The heat was stunning, and it was a relief to duck into the shaded galleries and interior stairways of the Roman ruin. A Byzantine church had been built in its midst in the Middle Ages; the whole place was a rock-pile jumble of two millennia. At last we emerged into a portal overlooking the entire site. The excavators had dug only partway down to the great half-circle stage, but it was easy enough to imagine, easy enough to move through time. When we finally clambered off the heap, I was grateful to our thoughtful driver who had found a water tap, which he ran for his parched inspectors of antiquities.

Then there was the local museum to see. It was across the street from a narrow beach at the sea's edge. I only had half an eye for the ancient statuary, for now I was longing for the Adriatic, which I could smell from there. "Where I come from," I said to Zef and Pavli, "it's considered good luck to dip your hand in the sea, if you're a visitor."

My hosts apparently felt we had fulfilled our duties as tourists and obligingly led me across the road. It was a scruffy bit of beach, pebbles and shells mostly, but the Adriatic stretched out before us in long, low layers of waves. I reached into it and wet my hand, scooping up some water to cool my face and head.

Since I'd displayed enthusiasm for this natural wonder, Zef and Pavli decided to show me the beaches at the south end of town. It was a five-minute drive. Down the wide stretch of sand was an area of resorts and hotels, where the workers and their families went for holidays and where, during the old regime, the country's few tourists had been permitted access in order to provide a source of foreign currency. We stopped at one of the hotels to get a cool drink. We sat in a cavernous hall that gave out onto the crowded beach below and the Adriatic rolling in, and sipped an orange-flavoured concoction.

Afterwards, the three of us strolled through the mob of bathers, families, groups of boys playing football in the sand, bodies everywhere. What struck me again, as it had the night before when strolling families had filled the boulevard, was the idea that when the ideological fog lifted, what remained were people — not the abstracted version, as in "the People," but the physical fact of them — and these people, the Albanians, were not so different from the rest of humanity, not dissimilar to the Italians or Greeks, who were on their own beaches that Sunday afternoon.

In the car again — now we were travelling inland and north, to Krujë — the image of that human flesh shimmering in the sun remained with me. I turned to Zef and Pavli, sitting in back.

"Communism never talked about the body," I declared.

"It never talked about the spirit, either," Zef countered.

"But it had an equivalent to the spirit," I replied. "It had the notion of revolutionary consciousness. At least that was a mental thing. But they claimed to be materialists, and yet, they didn't speak, except mechanically, about the body." To be fair, in the world I came from the body was relentlessly displayed, but for all its commodification, it was rendered almost equally meaningless, I added.

Of course, the return of the body is not the same thing as the birth of a citizenry, I admitted. The madman Hoxha had broken many bodies, but when the kingdom fell apart — for a variety of reasons, including the simple fact that it didn't work — the body of, say, old Trebeshina was, in a sense, replaced by that of the new generation to which Ilir belonged.

The bodies, left to themselves, form only the skeleton of a society — at best, the wisdom of the elders, at worst the gangs of the cities. Whereas the dictionaries Zef and Pavli made belonged to a culture, even a universal culture, out of which citizens might emerge where there were none before. I had no clearer idea of how it might turn out here than anyone else. But wasn't that true of so much of that new entity that we referred to by the old name of Europe? For the moment, it was simply bodies that impressed themselves upon me. Bodies that, as Pavli had said, no longer had to turn their heads to see if someone was following.

At Krujë, in the mountains, there was a reconstruction of Skanderbeg's castle and a sweeping view of the valley below. We dutifully toured the site. Nearby there was a little outdoor restaurant, and we sat in the walled garden by a fountain and feasted. Below us, at a table placed near the edge of a precipice, commanding a view of the valley, was a party of Italians. They were very jolly, yodelling out into the mountains, hoping to produce an echo. The waiter told us that, far from being the frivolous tourists we might imagine, they had taken in some young Albanian men who had fled to Brindisi — I remembered the footage of overcrowded boats I'd seen on TV the previous spring — and now they had come to visit the parents, to bring them news of their sons.

Sheep wandered about the garden, eating bread from our hands, nudging up against our knees, while we dug our fingers into their white, oily curls. But even as we feasted, dipping our bread into the dish of oil in which the olives soaked — Zef said matter-of-factly, "I haven't tasted olive oil in two years" — and as the Italians hallooed and yodelled, our talk strayed from the bucolic surroundings.

"What did you think the day Hoxha died?" I asked suddenly.

"It isn't very Christian," Zef answered, "but it was perhaps the finest day of my life."

"How did you hear about it?"

"We were not together at the time," Pavli said.

"First, there was only classical music on the radio," Zef remembered. "And we thought something had happened. And of course the only thing that could have happened was that he died. So we waited for the official announcement, which was on the twelve o'clock news."

"I was travelling that day, to my hometown," Pavli recalled. "I took my little daughter with me. I went to see my father, who was sick. On the way to the train station, I met an old journalist. He approached me with a sort of — I can't explain what his face was like when he saw me — but he desperately wanted to tell me something. He approached me with half a smile and said, 'He is dead and gone.' I got it immediately. When I reached home, I told my father, I gave him the news. He just rejoiced. 'I saw him go before me. I don't mind if I die now.' Those were his words."

Pavli fell silent. We listened to the water falling in the fountain.

Zef said, "We hoped that his death would be the end, but the regime lingered on for another six years."

"The true end of the dictator," Pavli continued, "was on that famous day when his ten-metre-high statue was brought down. My wife was walking with her bicycle in the square and she saw people gathering, rushing about, and the police throwing tear-gas bombs. Nobody cared about their lives, they just rushed toward the statue and managed to bring it down. Afterwards, a tractor pulled it to the campus, where the students were on a hunger strike. They cut off the head, which was sent to the students. And then the body —"

"— it was dragged along," Zef interjected, "like a dead crocodile."

"Without its head," Pavli added.

In the mid-afternoon we came down from Krujë, back toward Tirana. I would be leaving the next day, so, though there would be a farewell, this was in a sense the last of our conversations. And at the end, as we had begun, we spoke of dictionaries. It was as if they hadn't made themselves clear enough, hadn't got it right, and it was somehow important to them that I understand.

"If we had been hot-headed and just burst in a fit of passion and told them everything we had in our minds, we would have been content for a while, but our work would not have been done," Pavli said. "Dictionaries are not our work. It is something which belongs to the whole people, and people who make dictionaries are only a few idiotic, I would say, hard-working asses who take upon themselves the work of a lifetime."

"Eccentrics," Zef said, chuckling. "But it was some sort of justification."

"Or a revenge on our own selves," Pavli offered, alternatively. "After having humiliated ourselves, serving him so devotedly, we wanted to do something to atone for what we had done."

Zef disagreed. "I, for my part, didn't think of it as atonement. I considered it only as a reply to people who, after liberation — I was always hoping for liberation — to people who would ask me, 'And during these years, what have you done?' It was meant as a reply."

"So that you could say ...?"

"I did something useful," Zef concluded. The car pulled into the driveway of the Dajti.

I WENT DOWN TO the hotel veranda at five. Ilir was there, in a white T-shirt and jeans. When we went to the bar to get mineral water and soft drinks, he wouldn't let me pay; instead, he made some arrangement so that I was his guest. Upstairs, in my room, we sat on the little balcony facing the electric sign.

He was a dancer, it turned out. His father wanted him to study law, I think it was, but he wanted to dance. There was some difficulty with language. We used Zef's dictionary to get through the rough spots. I would think of a word we needed in English and translate it into German in my mind, and then look it up in the dictionary and show Ilir the corresponding word in Albanian. Then I would say the English word for it. Cumbersome, but a bit like a game.

He was in one of those folk-dance ensembles approved by the regime. But his passion was for ballet. Classical and modern dance, although he called the latter "abstract." "Ballet abstract," he said. He told me, in bits and pieces, the story of a ballet he was in at school, "The Silver Birds," written by his teacher, his "choreograph." And then I finally got it about "the rap." What he was interested in was hip hop dancing. He'd seen this fellow, MC Hammer, an American, who was a performer of hip hop, on Yugoslav television. And the famous Michael Jackson, of course. I hadn't paid much attention to any of that, but one absorbs it, since it's in the air, so I knew what he was talking about. I'd thought the sound of rap was like the staccato of a firing squad. But Ilir's idea was this: He too wanted to be a choreographer. And the ballet he wanted to create would be a combination of classical ballet and hip hop. Well, why not?

We sat on the balcony and chatted away for an hour before dinner. There were stories about family, politics, travels (he had been to Turkey). Ilir was outgoing, unselfconscious, a little breathless. Perhaps all the pidgin English, pidgin Albanian, made our encounter seem simpler than it was. I didn't think he represented the "spirit of Albania" or some such nonsense. I could feel the temptation to make that of him, but that's a dangerous sentimentality too. He was simply himself. But he was also of the place; he would have to live here when Vrioni and Don Quixote and the translators had gone on.

He might even make a ballet, if the place wasn't overtaken by chaos; if it didn't revert to hill banditry, blood feuds, mafias; if, against the odds, Ilir's musical talent and the "deliberate belief" (as Conrad calls it) of the dictionary makers could forge a citizenry, sustain a culture. He wanted to see me again the next day, before I left. He would bring me a *regalo*, a gift. He'd come at nine the next morning.

That evening I had dinner in the hotel, in a large hall at the end of the long corridor, beyond the bar and breakfast room that flanked its length. Through the dining room windows you could see the boulevard, filled with people passing up and down in the middle of the wide avenue. The pilgrims, myself included, were at their cutlets. The Texans were at a table on one side of me. I gathered they were off to Cairo the next day. Apparently they'd done a deal for oil rights down at Flore, to the south, below Apollonia, the old Greek town. And at the table on my other side there was another businessman, with a woman, earnestly lecturing a local fellow, who seemed quite deferential before the pilgrim's sermon on efficiency.

I took the air for a bit, among the strolling crowds, and then retired to my room. Before I nodded off to sleep that night, I glimpsed the end of it, of the story I was following here. I thought about the meeting with Ilir in the morning, the flight back to Berlin, but more than that, I saw how all the conversations, the places I'd seen, and the dictionaries came together. When you're vouchsafed, in advance, a glimpse of the tale in its entirety, you simply shudder with gratefulness to the god for whom the Greeks named that town of Apollonia.

Ilir arrived promptly at nine. The haze was just lifting from Mount Dajti. He had a plastic sack filled with *regalos*: a bottle of Albanian raki, another of wine, some candy, and a collection of video and cassette tapes — Beethoven and a local singer and MC Hammer, which he'd taken off the radio, and some TV footage of the visit of the American secretary of state to Tirana. There was also a snapshot of himself, so that I wouldn't forget him. He emptied his treasury upon me. Would I send him a music video of MC Hammer or perhaps Michael Jackson? "Yes, of course," I promised. "But there's one more *regalo* I'd like," I said. He was puzzled. What more could there be?

"I'd like to see you dance," I said. I knew my request was some-what presumptuous, even intrusive, but it was an essential part of the story.

"But where?" he asked.

"Here?" I said. At first he made the faintest show of resistance, but he was an artist and accustomed to performing. Beethoven is not really for dancing, he pointed out, even as he snapped the tape into my little interview recorder with the familiar dexterity of teen-agers everywhere.

He placed himself in front of the muslin curtain before the win-dow. It was embroidered with birds, and the faintest breeze moved the cloth. I pressed the button and the symphonic strains emerged. At first I didn't think it would come off. There was barely enough room to move between the bed and the doorway to the bathroom, three or four paces at most. I don't know what I expected — that it would be quite provincial or crudely amateurish, perhaps.

I needn't have worried. He struck a pose and quickly found room in that limited space to soar and plunge and turn. When the Beethoven ran out, he immediately found a female pop singer on the tape and danced a mixture of Turkish and folkloric movements. For the finale he performed a hip hop dance to MC Hammer chanting the refrain, "Can't touch this," repeated again and again. It was one of those boasting songs from American hip hop, full of aggressive sexual double entendres and self-acclaim for the performer's artistry. Although I'd only paid mildly irritated attention to it when I'd seen the video on television, I now got the point; I saw the art of it. Ilir viewed it as simply another form of modern dance. For him, the elements of the culture had no gaping spaces. For his needs, Beethoven and MC Hammer were contemporaries. And the tiny room was as adequate as the stage in the amphitheatre at Durrës.

At the end, he collapsed into the chair at my desk, heaving for breath. I offered him a can of cola. It was soon time for him to go; he had a test at school that day. We hugged farewell. "Can't touch this," I said, echoing MC Hammer. "Can't touch this," he repeated with a grin.

❦

THE RUBBER TIRES OF the plane squeaked down onto the tarmac at Tegel Airport in Berlin as I turned the last pages of Conrad's story. I was left at the end with Marlow, Conrad's yarn-spinner: "Marlow ceased, and sat apart, indistinct and silent, in the pose of a meditating Buddha."

I got up, reaching into the overhead luggage rack for my gym bag. Coincidentally — and this was one of those thousand things you couldn't possibly make up — my seat companion on the flight had been a riverboat captain, just returning from someplace in Africa where he worked for a German resource company. We wished each other well at the end of our respective journeys.

That evening, a cool, damp Berlin night, I had a drink at the Café Einstein. When I said to a friend I'd run into there that I was just back from Tirana, he made me repeat the name and then tried it out himself, as if uttering the name of some place on the moon. I extracted Zef's dictionary from my bag as evidence that I wasn't making it up. "But why did you want to go there?" he asked.

Borkowicz's Death
(Warsaw, 1990)

If there had been a graduating class photo of the dissidents who brought down the Communist regimes of Central and Eastern Europe at the end of the 1980s, Jan Lityński would be in the photo. Did someone say that to me, or did the thought simply arise on its own? Indeed, there *was* such a photo, or something very like it, illustrating an article by the Polish writer Adam Michnik in the *New York Times*, which Tom Sandborn happened to be reading as the transatlantic flight took us toward Europe in mid-March 1990, the first springtime of the decade, just three months after the overthrow of Communism in 1989. (Adam Michnik, "Notes on the Revolution," *New York Times Magazine*, March 11, 1990.)

The photo recorded a meeting of about two dozen Czech and Polish political activists, held at the border between their countries in the summer of 1988. They were posed in a wooded area in front of a small sign warning, in Polish, "State border, crossing forbidden" — an order they had lightly disregarded in the same way they had ignored or defied so many other dictates of the authorities over the years, with consequences that were in many cases not light at all.

I recognized a few of the figures in the photo. Michnik was there, of course; he was holding his fingers aloft, flashing a V-sign. The curly-haired Czech playwright and essayist Václav Havel was crouched in front of him, glancing off to the side, away from the face of History to which his Polish colleague was signalling. Jacek Kuroń, who had been among the first of the Polish intellectuals to challenge the Communist regime openly (and had paid for it with abundant prison time), was sprawled in the grass at the bottom of the photo, a brimmed cap atop his bulldog face, his hand slightly blurred as he waved at the camera. In the middle, standing next to Michnik, was a slight, greying man, hands delicately clutched together, wearing a ski sweater embroidered with stylized reindeer. That was Lityński, to whom I had acquired a note of introduction from an acquaintance at home. If it was a graduating class photo, how many of them — now sitting in newly constituted parliaments and editorial offices — could have anticipated the world they would be graduating into just a year or so later?

That, in fact, was what Michnik was attempting to come to terms with in the essay Tom was reading as we flew above the clouds. "The final days of 1989 brought with them the end of the Communist era," his article bluntly began. "The system that had proclaimed itself the future of the world was buried in the ashes of burning Romanian towns. No doubt there will still be police and military relapses ... But the idea has died. For Communism, it is the end. At last."

I too had been struck by the image of those burning towns three months ago. One day the previous December, I'd seen a news story on television about an insurrection against the heretofore impregnable Romanian regime, in the city of Timișoara, near the Hungarian border. In that *annus mirabilis* of 1989, in swift succession, the Solidarity movement in Poland (in which Michnik, Kuroń, and Lityński were prominent) had defeated the Communist Party in elections; the Berlin Wall had buckled, then come down; the Czechs — led by their philosophical playwright, Havel — had carried out a "Velvet Revolution" in Prague's Wenceslas Square; and now something had happened in distant Romania.

Romania was so remote that there wasn't even video footage immediately available, merely a voice crackling on a line from Budapest, reporting extensive shooting. A few days later the regime collapsed, followed by abundant and gruesome television coverage, pictures of the hasty execution of the elderly Communist dictator, Nicolae Ceauşescu, and his wife. For all the finality of those images, it was difficult to discern the character of events there. Was a "popular revolution" in progress (there were nighttime crowds on the screen, tanks, flags, the sound of gunfire), or was Romania experiencing an internal Communist Party coup (a prominent party leader had emerged at the head of the newly cobbled-together provisional government)? It was in an interrogative mood that I plotted my itinerary.

Or rather, *our* itinerary, since I'd immediately fastened on Tom as my ideal fellow traveller. Ours was the sort of long-term friendship in which I could call up one day and out of a clear blue sky announce, "We have to go to Eastern Europe." Shouldn't those of us who had lived in a world divided by the so-called Iron Curtain attempt to comprehend its epochal fall? Or, as one writer put it, "You might just decide that the most important thing in your life this year was to find out the truth about something." Tom agreed to arrange tickets and contacts for a whirlwind trip to a half-dozen Eastern European capitals.

The somewhat strident opening of Michnik's piece (for I usually thought of him as a writer especially sensitive to nuances of history and language) was succeeded by some reminiscences of people he considered particularly important to the stirring events of recent years: the Russian physicist-turned-human-rights-activist Andrei Sakharov (whose graveside Michnik had attended only months before), and such others as his friend Havel (who had lately become the president of Czechoslovakia) and Hungary's Janos Kiš, a philosopher who shortly would be standing for office (successfully, as it turned out) in the March 1990 election there.

"Today I can't help wondering," Michnik mused, "what gave those people the strength? What made it possible for Sakharov, Kiš, Havel to live for years the way they did live? Why did they abandon academic careers and sacrifice freedom, calm, and personal security for a hopeless battle against the Communist leviathan? Not one of them ever declared himself to be a man of religious calling or a politician.

And yet, embroiling themselves in politics, they bore moral witness. And they prevailed over the political professionals of police dictatorships. How was that possible?"

But for modesty, Michnik could have added his own name to that list. There had been a famous occasion several years before, when an angry mob in a small town near Warsaw surrounded the local police station and seized two or three thoroughly frightened policemen. The men's lives hung on the thread of the crowd's mood. The authorities had branded the opponents of the regime "anti-socialist elements," and with characteristic Polish humour the slander had been turned into something of a joke; teenagers wore T-shirts that mockingly said, "Anti-socialist Element." From that crowd threatening to become a lynch mob, Michnik leapt onto the roof of an automobile and announced himself to the enraged masses. "You know me," he said, "I'm an 'anti-socialist element'." The crowd laughed, and the lives of the policemen were spared. (Only months later, Michnik was back in jail.)

The more pressing question, however, was what sort of Europe would emerge from the cataclysm. "The European spirit," Michnik observed, "is struggling with the narrowly nationalist one. ... This European mosaic of nationalities could be swept by a conflagration of border conflicts. These are unhappy nations, nations that have lived for years in bondage and humiliation. Complexes and resentments can easily explode. Hatred breeds hatred, force breeds force. And that way lies the path of the Balkanization of our 'native Europe'," he warned.

"For now two roads lie open before my country and to our newly freed neighbours. One road leads to border wars, the other to minimizing borders, reducing them to little more than road signs; one road leads to new barbed-wire fences, the other to a new order based on pluralism and tolerance; one road leads to nationalism and isolation, the other to a return to our 'native Europe'."

But what did that idea of "a return to our native Europe" mean? "A commitment to certain attributes of European culture," Michnik explained. "It means replacing the totalitarian dogmas with an attitude that presupposed a critical distance towards oneself, and it means respecting tolerance in public life and skepticism in intellectual matters."

I HAD BEEN TO Warsaw before, in 1981. I'd spent a week there at the end of a lengthy visit to Gdańsk, Poland, to record the stories of the workers at the Lenin Shipyard. Led by Lech Wałęsa, they had gone on strike in August 1980 in order to secure recognition for Solidarity, the first independent workers' organization in the so-called workers' states of Central and Eastern Europe.

Now, nearly ten years later, Tom and I stood at the entrance of a dogleg, dead-end lane lined with four-storey apartment buildings, tucked into a maze of narrow streets just a few blocks off Marszalkowska Boulevard, the main thoroughfare of downtown Warsaw. We had been travelling and gathering material about newly post-Communist Europe for several weeks, and had arrived at our last working stop, Warsaw, in mid-April, after a long train ride from Bucharest.

A crabapple tree, bursting with pink blossoms, stood at the corner of the tiny street. While we waited at the doorway of a building about two-thirds of the way down the lane where we had secured a sublet, we could hear, floating from a nearby open balcony, the sound of someone playing Chopin.

Peter Borkowicz, a furniture-maker and friend of ours in Vancouver, had arranged the apartment for us. It belonged to the Titkovs, who had been long-time friends of Peter's recently deceased father, Leonard Borkowicz, and who were on holiday in Israel for a month. Peter was friends with the Titkovs' daughter, an actress named Olga, who would be looking after us. So already there were a couple of generations whose connections we would have to sort out — brothers, husbands, an aunt of Peter's whom we had promised to visit, in-laws, ghosts, the lot.

For that matter, there were our own ties to Peter. I had met him years before, at a talk I was giving on Polish politics. Since political circles are famously intertwined, Tom too had in due course gotten to know him. Tom had been friends with the woman Peter married and with whom he'd recently had a child. Peter had started out in the theatre world, but was now working in hand-crafted furniture, a career shift that had to do with making a more secure living, given his new parental responsibilities. I didn't know him well, but I intuitively responded to the frizzy, lively energy and intelligence that seemed to match his frizzy hair. In any case, it was only natural that Tom would contact Peter about our trip to Poland, and ask him to put his connections to use. He'd come through, and eventually — gathered around a dinner table in Vancouver — Tom and I would report back to Peter.

The apartment in Warsaw was on the top floor. The living room, which also contained a couple of beds, gave out onto a balcony overlooking the storybook lane below. It joined a dining room (I immediately claimed the table as my writing space) that had a view into a tangled courtyard out back dominated by a large chestnut tree, its candle-shaped heaps of white blossoms in bloom. On the far side of the small kitchen, adjacent to the dining room and just off the entrance corridor, was a tiny child's room, with a narrow bed. It looked like a monk's cell, and I decided to sleep there, while Tom staked out the front room as his quarters.

"You must be Olga," I said, when she appeared at the door that afternoon. She was a fine-featured woman of about forty, and her long dark hair had a mahogany glow. "Peter sends his greetings."

"How are you?" she asked as we shook hands, smiling in recognition at the mention of Peter. "Was the train ride tiring?"

"No, it was all right," I said, and then, out of nowhere, I added, "But I've been thinking a lot about death."

While waiting for her, I'd found a copy, on her parents' bookshelves in the front room, of Tadeusz Konwicki's *A Minor Apocalypse* (1979). I happened to have brought along an English edition of it in my luggage. It was a novel written the year before Solidarity, in which the narrator, a version of Konwicki himself, is visited by two old comrades from the opposition who propose that he set himself on fire in front of the Communist Party headquarters that evening. "Here comes the end of the world," it opens. Perhaps it was thumbing through the Titkovs' copy that had produced the odd mood that led me to announce my brooding thoughts.

Olga took it in stride. She replied — even before offering the usual visitors' orientation about which key worked for which door, and what our duties might be (they consisted of nothing more elaborate than remembering to water the geraniums on the outside landing) — with a prefatory remembrance of how she had gotten to know Peter. He had arrived in Poland to work in a theatre company, and since she was in theatre, they had inevitably met ... which led to something of an explanation of the relationship between Peter and Leonard Borkowicz, whose first wife had immigrated to Canada long ago, taking Peter with her, so that it was only as an adult, really, that he had met his father.

Somewhere in that description of the family tree, which included the interlinked roots of the Titkovs, Olga remarked in passing, "You know about Borkowicz's death, of course." Though I didn't, I merely grunted, sensing that there was something hush-hush about it which one should know, but which one couldn't really admit to not knowing. Perhaps it would come out over the next days. She went on to describe some details of Borkowicz's funeral the previous autumn, which Peter had flown to Warsaw to attend.

After providing the household instructions, Olga had to dash — she had a rehearsal that evening. We would have dinner with her in a day or two, she promised, at which we could meet her brother, Andrzej. Unfortunately, her husband was in New York trying to sell a musical. Yes, she could make contacts for us with some of the people we wanted to talk to. I gave her — rather impetuously — a copy of a book I'd written about homoerotic desire; she knew a gay rock singer I might be interested in meeting. And then she was off to recite lines — by Chekhov, I think.

❧

IT IS NOT ENOUGH (or is even slightly deceptive) to say I had been in Warsaw before, and leave it at that. In fact, nearly ten years before, in 1981, I became friends with the singer in a rock band. The band was called, appropriately enough for the times, Crisis, and the singer's name was Mirek. Though it had been a long time ago — and what significance could one claim for a brief friendship? — nonetheless, when you return to a place where you've been touched by something emotionally important, it's almost as though the feeling is still there.

As soon as Tom and I arrived in the city — we were walking through the underpass beneath the intersection of Marszalkowska Boulevard and Jerozolimskie Avenue, the main crossroads in Warsaw — the familiar dank odour of the pedestrian tunnels beneath the city traffic evoked a whiff of nostalgia. During the week I spent in the city in 1981, Mirek and I had used that underpass to get from the Forum Hotel on one side of the Marszalkowska, where we ate late-night desserts, to the Metropol on the other side, where I had a room, and at whose lobby entrance he said good night to me.

Mirek and I met in Gdańsk. I'd arrived on a Thursday night, the eve of May Day, and put up at the hotel across the street from the train station. From the hotel room window I could see the dinosaur-like cranes of the shipyard looming in the shadow of streetlamps. I quickly struck up an acquaintance with a French journalist named Christine. She promised to take me out to the union's headquarters in a suburb on the edge of Gdańsk the following Monday, right after the weekend holiday.

Whatever conceptions or illusions I had about the great workers' holiday were immediately dashed. No Red Square parades (images stored in my mind from a repertoire of television clips) in this coastal city, where the workers had rebelled against the workers' state the summer before. Instead, the first day, I found myself on a union bus that drove out to Gdynia, the next shipyard town up the coast, where I was a half-comprehending witness to a flower-laying ceremony marking the deaths of workers a decade earlier, in one of the proto-rebellions before Solidarity.

I had the weekend to wander around. The real holiday, it turned out, was on Sunday, which commemorated the Constitution of 1791. That scrap of parchment had been Poland's bid to make common cause with the quasi-democratic Enlightenment, an ill-fated venture that resulted in a partition of the country that removed Poland from the maps of Europe until the end of World War I. In any case, I stumbled onto a crowd of maybe 25,000 people, and followed it across the square named for King Jan Sobieski as it moved toward the capacious St. Brigid's Catholic Church at the far end.

In the jostling but sombre crowd, I found myself alongside a young couple, Mirek and Barbara. He was in his early or mid-twenties, frail in a waiflike way, with short blond hair chopped in a semi-punk style. He wore jeans and a black suit jacket. She was his age, but more conventionally dressed in an understated polka-dot dress, and with a stylish hairdo. Both of them had enough English to explain what was going on as we were pressed together in the emotional crush of people — it was the first time the Communist regime had been forced, in response to the Solidarity union strikes, to legally permit Constitution Day ceremonies. The year before, people had been arrested when they tried to assemble for the commemoration.

We latched onto each other for the day. A crammed 11 a.m. mass in the church, speeches in the plaza, red and white wreaths of carnations draping the equestrian statue of the king, late lunch at the hotel restaurant, and by evening we were sauntering through the now-deserted Sobieski Square, the carnations shimmering with dew at the foot of the bronze mount. It was at that moment, I think, that I knew Communism was doomed. Not that I had any prescient insight about its exact demise — the Iron Curtain still seemed permanent — but simply that I had incontrovertible, firsthand evidence that people didn't believe in it. I still retained, as a self-defined leftist, an unrealistic hope that some genuine reformer would rescue the dream of socialism from which Communism had arisen, but the possibility seemed increasingly unlikely.

I don't recall if Mirek and I saw much of each other over the next few weeks. I was preoccupied with recording the chronicles of the shipyard workers who had organized the Solidarity movement, doing interviews for a book I was writing, *At the Lenin Shipyard* (1981). But when I arrived in Warsaw — I'd finished interviewing — I spotted a poster announcing a rock concert in which Mirek's group, Crisis, was fronting for a better-known band called Perfect.

At the end of Mirek's set, I went over to him. He seemed surprised and pleased that I had gone to the trouble of finding him, and immediately detached himself from the inevitable gaggle of admiring teenage fans. We went for coffee at the Forum, talking about everything from Poland itself (he was slightly cynical — the cynicism of a people whose hopes had been dashed throughout history) to the lead singer of Perfect (we agreed that he was a terrible narcissist). Among other things, I saw Mirek as emblematic of a new generation of Poles, cautious but decidedly curious about what might be a next, slightly different world.

After that, we saw each other frequently until I left. We took walks, ate at the hotels, and strolled through the tunnels of the underpass. Sometimes we went to the apartment of one of the musicians in the group, which was just a couple of blocks up Jerozolimskie. His name was Zbigniew and he was the leader, manager, and boss of the band. He had a tape of the recent concert, which he played on a primitive reel-to-reel recorder that had to be rewound by hand. "Just look at this," he said disgustedly, sneering at the tape deck as if it represented the entire mess of Poland. Then he'd bawl out Mirek for singing off-key, or not practising enough. Mirek endured these harsh criticisms while I, slightly embarrassed for him, gazed out the window at the gothic-Stalinist Palace of Culture and Science — an unwelcomed fraternal gift from the Soviet Union — that dominated the city as much as the Russians did Poland.

One evening, Mirek took me there to see a movie. It was by the Russian director Andrei Tarkovsky, and had been banned for some years but was now, in the Solidarity-caused thaw, suddenly available for viewing. Its story took place in the late Middle Ages — the soundtrack was in Russian and there were Polish subtitles — and what remained in my memory was an improbable canvas balloon or dirigible on which the movie's protagonist, clinging to its surface, careered over his peasant village. That image seemed emblematic of contemporary Poland, too.

Inevitably, one night Mirek said a final goodbye to me at my hotel entrance, and went off to join his friends. I went up to my room and stood at the window, trying to pick out, among the figures walking on the far side of the boulevard, his form as it disappeared into the crowd. Before the year was out, martial law was declared in Poland to forestall a threatened Soviet military invasion and the Solidarity movement had been driven underground. Now it was almost a decade later, and the future of Poland I'd glimpsed in 1981 had arrived.

ANNA S. LIVED IN a tiny apartment in an indistinguishable row of concrete blocks of flats on the far side of Warsaw. In the early evening, the taxi driver had to cruise slowly up and down several rows of those identical blocks before we were able to pick out the dimly lit number we were seeking. I had her name from the same person who had provided the note of introduction to Jan Lityński.

She was a woman in her late thirties, married with two children, who worked as a translator. Her husband, an academic of some sort, was in Dubrovnik, Yugoslavia, at a conference, earning some much-needed foreign currency. She settled us in a cramped, book-lined study. The older boy, Milosz, about ten, presently wandered to another part of the flat, while the younger one, Karol, a six-year-old, crawled over her, demanding attention. Anna's hair was drawn back in a bun; she rested her chin on the palm of one hand, her fingers nervously stroking the side of her nose beneath the rims of her glasses. She looked tired, as if she was drawing on depleted reserves of energy to see us.

She wanted to know, reasonably enough, who we were, what we were going to do with the material we were gathering, whether we were connected to a newspaper. "And are you going to use my name?" Anna asked.

"It would be up to you," Tom said soothingly. He had the same habit as Anna, I noticed, of absently stroking the side of his nose.

"Well, I don't know," she said. "My opinions and my views about the situation in Poland are not very popular, and are very pessimistic on the whole."

"Fair enough," I assured her.

"We'll see," she said. "We'll see what happens, and what I'll say." And then she briefly laughed, as if amused by the thought that what she might say was unpredictable. "So, I'll make you coffee," she said, rising. "Do you take sugar?"

"You said that some of your opinions are unpopular," Tom reminded her, after she returned from the kitchen and had shunted off the younger boy to join his brother.

"Yes, well, all criticism against the present new government is unpopular," Anna replied. "If I talk to people and I say, 'I think there is something wrong with the situation of books,' for example — there are so many taxes on them. Because what the government did, they stopped all the subsidies; culture is treated like factories, everybody must earn for himself, so books have suddenly become very expensive. But if I say that in some cases this policy is no good, everybody says, 'But how should it be?' I don't know how it should be" — she shrugged — "because I am not an economist. I only see how this situation is very hard for people."

She and her husband, she emphasized, were better off than most people, because they had access to foreign earnings, but still, "we eat all the money we have, because food is so expensive; we buy fewer books than before. Definitely fewer."

Anna was reacting to the newly imposed post-Communist economic program, a shock-treatment transition to the free market, recommended by the foreign experts from capitalist countries. But her complaints were not at all ideological; they were literal, emanating directly from her experience — almost, one could say, from her body, which sagged with a touch of exhaustion and anxiety, even as her younger child came back into the cramped study and clung to her.

"Today I went to the bookshop that has all the interesting books," she said, "the ones that either haven't been published before, or were published in the underground. I wanted to buy a book or two, but the price is 16,000 złotys, or 18,000 even, for a thin book. Well, it's too much."

"And the price before?" I asked.

"Six months ago, it was less than half — 3,000 or 4,000 złotys. And of course all the wages are blocked: they are raised very, very slightly each three months. I agree that maybe it's the way of starting a new economic system, a new political system, but I'm very pessimistic about the results, because now we have 'world prices,' it's called." And the "world prices" didn't get you very far on an average wage of 500,000 złotys monthly (about $50 USD).

"Now they are planning to put the prices of the apartments up," Anna added.

I asked what the current rent was.

"For this flat here, we pay — let me think, it changes almost every two months, it goes up — but now it's about 60,000 złotys. If the plan is realized, I think it will be 300,000."

"But if the rent goes to 300,000 and a person is making 500,000, how can they ...?" I wondered.

"Well, exactly," she said. "What they say — I heard it on the radio the other day — is that people will stop paying rent, like they do in Brazil. In fact, it's becoming more and more the general opinion that we are going into not the kind of capitalism in the U.S.A., Canada, or Western Europe, but the kind in Brazil."

I noticed I was of two minds about what she was saying. I liked the precision with which Anna presented the concrete details of her own daily life. The actual prices of things, the calculation of those prices against the monthly wage, the ominous anticipation of the next phases of the "economic shock therapy," as the plan, now only a few months old, was described. Yet, at the same time, even though it was illogical on my part, I was resistant to her justified criticisms. I had scant loyalty to the capitalist panacea of the marketplace, yet I found myself cheering for the success of the plan, which had been dreamed up by an American professor and the Solidarity economists. I didn't want to hear Anna's apprehensions; I put some of them down to the class snobbery of intellectuals, and dismissed others as the inevitable temporary glitches of a vast transformation. Still, as she spoke, I gradually built up a picture of this intelligent, worried woman, more or less housebound with her children, listening to serious radio and television programs as she did household chores, developing her own opinions.

Anna was also dubious about the capacity of Polish workers. "It's always been one of the characteristics of the Polish people," she insisted, "this not wanting to work, trying to get as much money from nothing as possible."

"But all of my Polish friends here work very hard," I objected.

"Well, yes, but you move in certain circles," she replied.

"The most popular theory," Anna continued, "is that it started in the years when Poland was divided between Russia, Prussia, and Austria, that not working for the occupiers was all right. There were only about twenty years in between. Then came the German occupation, then it was the Communist system. Nobody works for himself. The people in the shops, they got paid, no matter whether they sold anything or not, so why bother?" She straightened up into a shrug, and spread her hands in a gesture of helplessness.

And that wasn't the worst of it, in her view. "There is something very frightening that is now coming up ... always hate for people that are different. There are many more slogans on the wall against, for example, Jewish people" — her eyes widened to emphasize the absurdity of it — "and there are basically no Jews in Poland. A few hundred."

She offered the example of people with AIDS trying to establish a hospice in Warsaw who were almost killed by people in the neighbourhood. "Even the doctors don't want to take care of such people. If the doctors have such attitudes, then ordinary people are absolutely sure that breathing the same air and drinking water from the same well gives you AIDS. I don't know, I'm not very happy about my children growing up in this country," she added, subsiding into her chair.

I was interested in what she had to say about Jews and people with AIDS. It is a reporter's (or an anthropologist's) rule of thumb that when you go to a place you don't know, one of the best ways to learn about it is to ask about the status of that society's scape-goats. In many European countries, especially Catholic ones like Poland, the people to ask about are Jews and gays. In others places you ask about the Roma, or about the status of women. The state of the scapegoated is one of the more reliable measures of the conditions of a given culture.

When I asked Anna further questions, she pulled herself out of her weariness to deliver an additional litany of worries: crime, drugs, poverty, nationalism, the Catholic Church's backward views on abor-tion. "I'm afraid of the atmosphere of this country that my sons will be growing up in," she said.

"People in North America," I suggested lamely, "are also com-plaining about crime and drugs and homelessness."

"Well, then, these are about the only things in which we are nearer to the West," she said.

At the end, as we were gathering our things to leave, Anna's mood lifted in a sudden moment of reminiscence. "The best time was the last part of 1980, and 1981, when Solidarity started, because then — well, I was ten years younger." Tom and I laughed with her, acknowledging that so were we. "It seemed so wonderful," she said. "Everything was wonderful, and it didn't matter that there was nothing in the shops, that you couldn't buy anything. I remember once I was talking with my best friend — we were pregnant at the same time, she with her second child and I with my first — and we were sitting and talking. There was some strike going on, and we were saying, 'What happens if the Russians come?' and her husband said, 'You shouldn't worry, any Russian tank will take you to the hospital for half a litre of vodka.'" She remembered when they had made jokes, but quickly added, "Then came martial law."

I too remembered it that way. When I had been in Poland before — only months before the military coup ordered by the new party boss, General Wojciech Jaruzelski — it had been a time of dreaming, of tales of heroic deeds in the shipyards, of young artists who sang punk songs. When I left Gdańsk, I'd hosted a farewell dinner for the friends I'd acquired during the weeks of interviewing. We ate at the Grand Hotel on the beach at Sopot. That evening someone spoke of the legendary wild white boars who were reputed to wander the dune grasses at night. We had walked out onto the long wooden jetty that looked across the Baltic to Sweden, and for a moment it felt as if we had left the century — as if, amid the beaches, the imaginary beasts, the grandeur of the old hotel, we had been transported to an earlier time, from which we would be able to chart a course that might avert the horrors Poland had experienced across the twentieth century.

THE MOMENT I SAW Slawek Starosta — the gay rock singer Olga had suggested I meet — I recognized him as an updated, post-Communist version of Mirek. Starosta poked his head into the cubbyhole at the University of Warsaw where we were waiting for him, to assure us he'd be along in a few minutes. I got a glimpse of a young man, mid-twenties, with a blond brush cut — one lock of hair artfully falling onto his forehead — fashionable gold wire-rimmed glasses, the high collar of an embroidered white Russian peasant shirt.

Until that moment, I had harboured the absurd fantasy that I might run into Mirek again. Instead, the new era was providing a contemporary counterpart in his place, someone more confident, more ambitious. Mirek belonged to another time, a time that was gone and, I intuited, whose passing had taken him with it.

The manager of Slawek's two-person group, which was called Balkan Electric, brought Tom and me coffee as we waited in the high-ceilinged, narrow room that was one of a warren of offices in the student building. I sat next to a tall window whose long wooden shutter had been turned back, providing a view onto Nowy Świat, the busy avenue outside the university. The manager introduced himself as Jarek. He was in his late twenties, a graduate student in political science, with a closely cropped reddish beard and a dark shirt buttoned to the collar. Slawek was momentarily tied up with the arrangements for a concert that night, Jarek apologized.

Instead of waiting around, dawdling over our coffee, as I'd expected, the three of us immediately plunged into a conversation about the very thing Tom and I had puzzled over when we joked about being "leftists — whatever that means." It began with the usual dissection — at least usual when you're talking to Polish intellectuals — of complex elements of Polish society and their effect, in turn, upon the equally complex current situation.

Jarek's starting point was the modern formation of the working class and the rapid movement of the peasantry to the cities after World War II. I remembered Anna's unhappy remarks about workers, though she had qualified her criticisms with a historical explanation of the resistance to working for the enemy. "During a very short period," Jarek said, "they became workers in states in which the working class had a special status. They heard from everywhere that this special class should rule the country, should rule the world."

Oddly, it was the success of the Communists in instilling working-class consciousness — even as the workers saw that it was the Party and not themselves who were doing the ruling — that had given rise to Solidarity. "In 1980, Solidarity as a workers' movement was acting against what they rightly saw was not the workers' party, but a bureaucracy." And the same was true in the past year, when the Party collapsed. "But this year," Jarek continued, "we can say that what is happening is really against the working class."

When I looked up from my coffee cup, a bit puzzled, he elaborated. "Nobody is going to say, 'You should have a social service because you are a worker.' Nowadays, it's, 'We should handle our own business ... and we should help ourselves.' And it really means that egalitarianism, which was very popular in 1980 and which created the movement against bureaucracy, is not valued anymore. It's a real break, a big change in society." Was that his personal feeling too? He began by demurring — "I have no opinion" — but then he added, "It is not possible within a few months to come out of real, bureaucratic socialism into very poor and very aggressive liberalism, which means you can die in the street if you aren't able to work."

I noticed that Tom had suddenly perked up, and I was feeling it too. What had begun as a polite conversation to pass the time was unexpectedly revealing itself as fully engaging in its own right. The habit of interviewing often produced pleasant surprises. The Polish word for "interview" — *wywiad* (pronounced "vivyat") — seemed to hint at such intellectual pleasures; its sound suggested the English word "vivid." The interview was a relationship in which a kind of vividness might be achieved by virtue of the unspoken permission to say things that strangers wouldn't normally say to each other. While it courted the danger of superficiality (of course we wouldn't come to know each other in an hour or two), it harboured the possibility of unexpected vivacity. Identities shifted — the rock band manager became an astute political observer; the foreign journalists were not merely journalists but also participants and familiar with the references, the vocabulary.

"I was not a Communist," Jarek began again. "I was working in an organization which was socialist." We didn't interrupt to determine the distinction between Communists, socialists, and whatever other shadings might exist in his political vocabulary. "Many people who were non-socialists were members," Jarek went on. "But I was a leftist — and what really happened in our country in the sixties and seventies is that leftists were destroyed."

It was the first time I'd heard someone in Eastern Europe use the word "leftist" in its familiar sense. A decade ago, when I'd asked about the meanings of "left" and "right," my Polish acquaintances had taken great pleasure in sending up those terms. "Okay, let's begin with the Communist Party," they began. "Now that's" — there was a significant pause, as if they were trying to locate it — "the far right." And then everyone broke up in laughter.

"To be a *leftist*" — in some official or practical sense, we understood Jarek to be saying — "meant to be a Marxist-Leninist. Anything which was not linked with the official ideology of the Party should be stamped out and persecuted as illegal activity against the state." With the entire space for leftism occupied by the Party, there had been no room for alternative versions of a non-capitalist politics, and leftism in general withered.

"At the same time, the Communists knew that social support for the regime was dropping. So they began to negotiate with the Polish Catholic Church, which really meant that Communists killed leftists in our country, and gave special privileges to the rightists," Jarek said.

But wasn't the present government — the Solidarity regime of people like Michnik, Lityński, Kuroń, even the weary present prime minister, Tadeusz Mazowiecki — "leftist"? "Yes," Jarek was prompt to concede, "it's a good centre-left government at the moment, but then you have to take into account the currents and tendencies within Solidarity. You see, the Solidarity 'court' in Gdańsk is dominated by rightists, who also want the Church to have power."

"Court?" I repeated, to make sure he had used that word in the royalist sense.

"Yes, the entourage around Wałesa," Jarek said.

So, even if the present Solidarity figures in government were centre-leftists, while Prime Minister Mazowiecki represented the tradition of intellectual Catholicism, both the economic circumstances of the country and the fractures within Solidarity meant that they found themselves as advocates — or, more than advocates, administrators, even legislators — of a "fast track" transition to the free market. In the long litany of ironies that make up Polish political history, the workers' movement that had ousted the "workers' party" was now issuing layoff slips to the workers.

Just as Jarek was about to go on, Slawek arrived.

There was an abrupt shift of mood and subject. Jarek and Slawek briefly talked business and about that night's concert, and then Slawek turned to us, ready to fulfill the combined obligations of rising rock star and gay activist.

"Can you come to the gig tonight?" he asked.

"Sure," I said, picking up a nod of agreement from Tom. "But first I'd like to know something about the gay movement in Poland."

Slawek sighed, tossing back his head, allowing the one long lock at the front of his brush cut to bob up and flop onto his forehead.

"Does everyone from the West ask you that?" Tom chuckled, half apologizing for our obviousness.

Slawek laughed, took a breath, and said, "So, from the beginning ..." And since even the two or three years to be recounted seemed like an eternity to someone his age, he sighed again. "The beginning ..."

THAT AFTERNOON, I WAS on the telephone to Olga from her parents' apartment. "We saw Slawek this morning," I reported.

"Oh, good. How did it go?"

"Fine. Tom and I found him very charming. Ambitious, but charming." Tom had remarked, when we'd finished the interview with Slawek and Jarek and were on our way to our next appointment, "Well, he's full of himself, but they all are at that age."

I laughed, as much at the avuncular heights from which we viewed the young these days as at the accuracy of his observation. "Though not offensive," I amended. "Not offensive," Tom agreed.

It turned out that Olga and I had a few minutes to chat — our dinner wasn't for an hour and her crowded schedule also happened to have a gap in it.

"We're seeing them for an early dinner tonight, and then we're going to Balkan Electric's concert."

"Did you meet the other singer?"

"Violeta?" I said, recalling the name of the curly-haired young Bulgarian woman (hence the "Balkan" part of the group's name) who was Slawek's stage partner. "Just for a minute. And we had a talk with the manager."

"Slawek's boyfriend," Olga said. Until then, it hadn't occurred to me that they might be lovers.

"Oh, and we saw Peter's aunt afterwards," I suddenly remembered, even as I did a quick mental double take to reconfigure Slawek and Jarek's relationship in my mind.

"Yes. Maryla. How was it?"

"A comedy of errors," I said. "She had a message for Peter in Polish which we recorded on the tape, and that was fine."

"That's for the papers Peter has to sign. He should've done it when he came for his father's funeral, but it was all such a hurry, you know." Olga knew all about it — the details of familial property settlements.

"But I had gotten the idea, from Peter I think, that Aunt Maryla was in favour of the Party, still, so all my questions were designed to get her to explain why she believed in Communism."

Olga burst out laughing.

"It was a disaster, of course," I admitted. "At one point, after I asked a bunch of questions about Marx, she said, 'I suspect you're leftists.'"

Olga thought that was very funny — the bumbling truth-seekers versus the wise old aunt. I can't remember how we got onto the next thing. Perhaps we were talking about the time Peter first returned to Poland to get to know his father, Leonard, but she said, referring to old Borkowicz, "… and he had just been retired from his job."

Olga was about to go on to another thought when I interrupted. "What do you mean, he'd just been retired?"

"Well, in 1967, when the Arab-Israeli war broke out," Olga began. "Just a second, I have to turn the kettle off," she said. "After that war, in 1968," Olga continued when she returned to the phone a couple of minutes later, "there was a very big wave of anti-Semitism in Poland, and all of the intelligentsia, and most of the Jews who had any kind of post in the Party or government, were immediately relieved of their positions. You know, they were accused of being Zionists and … well, any kind of Jewish background."

I suddenly recalled that Olga's parents, whose apartment I was in at that moment, were on holiday in Israel. "So, your father too?"

"Oh, yes, of course. I mean, Peter's father, Leonard, wasn't a practising Jew, or anything like that, but he had a Jewish background, and for anti-Semites, you know, it doesn't really matter."

"So old Borkowicz was basically a Party figure."

"And a very distinguished one," Olga said, launching into an account of Leonard Borkowicz's career. As early as his teenage years, Borkowicz had been imprisoned for being a Communist activist.

Before World War II, he had already spent perhaps a total of seven years in jail. When the war broke out, Leonard ended up in the Red Army that was being formed in Poland — he, his brother, and his sister.

"You mean Aunt Maryla?"

"Yes," Olga confirmed. The brother died at the battle of Lenino; meanwhile, Borkowicz worked his way up the ranks to a fairly high officer's position, colonel or lieutenant colonel. After the war, the party appointed him governor of the district of Szczecin, a sizeable province along the Baltic that had been part of Germany but was now allocated to Poland as part of the war settlement. It was a complicated situation, involving both the resettlement of Germans and extensive reconstruction, and Borkowicz had apparently made a success of it. There was a book on the subject, and even a documentary film.

Afterwards, Borkowicz became the Polish ambassador to Czechoslovakia and was stationed in Prague for a couple of years. But the happiest part of his life was after Prague, when he was appointed head of the Polish film industry, a job he'd evidently enjoyed thoroughly. Peter had told me how, even after his dismissal, his father had maintained his contacts with artists, so that when Peter went to Poland as a teenager to meet Leonard, the renowned director Andrzej Wajda turned up for dinner one night.

The end of Borkowicz's career had been abrupt. The 1967 Arab-Israeli War coincided with one of the periodic convulsions within the Party and the country. The Israeli connection, however spurious, provided an excuse to make officials of Jewish origin — they had a long history in the party and were irrationally resented, both inside and outside of its ranks — the scapegoats for the crisis of the moment.

"They retired him instantly, just like that," Olga said. "And he was still a young man, you know. He would have been ... well, he was seventy-seven when he died in 1989, so he would have been —"

"Mid-fifties," I said. "And was your father also thrown out?"

"That's right. My father was the minister of health. He and Leonard had been friends since the war. Actually, my mother was in the Red Army with Leonard. But the whole thing was much harder on Leonard. You know, my father was a doctor, so when he was thrown out he was able to go into private practice. But with somebody like Leonard, who was a professional bureaucrat ... well, it was very hard. In Poland in those days, everybody had a job, and that was one of the ways the state used to punish people. So basically he was left with unemployment, with nothing."

I couldn't recall if I had seen photographs of Leonard Borkowicz at Peter's house, or if Tom had once told me about a dinner at Peter's when the elder Borkowicz was visiting from Poland. In any case, I had an image in my mind of a lean, fit man with a rakish moustache, resembling Peter and similarly animated. Talking to Olga now, I had to take into account that beneath the present surface — rock musicians, Anna's thoughtful worries, the new entrepreneurial spirit — there were also long, tangled histories like those of her and Peter's fathers, lives of a generation now coming to an end. The dream, as well as the nightmare of the dream, whose responsibility they had accepted, had ended. They had awakened to its emptiness, or had turned to other faiths (did that explain the Titkovs' holiday in Israel?).

"Look, I have afternoon rehearsals this week, and I'm due there now," Olga said, "but why don't you and Tom come for dinner tomorrow night? My brother Andrzej will come to get you around six. Is that okay?"

SLAWEK AND JAREK PICKED us up at the Titkovs' and — all of us crammed into their Polski Fiat — we drove to a Vietnamese restaurant they liked. Slawek was wearing an outlandish, multicoloured, bright pastel costume, a sort of jumpsuit made out of flimsy polyester. The shirt part had only one lapel-wing on the collar; the other half was in the style of Russian peasant smocks. I figured it was something he'd be wearing on stage that night.

"Yes, but it's part of Balkan Electric's clothing line," the rock singer explained. He stood up at the table in order to turn around and show us what I took to be a large, garish designer label, in Polish, on the back.

"It says," Jarek translated, "' ... and it's cheap, too.' You know, like, you can afford it."

"Well, Balcerowicz would approve of your industriousness," I teased, referring to the finance minister and his plan to encourage exactly such entrepreneurial ventures.

They ignored me and went on to describe their idea of setting up a bed-and-breakfast arrangement for gay tourists in Poland. And then there was talk of record contracts, foreign tours, making the hit charts. They were, in that way, just like young, ambitious music producers in Paris or London or New York. They were not at all like the lost Mirek, who sang, not toward any horizon of success (no such horizon existed then), but simply to say something about how things were at that moment.

We consumed the spring rolls and wonton soup, and while we waited for the pork brochettes we went on to discuss the presidential ambitions of Lech Wałesa — it was what everybody was talking about at the moment. Anna had declared her disapproval to us. So had Peter's Aunt Maryla. "He's not the right person," she had said. "He should be the leader of the trade unions, not the president."

For a moment, I tuned out of the chatter about the charismatic Wałesa. Instead I was recalling what Maryla had said earlier in the day, at the end of our conversation. It had almost slipped my mind.

An image of her tiny apartment — coffee cups and sugar-crusted cookies on a clear glass plate laid out carefully on a small table — reappeared before me as well as the sense she conveyed of her own dignity. When I asked her if she had ever expected the end of Communism, she said, "I never thought I would live to see this."

"Do you feel a great disappointment in terms of your own life?" I asked. All those years in the Party, the anti-Semitic dismissals, a minuscule, nearly worthless pension at the end. Again, it was one of those "rude" questions you would only think of asking in an interview.

"My own?" she asked.

"Yes."

"No. Goethe said that to be sorry for what you've done in your life means to betray yourself," she replied.

"Well, once Goethe has been cited ..." I said, trying to turn her remark into a what-more-can-be-said pleasantry to conclude our chat. But to her, it hadn't been a mere pleasantry.

"Wałesa says he doesn't want to run to become president," Jarek was saying when I returned from my reveries. "He says he's running only because he wants to make the changes faster. This is not true. He wants to be a president."

In the car on the way to the concert, Slawek mentioned that he'd be performing his latest song that evening. It had been occasioned by a project he'd undertaken on AIDS education.

"I decided to write a song — just a love song," he explained. It was called "Do Love, Don't Kill."

"Like 'Make Love, Not War'?" I asked.

"Yeah. It's really our first song in Polish, even though the title's in English, because I wanted people to understand what we're singing about. The song, actually, is not about safe sex. It's more general, about love and ... there's one small fragment in the text where you can find out that I'm singing this love song to a guy."

I'd wanted to know how explicit or "out" he was. "You and Jarek seem to be pretty discreet as a couple," I observed. "But are there times when you've had to make clear your sexual preference?"

"Well, *clear*," Slawek replied, drawing out that word. "I mean, I don't like to be over-homosexual. I don't like anything that is too clear. That's straight, or that's serious. So no, I never gave an interview where I said, I'm gay, or I'm homosexual. But always I make some remark, like I gave an interview and said, 'Balkan Electric loves young and handsome men.' I think it's clear enough."

I wasn't sure what I wanted from Slawek, or what I was looking for. Well, I did know. I was nostalgically looking for Mirek, and, for better or worse, Solidarity as it had been. Back when I had interviewed the workers at the Lenin Shipyard, they had joked about the impossibility of "privatization" and instead were groping toward a notion of industries run by a "workers' council" within the context of a semi-socialist economy. "After all," they said, "we can't return the shipyard to the Lenin family." But the present moment was deromanticized: the working-class hero had become a populist with demagogic possibilities; the gay young rock star, for all his daring in a context like that of Poland, managed his identity with a self-aware, understated, fashionably entrepreneurial touch.

"You know, for me it's like I went through twenty years of the gay liberation movement in six months," Slawek said. "I mean, coming out to my parents, the gay-is-good thing, militancy, the infighting of gay politics, AIDS, everything. It was all speeded up." I sensed that everything in Poland had been speeded up in the same way — democracy, capitalism, individual lives.

Jarek found a parking place in front of the Remont student club. Early arrivals were standing around on the sidewalk. Going down the steps into its semi-basement past a ticket taker, I recognized the club as the one in which I had heard Mirek sing. Jarek and Slawek went into the hall to set up.

There was a large foyer, with walls painted black, to hang out in before the show began. Along one side was a bar where you could get beer and soft drinks. Tom bought me a mineral water. Most of the space was taken up by a raised lounge area with table and chairs; some kids sat on the ledge of the platform. A couple of televisions were showing safe-sex educational videos made in Norway.

Once we were inside the auditorium, people pressed together in the darkness, standing. Slawek and Violeta, accompanied by synthesizers, tambourines, and rattles, appeared on stage and performed a set of rock songs; lilting Bulgarian folk melodies meshed with the percussive thump we'd all been raised with. We were swept into the rhythms. Someone released a beach-ball-sized balloon that bounced over the crowd, an occasional hand punching it back up into the air when it drifted close enough to touch.

JAN LITYŃSKI'S OFFICE WAS in a corner of a chunky four-storey labour ministry building in one of the side streets of downtown

Warsaw, just behind the Forum Hotel on Marszalkowska Boulevard.

Lityński was sitting at the far side of the room, in front of a glowing green computer screen, when the assistant ushered us in. He detached himself from the machine and came over to join us. We sat on opposite sides of his work table. The ski sweater had been succeeded by an inexpensive, somewhat shabby suit, but he was recognizably the slight, greying man, worn beyond his forty-five or so years, whom we had seen in the *New York Times* photograph.

Despite his accountant-like appearance, during the 1980s — from the inception of martial law in 1981 until the resurfacing of the opposition at the end of the decade — it was people such as Lityński who were arrested and tried, who served time in jails and internment camps, escaped, and issued declarations from the underground. They had, in Michnik's phrase, borne "moral witness." In the West, we had almost forgotten about them.

"It was a strange and interesting time," Lityński reflected, when I asked him about it. "The struggle between the government and Solidarity was like a positional war. It was obvious that nobody was able to win. And in some sense," he added, "it was a lost period. Because under the cover of martial law, the Communists tried to make economic reform. But they failed. They destroyed the whole system, the whole economy, practically, with martial law, but they didn't build any other system."

"But wasn't it also a lost period personally for many people?"

He made a clearing sound in his throat as he considered how to revisit this past.

"Do you remember where you were on December 13, 1981?" I asked, slightly shifting tack; this was the date that martial law had been declared.

"I'd just come back from some lectures in the south of Poland," he answered. "We were forming what were called self-management clubs. When I got to Warsaw, the telephones had been cut off. I returned to my flat and the police were already there."

There was a soft knock at the door. It was the assistant, bringing coffee and a sheaf of papers, which Lityński thumbed through.

"These are the month's unemployment figures," he explained, pushing the papers in my direction. There were columns of numbers listing the jobless by cities and regions. The total came to about a quarter of a million people. "We're trying, according to the plan, to hold the figure to about 400,000."

Though we were urged by the present — fluid, troubling, unknowable — it was the lost years of the past that drew me. What had he thought then?

"I felt from the very beginning that it was a kind of tragi-farce. In the internment camp the conditions were quite good. We had books, we could write. Some people said they were tragic conditions, but it was not true," he testified. "But it was also a comedy. In the street, people were being arrested for wearing Solidarity badges."

Lityński had gone on trial, along with Michnik and Kuroń, in the fall of 1982. "We were sentenced to two and a half years." But he'd escaped the following year and melted into the Solidarity underground in Warsaw. They had been desultory years. The structures and committees they attempted to organize, the occasional demonstration they set up from the shadows, the manifestos that were issued, had a certain futility to them. "But we signed our statements with our names," Lityński quietly insisted.

"Did you have to move around?"

"It was a very complicated system of changing flats, but we practically lived a normal life. Yet it was a very bad situation. It was normal life without normal responsibility. Very demoralizing," he said, then added, "It's much easier to be in prison and afterwards get back into normal life than it is to return from the underground."

The phone rang. While Lityński talked to someone at the other end, Tom and I exchanged a connecting glance as we listened to the traffic outside in the sunny spring forenoon. We had developed a sort of telepathy while conducting interviews, a delicate sensing of which one of us ought to "lead" the questioning. I appreciated Tom's patience with my drawn-out pursuit of the details of an old story.

"That was from Gdańsk, a friend," Lityński explained, when he'd hung up. Solidarity was holding its first congress since the fall of

the Communist government — actually, its first congress since just
before martial law was declared nearly a decade ago.

"How's it going?" I asked.

"My friend said it's very boring," he chuckled, and we, veteran
meeting-goers ourselves, laughed with him.

Solidarity had outgrown its trade-union origins long ago, but now
its character as a civic movement — born at a time when the notion
of civil society had been repressed — was coming apart at the seams.
Proto-parties were emerging from its factions. "Wałesa is a real
problem," Lityński remarked. I was still interested in why, and how,
Communism had fallen.

At the end — in late 1987, through 1988, and into the spring of
1989 — power had changed hands at a series of "round-table discus-
sions," as they were called. The process had been imperceptible to
observers outside the situation. Lityński had been part of the sub-
table negotiations concerning the mining industry. I asked him if
it had been obvious at the time that Jaruzelski's government would
have to make concessions, allowing the re-legalization of Solidarity.

"To me it was quite obvious, and to many of us, that we weren't
paying anything," Lityński said, "that every agreement was to our
benefit." He shrugged. "We had nothing to offer. It was obviously
the beginning of the end of the system."

"But surely Jaruzelski's aim had been for the Party to retain
power," I said.

"They had no choice once the process started," Lityński said. "Of
course, nobody predicted it would develop so fast. And yes, they
hoped that they could save the power." But the Party made mistakes
— technical mistakes, Lityński called them — when they agreed to
the first partial elections, which would permit Solidarity to gain
parliamentary representation while the Communists retained their
formal majority. They hadn't anticipated that the results of the election, technicalities aside, would spell the party's doom.

"Had the Party abandoned all ideological beliefs by then?" I
wondered.

"They had lost a sense of their existence. In the election they tried to attack us on TV, but it was ridiculous. Of course, it didn't seem so ridiculous then," he amended. "The campaign was a struggle about memory: they tried to remind people of the disorder of the last period of Solidarity, before martial law, and we tried to remind them of the first period of Solidarity, of hope."

We went downstairs and walked toward the nearby Forum Hotel for lunch, through the falling petals of the blossoming fruit trees that lined the side streets. Lityński asked how we were getting on in Warsaw.

"We were at a rock concert last night," Tom reported.

"Oh, yes. Which one?"

"A group called Balkan Electric."

"Oh, they're one of the best right now," Lityński said. Tom and I exchanged a surprised glance.

"You listen to rock music?" Tom asked him.

It turned out that our shy labour ministry official was rather thoroughly knowledgeable. As we strolled toward the hotel, he recalled that during the days of the underground he and a co-fugitive — a man named Bujak, who was the head of the Warsaw underground — found themselves in a strange apartment, headphones in place, lost in the sounds of the Beatles' *Abbey Road* album. We laughed at the incongruity of a world in which the authorities scoured the streets for opponents who had disappeared, borne away on rock 'n' roll.

The ground-floor lobby of the hotel was unexpectedly crowded with noisy teenagers. They appeared to be in some sort of uniform, and most of them had knapsacks. As we threaded our way through their loud chatter in various languages, I saw that it wasn't exactly uniforms, but that they were wearing similar clothing, lots of short-sleeved white shirts and blouses, and then I noticed that most of the boys were sporting yarmulkas, and that there was a scattering of blue-and-white Israeli flags. They were young Jews.

We'd been haunted by the presence of actual and remembered Jews in the last days: Anna's complaints about the absurdity of the current anti-Semitic remarks — "and there are, basically, no Jews in Poland, a few hundred" — the stories about the party purge of old Borkowicz and Titkov decades ago; Olga, her brother Andrzej, Michnik himself. Still, finding a group of Jewish teenagers in the hotel lobby, in sudden profusion, was like happening upon a herd of unicorns.

It was some sort of Israeli-sponsored youth convention in which the youngsters — according to the banners and signs that Lityński translated for us — would be travelling to Auschwitz-Birkenau to tour the concentration camps. Their natural ebullience jarred against the grisly prospect that awaited them.

But the young Jews were not the only mythical creatures on view. There was one last ghostly apparition. At the door of the restaurant, a man was coming out as we were going in, and we squeezed past each other.

Once seated at the linen-covered table, Lityński remarked, "That was my secret policeman."

At first I didn't know who he was referring to, then I tried to recall the nondescript figure we'd passed a moment before.

"Your secret policeman?" I asked, puzzled by the possessive pronoun.

"Yes, that's the man who was assigned to keep me under surveillance." Lityński seemed amused that history had contrived to make them diners at the same restaurant. We glanced back at the empty doorway.

The matter of belief continued to nag at me, even as lunch was drawing to a close. Perhaps I was only wondering about my own convictions. If the Party had ended up without belief, wasn't it nonetheless possible that the ideas in whose name they had ineptly ruled still meant something? "Or has Marxism become utterly meaningless?" I asked.

Lityński didn't answer immediately. He lit a cigarette and, through exhaled smoke, finally declared, "Yes, it's the end of Marxism as an ideology." He paused. "All over the world. Not only here. I think that Marx is a very interesting thinker, but not a man whose ideas can create political movements. Now Marx finds his proper place in history as a philosopher."

"A philosopher?" I repeated.

"Yes, understood by specialists," Lityński confirmed. "Nobody knows what the 'left' is —" Once more, the puzzling definition of ourselves appeared before us.

"I think of Kuroń and Michnik as the left," I interjected.

"They are described as leftists, but what does it mean today?" He shrugged, perhaps including himself in that fading definition. "Of course, there is a difference of attitude between various groups," he granted, "but the left is no longer a reality, as it still may be in the West. Here everybody simply connects it with the former system."

"So if Marx returns to philosophy, Lenin simply returns to history," I suggested. I recalled Konwicki's mockery in *A Minor Apocalypse*, describing how, from the aging party building "already showing cracks at various spots," a vast white banner fluttered in the breeze, hysterically proclaiming, "We have built socialism!"

Lityński seemed willing to let it rest there. "Lenin returns to history," he exhaled.

IN ADDITION TO THE interviews, collecting individual histories, and the rest of our "gathering material" activities, Tom and I had our own lives during our stay in Warsaw, moments when we weren't on the job.

Tom was diligent. In the morning he hopped into his grey jogging sweats and went off for a long run. Though I'd never seen him at it — only his going and coming back, coated in sweat, peeling off his gear on the way to the bath — I imagined his running to be peaceful, something like the flight of birds.

Meanwhile, I was left at the dining room table, hunched over a book (Konwicki's novel), drinking coffee, wreathed in cigarette smoke. I had been up for some time, having risen from the narrow child's bed in my room (had Olga once slept here? Or her brother?). As I stumbled through my morning routine, and boiled water for coffee, I gradually woke up — it took me hours — into the city re-imagined by the Polish novelist. In fact, in each place I went to

I seemed to acquire a sort of muse or guide. Konwicki's Warsaw required no less than a Virgil to lead you through its surrealistic, decaying, mouldering inferno. In the present bucolic Warsaw, outside the French doors on my left, a chestnut tree filled most of the space in the semi-courtyard, almost growing onto the wrought-iron balcony (had I ever seen such a tree before?). Inside, I gazed, as I had for days, at a painting on the wall before me of a woman walking toward me on a white gravel path.

But in Konwicki's Warsaw, rising up in my imagination, the Palace of Culture and Science was mildewed, lichen-covered, sweating; trams inexplicably broke down in mid-route; the careening police cars always had a headlight out; "a great cloud of virulent exhaust fumes from poorly tuned motors floated down the shallow ditch that was Nowy Swiat Street." In his apocalyptic Warsaw, bridges collapsed into the sewer of the Vistula River, chunks of facades tumbled from buildings ("Suddenly a slab of sandstone went flying off the Palace of Culture, taking a wreath of lightbulbs with it as it fell"), planes casually crashed ("something had gone wrong, some defect, and the silvery, moth-eaten machine began plunging toward the beach on the other side of the Vistula with the obvious intention of nose-diving onto the golden sands of that broad shore").

Amid the foamy water from burst water pipes, the liquefying asphalt of the streets, the senile, lumbering figures of the Party congress whose antics appeared on ubiquitous television sets ("Someone had turned off the sound as people always do when programs like that are on"), "Suddenly and for no special reason," announced Konwicki, "I felt like looking at the world around me, to see nature ... which, it seems, is dying out and had been mourned for years before indifference was finally victorious ... I was looking in the direction of the Poniatowski Bridge, which had unfortunately collapsed a few hours back. It was no great catastrophe, there were other bridges. Anyway, I was looking toward the Vistula and I could see the blackened tops of the houses on the shore, I could see the poisonous mouth of the river ... A crippled landscape, ugly yet at the same time beautiful, because it was all we had left, and so that dolorous sight, gale-tossed and lashed by hail every quarter of an hour, still gave me some heart." At the end, my crotchety muse simply sighed, "... this city of ours, this dying microcosm in the middle of Europe."

ANDRZEJ LED US FROM our nest of narrow streets to a similar tangle of meandering lanes nearby, where Olga and her husband lived. Her brother was a small, delicately built man whose temperament seemed at once sweet and melancholy. He worked as a film director, making both documentaries and dramatic features.

"Olga said that perhaps you might like to see something," he shyly offered.

"Very much," Tom said.

"Well, there's a video machine there. We'll see." He was more interested, he warned us, in the psychology of relationships than in anything political. Tom and I liked him immediately.

Olga's apartment was comfortable, spacious, and thoughtfully arranged. She was at the stove in a large, open kitchen; an island work counter separated the cooking area from the table, which was already set. An uncorked bottle of white wine awaited us.

Yet I had to take only one look at Olga — even as we were in the midst of greetings, and she was asking, "Shall I pour you a glass ...?" — before I interrupted, asking, "What's wrong?" The uncanny intimacy I experienced with her, as if we had known each other for a long time, suffused our brief relationship with sudden intuitions.

"Last night, at the theatre," she replied without preamble, "minutes before we were to go on, the assistant director had a heart attack and died." He had been a young man, only forty-two, and they had known each other for years.

For a moment the four of us were caught in a pall of silence, Tom and I captured by a grief that wasn't ours, but that touched us nonetheless. Then the small pleasures of the living, suddenly magnified, summoned us; we must continue. Olga invited us back from the sharp edge of mortality, lifting the beaded bottle of wine and filled our glasses. The image of the dead man returned to her private sorrow.

After dinner, she urged Andrzej to show us some of his work. I noticed that she displayed a protectiveness toward her brother, and guessed it might have something to do with her commercial success, or her husband's; perhaps she feared that Andrzej's work would be in some way overshadowed.

In the living room, Andrzej slid a cassette into the machine. It was a documentary he'd made recently about a Gestalt therapist. Although I couldn't follow the bearded group leader's version of therapy — it was in Polish, of course, and took place in a forest — Tom, who worked as a therapist among his various occupations, didn't have any trouble understanding what was going on.

Then Andrzej showed a second film, one that required no linguistic or therapeutic skills for comprehension. It was an intense, brief portrait (no more than ten minutes), without dialogue, of the old Jewish section of the city of Kraków, in the south of Poland. There was simply a succession of images of its present streets, eerily depopulated, with patches of cracked plaster walls, light on the narrow brick lanes, bits of colour, a doorway. Interspersed with those mundane scenes were stretches of historical footage from the 1930s, in black and white, of Krakow's ghetto. From that other world, men in long dark coats, women, their children, shuffled into groups, herded toward an impending horror. I strained to catch their fleeting faces as if I were trying to spot a relative arriving in the crowd at an airport. In the space between their innocence and our knowledge of what happened, a reflection of clouds rushed across the face of a tombstone in a time-lapse sequence.

Later in the evening, when we had drifted back to the kitchen table and Andrzej had opened another bottle of wine, I asked Olga, "Well, what exactly happened?"

She had been at the sink, rinsing a glass, and was coming to join us, drying her hands on a dishtowel.

"One morning, Leonard Borkowicz called my father and said to him, 'Come over at ten-thirty,'" she began, again in no doubt as to what I was asking about. "My father said, 'Why?' 'Just come over,'

Leonard tells him. So my father comes over at ten-thirty, and Leonard is dead."

"No," I murmured. So this was Borkowicz's death, which Olga had alluded to that first day.

Leonard was in his bed, the poison or pills (I didn't ask which) having fulfilled his intentions. Olga paused to shade in the complications. There was a second wife — "she didn't live with him" — and a girlfriend, or mistress perhaps, due to arrive at noon — "He didn't want her to find him; and there's a daughter and, well, you know ..."

"Families," I said.

"Families," Olga repeated. "So you know what it's like. He wanted it done that way and that's how it turned out. You know, since my father's a doctor, he would see Leonard's body, take care of it ..."

"So your father found him ..."

"Yes, he finds him. No pulse" — she shrugged — "so he calls an ambulance. Well, you know, they take forever to come. So Uzek comes —"

"Uzek?"

"One of my father's friends. He used to be in the security service. So he says, 'I'll call the minister of security' — well, actually it's the ex-minister because —" Olga made an impatient gesture with her fingers to signal the inevitable tangle of relations and assumptions that undergirded even the simplest anecdote — in this instance the whole group of retired and purged and pensioned-off former officials. "So Uzek calls the ex-minister, the ex-minister calls the present minister, and he sends over some agents to handle this, because the police and the ambulance aren't coming, you know, it's just a corpse. But for the Party, it's a delicate matter, so they send these guys over. And there's a note."

"Borkowicz left a suicide note?"

"And he wanted to show them the note —"

"This is your father, now?"

"My father and Uzek. They don't, you know, want to be accused of murder or whatever. So they show one of the security agents the note."

For a moment the apocalyptic comedy of my muse Konwicki began to leer. His catastrophic, crumbling Warsaw seeped into the tale: the missing ambulance, bumbling party hacks stumbling around the furniture, the stillness of the body that was once the living Borkowicz.

"So he starts reading the note out loud."

"The agent?"

"Yes. And then he comes to the last part of it, and — it's a very short note, I've seen it, and it's mostly instructions for my father to handle the burial, and so on — and the agent gets to the last part of it, the last sentence. And it says, 'Just so there's no misunderstanding: I am glad to have seen the end of Communism.'"

"That's the last line?" I said.

"He just put that in, 'I'm glad to have seen the end of Communism.' Well, this guy's reading this, and he's like, Oh, God!"

We laughed with Olga as the elements of the "tragi-farce" — was that what Lityński had called it? — collided once more. There were motives, consequences, intentions to sort out, and for a few minutes we awkwardly asked the usual questions. There wasn't a "reason" for Borkowicz's suicide, at least not one that was sharply delineated; he was seventy-seven, he had seen enough … well, there was whatever there was. The last line of his note, however, had a practical import. If it was the intention of the Party to use his death, by means of a public funeral for an "old and honoured comrade," then, in the struggle over memory, Borkowicz's note effectively forestalled it.

But underneath it all — the contested politics, the absurdities, the aspect of mortality that is always grotesque — there was Borkowicz himself, at the end, alone, writing a note that was also a testimony, a declaration of "moral witness," as Michnik had put it.

Both then, at the moment of Olga telling us of it, and much later (after we had seen Peter and gone through the story again), my breath was taken away by Borkowicz's suicide note. It was as if I had come all this way to hear a shaggy-dog story, one drawn out over days, weaving its way through other conversations, events, reflections, before delivering its punchline. At times — after Olga had first remarked, "You know about Borkowicz's death, of course" — I had simply forgotten about it, filed it away (under the heading, "If you think of it, remember to ask Olga"), consigned it to the casual details that knit together the familial web of Peter's kin.

"Just so there's no misunderstanding," Borkowicz had written. But what was our understanding? You come to a place, irrespective of what you may know (having read Michnik's essay, Konwicki's novel, having loved someone), in a state of more or less thorough ignorance. And there's an initial insight that whatever you encounter is, more or less accurately, a core sample, that it constitutes a representation of all there is. Anna, Balkan Electric, Lityński, Borkowicz's death. Just a moment of understanding before becoming ignorant again — now profoundly rather than naively ignorant — upon recognizing the complexity of what there is.

Afterwards, Borkowicz's death would remain with me, stay in my mind, seem to be one of the essential features of the idea of "the fall of Communism." It fell because a man, in the penultimate act of his life, could declare, "Just so there's no misunderstanding, I am glad to have seen the end of Communism."

I STOOD ON THE crowded platform of the railway station, waiting for the Warsaw–Berlin train to begin boarding. The long line of dun-coloured passenger cars stretched down the track under the vaulted roof of the gloomy terminal. Tom and Andrzej had gone off for a minute to check our booking. Andrjez, though he was in the middle of shooting a play for television, had sweetly come along to see us off.

The woman who happened to be standing next to me — she was heavily made up, and generously filled out her floral-patterned silk dress — told me her brother lived in West Berlin. "But they're trying to deport him," she said. "They treat Poles badly." On the other hand, she couldn't really blame them, because many Poles — and here she indicated the nervous crowd about to pack the train, many of them travelling to Germany to buy goods that could be

resold on the Polish market — were loutish drunks, avaricious, etc.
I lost a sentence or two as I lit a cigarette. "… and the Jews," she was
heatedly saying.

The crowd surged onto the high metal stairs, mounting the train
cars. Andrjez and Tom turned up and we began wrestling with
our oversupply of baggage, clutching tickets, saying farewell. I was
halfway down a crammed corridor, trying to locate a compartment
number. Tom was at the far end of the car, where Andrzej was passing
him the last of our luggage from the platform.

The rest happened both very quickly and in aqueous slow motion.
I was partway into a compartment, jostled by several people behind
me who were insistently shoving to secure places. I attempted to
heave my suitcase onto a baggage rack, at the same time half turning my head to offer verbal reassurance to the figures behind me,
bulky men, a mass of bodies in an oozing scrum that surged along
the narrow corridor.

As I twisted, I caught a glimpse of Tom, at the end of the car. He
was bellowing, a fearsome wounded sound coming out of his throat,
his face contorted with rage and pain, screaming, hoping that making as much noise as possible would somehow save us.

"They've got everything," he yelled, seeing me. I reached for
my wallet. It was gone. Tom had the passports, travellers' cheques,
tickets. They were gone, too. For a second I anticipated the mess of the
next several days.

Outside the car, on the platform, a blur of running figures surged
past Andrzej's vain efforts to stop them. I watched through a dusty
window as his slight body, one arm outstretched, toppled to the
ground. For the briefest instant, as though it were the sort of freeze-
frame he might shoot in one of his films, I saw Andrzej's falling body
caught in the not-yet-created world after the end of Communism.

Árpád's Horsemen
(Budapest, 1990)

> *How do we distill ourselves*
> *into a text, how does the text*
> *arise from our texture?*
> GYÖRGY KONRÁD, *ANTIPOLITICS* (1984)

Several times during our conversation that Sunday evening in Budapest, András B. Hegedűs referred self-reflexively to the room in which he, Tom Sandborn, and I were talking. Hegedűs also insisted on the middle initial so that we wouldn't confuse him with a former, discredited Hungarian prime minister of the same first and last name.

"In this room ..." Hegedűs said, and then later, in reference to something else, "Yes, right here, in this room," and once again, toward the end, when the grandfather clock in the corner chimed the quarter hour before seven in the evening, reminding us it was time to go, one of us asked (I can't remember if it was Tom or me), "Did that happen here?" and he said, "Yes, in this room."

It was a long, high-ceilinged, sumptuous room, lined on three sides with overfull bookcases. It was the centrepiece of Hegedűs's fourth-floor apartment, which overlooked the interior courtyard of the building. Hegedűs had lived there for decades, from the days when intellectuals, engineers, and other members of the secure middle class were able to live in spacious, comfortable dwellings in solid nineteenth-century buildings. As a Communist Party member, he had retained the apartment during the Communist period, when housing became scarce and people scrambled for tiny rental flats, often subdivided from previously larger apartments. The door, bearing a small metal nameplate with the distinguishing middle initial, gave onto a dark wood-panelled foyer inside. The large library room was on the right, the personal living quarters off to the left. In the middle of the room there was a big work table with piles of documents spilling over — the work of the Committee for Historical Justice, of which Hegedűs was the secretary — and beyond that, comfortable armchairs and a low coffee table upon which cups, saucers, ashtray, notebooks, and tape recorder were eventually assembled. In the near corner, the elegant standing clock chimed the quarter hours and, more lengthily, the hours themselves.

Hegedűs, a man of about sixty with long, swept-back grey hair, wore a plaid shirt, tan corduroy pants, and slippers. He was a veteran of the defeated Hungarian Revolution of 1956, a revolution meant, minimally, to reform the Communist Party government. There could be few more poignant moments to think about the event that had figured so largely in his life than on this particular Sunday evening toward the end of March 1990: Hungarians had gone to the polls in the first post-Communist election. The election had been the first genuine multi-party contest in almost half a century.

Tom and I had spent the morning and early afternoon with a woman named Vera Zelenyi, who was our guide to the city. We observed her casting her ballot that morning; afterwards, she took us sightseeing and we ate a chestnut purée confection in a café in the hills overlooking the Danube river, which divides Buda from Pest. We had arranged to meet Hegedűs, to whom we had an introduction from an academic friend back home in Vancouver, in the early evening, and from there we would go to one of the election headquarters to get the first returns.

Once more, here in Budapest, as elsewhere in Central and Eastern Europe on similar occasions in the wake of Communism, names of the dead were invoked, names that meant something only to Hungarians and a diminishing circle of international intellectuals. Of all the Communist states in Eastern Europe after World War II, few had a more brutal inception or a more deceptively soft decline than Hungary's.

The country had never experienced anything resembling twentieth-century democracy. In the entirety of its thousand-year history, from mythical tales of the adventurer Árpád and his horsemen sweeping in from the Transylvanian hills to the collapse of the Austro-Hungarian Empire at the end of World War I, its sole bright political moment was associated with the proto-democratic revolutions of 1848, which sent a momentary tremor through the European monarchies. In a taxi that scooted along the shore of the river — it was on the day of our arrival — we'd caught a first glimpse of the statue of Sándor Petőfi, the young poet whose death was linked to the events in Budapest in March 1848.

Unlike Czechoslovakia's incipient democracy, or Germany's social democratic, if chaotic, Weimar Republic, between the great wars of the twentieth century Hungary drifted from the aristocratic conservatism of Admiral Horthy's regency to its own brand of Arrow Cross Fascism, complete with virulent anti-Semitism. In the end it sided with Hitler, and suffered the fate of the Nazi debacle.

After the country's consignment to the Soviet camp at Yalta, the gyrations of Soviet affairs determined political life in Hungary. By 1947, any nascent semblance of postwar democratic government had been squeezed out by the Communists, led by Mátyás Rákosi and the Muscovite faction of the Party. When Tito's Yugoslavia broke with the Soviet Union in 1948, an enraged Stalin demanded the unearthing of conspirators throughout his extended empire. Rákosi, who proudly dubbed himself "the best pupil of Comrade Stalin," readily complied, producing as the chief secret Titoist traitor László Rajk, the minister of the interior he had appointed to replace Imre Nagy, one of his rivals. Rajk was tortured, made to confess, and executed. In the terror that followed between 1949 and 1953, some 150,000 of Hungary's ten million citizens ended up in prison or in labour camps. Rákosi purged his own ranks, ensuring an atmosphere of suspicion and the penetration of a corrosive cynicism into every level of society.

When Stalin died in 1953, and was succeeded by a leadership dominated by Nikita Khrushchev, the internal rivalries of the Hungarian Communist Party were thrashed out in Moscow politburo rooms. The ensuing unsatisfactory compromise permitted Rákosi to retain his party post, but elevated Imre Nagy to the office of prime minister. Yet the local Party apparatus, jealous of its privileges, resisted, even as Nagy enforced a general liberalization that included the release of imprisoned former Party members (the most prominent being János Kádár), tolerance for a group known as the Petőfi Circle, and even an attempt to form an extra-party "patriotic front" to oppose the power of the Party apparatchiks. Rákosi counterattacked. Within two years Nagy was ousted, though the Soviets would not allow Rákosi to reimpose a reign of terror.

Again external events intervened. The Soviet decision to patch up its feud with Yugoslavia in 1955 effectively doomed Rákosi. In February 1956, Khrushchev delivered his secret denunciation of the crimes of Stalin to the Soviet Party Congress. By June, Rákosi was retired to the Soviet Union, replaced by a long-time henchman. That autumn there was the first of a sporadic series of political eruptions in nearby Poland, and in October the Hungarian Party reburied a posthumously "rehabilitated" László Rajk. Two weeks later, university students and workers demonstrated in the streets of Budapest, demanding reform. Stalin's giant statue was toppled. The secret police opened fire. The Hungarian Revolution of 1956 had begun.

"The Petőfi Circle," Hegedűs explained, "was a discussion club of young intellectuals. The first times there were a few people, then hundreds; at the climax, there were some thousands. The problem was, do we have a possibility of reforming the whole system or not? We have to say that we thought, between 1953 and 1956, that the system was reformable."

"This was reform within a Marxist context?" I asked, uncertain of his Party status at the time.

"You can say within a Marxist context," Hegedűs said with a shrug, "or in a socialist context. But all right, I can say within a Marxist context. Between 1946 and 1956 I was of this Party, naturally, as was everybody who was on the left. I was very active in 1956. Not in the revolution," he carefully noted, "but before the revolution. I was never in the fighting."

The Hungarian Revolution was crushed by a Soviet military invasion in November 1956. Imre Nagy and several of his associates were executed, then secretly buried in unmarked graves. János Kádár was installed — the beginning of a thirty-year regime — by his Russian masters. How ghostly to hear Hegedűs, in his richly accented English, mention the names of Rákosi and Rajk and Nagy in passing, presuming a rudimentary knowledge on our part. To me, as a fifteen-year-old, the Hungarian Revolution had meant little more than a photo spread in *Life* magazine. I tried to recall the images. Was there a tank in a cobblestone-paved square laced by metal tram tracks? And people photographed from above, running diagonally across the glossy sheet — blurred traces of them, like birds darting through one's field of vision?

"How did you live all these years?" Tom asked, bringing me back to the man in the room.

"I did a lot of things," Hegedűs replied. "I was arrested, two years; after that I did everything. From 1963, I was for fifteen years a mechanical-industrial economist. That was not bad, it was a normal life."

"You talked about making politics in this room," Tom prompted him.

"In the sixties, the seventies, I was passive, because we had no possibilities. I went back to politics in 1979, when there was the signing movement for the Czech Charter 77. I undersigned this declaration for Václav Havel. And after this action, this absolutely minor action, I lost my job, but I got my salary. I was banned from the institute, I didn't work. That was very bad psychologically, it was a hard situation," he admitted.

In the late 1980s, as the Kádár regime quietly expired, Hegedűs and some colleagues formed the Committee for Historical Justice. The committee had sought what Hegedűs called the "rehabilitation of '56" — that is, political recognition that the revolution was not merely an outburst of "Fascist hooligans," as the Party had long branded it. It also proposed the reburial of all those who had been executed, whose memory had been effaced. In the past year, the veterans of 1956 had succeeded beyond their wildest expectations.

In June 1989 the committee conducted the reburial of Imre Nagy, more than thirty years after his execution. An ailing Kádár died three weeks later. The reburials of the others were continuing. In fact, a reburial a few weeks before had been attended by Václav Havel, who had inspired Hegedűs to sign Charter 77.

"I never thought when I signed it that I would be with Václav Havel ten years later. I never thought that Havel would be President of Czechoslovakia. So, that was really a nice moment." Then he added, "Morally, it was not uninteresting."

The phone rang. Hegedűs got up and fished among the papers on his work table, pulling out a cream-coloured cordless telephone, and then ambled through a doorway I hadn't noticed in the book-shelves on the far wall.

Hegedűs's son Istvan, a man in his early thirties whom we'd seen at a press conference the day before, was a parliamentary candidate for the youth party — Fidesz, or the Young Democrats. It, along with the dissident-based Free Democrats, the centre-right Hungarian Democratic Forum, and the reformed but discredited Socialist Party, was among the likely contenders for the night's vote. When Hegedűs came back into the room and mentioned that the call was from Istvan, I asked him about his son's party.

"Fidesz is a hard question," he allowed, "because — well, that's my son. What's my opinion that my son is a candidate? I think that the new generation has the right to shape its own image, and we, the older generation — not only those in their sixties, but those in their forties too — are full of personal and political contradictions. Of course, I'm very far from my Petőfi Circle ideology, but I have a nostalgia for the generation of 1956. Fidesz are very well educated, very talented — but it is also my son, what can I do?" He offered a fatherly shrug. "We discussed, in this room, the problem of his being a candidate. I think I trust this generation, they have to try it. I lost trust in my generation. That's the reason."

"What made you sign the declaration?" I asked.

"Pardon?"

"What caused you to sign in defence of Václav Havel and the Charter 77 people?"

"Why did I sign it?" There was a longish pause. "It was a must," Hegedűs finally said. "I think it was a psychological must. Two young gentlemen came in this room, and it was … I thought it would be a shame not to sign." He was silent again. "Sometimes we have to say a yes or a no to something. Even if it has eruptive consequences."

As we stood in the foyer putting on our jackets, Tom and I had a last backward glance at the room in which Hegedűs had lived and worked for more than three decades. In the long absence of public places, it had provided a private space for public affairs. No doubt it would be used again, if not with the same urgency. The grandfather clock chimed once more.

THE YOUNG DEMOCRATS' ELECTION return centre was a large third-floor meeting room in a building on Molnar Street, with cubbyholes on the floor above for press interviews, and a general bustle on the floors below. There were a couple hundred people crowded into the room, the majority young men, most of them pressed toward the front, where the election results were being presented amid a bank of monitors and microphones.

While we watched the returns I got into conversation with a dark-haired young man I happened to be standing next to. He was with a younger friend, a plump boy who had costumed himself in a tuxedo shirt and bow tie worn with jeans for the evening's festivities. The young man with longish jet-black hair that he tossed back from time to time with a flick of his head had good English, so we chatted easily. Between the running narrative of the election returns that he provided, punctuated by cheers when the crowd was pleased, we exchanged the usual information common to people meeting for the first time.

"Szabolsc," he said, when I asked his name. He had to repeat it a couple of times before I got the pronounciation approximately right ("Za-*bolsh*"). I had been standing alongside him for a few moments when we happened to turn to each other.

His functioning eye was dark brown, a rich, glowing colour; the other was a milky blank, like a dully lucent moonstone. There was the faintest circle of grey where the pupil should have been. Upon seeing it, I experienced a tiny wave of unease as I imagined what it would be like to lose the use of one of my own eyes.

I hadn't heard the name Szabolsc before.

"It's old Hungarian," he said. His family, he added, had originated in Transylvania.

Szabolsc was unselfconsciously outgoing, friendly, at ease with foreigners. He was a student of economics and wore a loose-fitting white T-shirt and worn jeans. He seemed to convey or even embody — through his remarks, his interest in politics, his cosmopolitanism — a sense that Hungary was entering a new and larger world that evening, and that he was one of the young New Europeans determined to be part of it.

When he was temporarily stuck for a word in English, his face creased with annoyance, his hand plunged into his mop of black hair and he scratched furiously, as though he might extract the missing word from his mane. When he went off on a brief errand, his younger pal in the mocking tuxedo top trailed after him.

I returned again and again to that eye with its milky lucence. Unlike the squinting slit of a missing eye, or the fixed gaze of a glass eye, this one declared its absence of vision openly.

The crowd was excited, but the initial returns were less encouraging than might have been hoped for. The centre-right Democratic Forum led with about a quarter of the counted vote, followed closely by the Free Democrats. A party allied to the patriotic-religious Forum, the Smallholders, was next, while the revamped Socialists and Fidesz (the Young Democrats) were neck and neck with about ten per cent each. Under the proportional representation scheme of the first post-Communist Hungarian election, all of the main parties would have voices in Parliament.

We were there for a couple of hours. The final results wouldn't be known until the following afternoon. As Tom and I were leaving, we ran into Szabolsc and his friend, and I stopped to say goodbye. He gave me his phone number and we made a tentative dinner date for a few days later.

In the cool night air, Tom and I made our way along the river toward the sublet apartment where we were staying. There were lights on several of the bridges that spanned the Danube, and the castles and the Matthias Church high up on the ramparts of the Buda side were bathed in an illumination whose golden reflections played on the river. I thought about the distorted vision of the generation Hegedűs no longer trusted, and the optical illusion with which Szabolsc had surprised me. In the country of the blind, I wondered, is the one-eyed man still king?

OUR SUBLET WAS ON Ráday Street, a narrow lane located a couple of blocks back from the river, and near the fume-spewing traffic roar of Boráros Square. The apartment had been obtained for us through the same academic friend who had provided our introduction to Hegedűs. He'd put us in contact with a friend of his, Vera Zelenyi, who had arranged for us to sublet the place of a friend of hers, Klara, who would meanwhile stay with Vera. We arrived on a Friday morning and were slated to meet Vera, who would be our guide to Budapest, in the afternoon.

The building was a five-storey nineteenth-century apartment building. From the street, packed with traffic, we entered through a small door into the welcome hush of an enclosed courtyard. Klara's place was a two-room flat on the third floor. The morning we arrived, I sank into an old ochre-coloured armchair, determined never to be dislodged, while Tom, more energetic, boiled water for coffee, unpacked his bags, made forays into the square for food, and decided on morning jogging routes that would allow him to avoid asphyxiation from exhaust fumes.

When we met Vera that first afternoon in the lobby of an art-nouveau building being used as an election press centre, she told us, "This used to be the club of the secret police." Vera was employed by a Jewish film festival or magazine, or perhaps both — in the tumult of the Hungarian economy, everyone who worked seemed to have three or four jobs, and translating for the foreign press was only one of Vera's. She was separated from her husband, but their child lived with her. She had arranged a little party for the following evening, Saturday, where we would meet everybody.

In the second-floor theatre of the press centre, decorated with plaster putty and an art-nouveau goddess whose flowing hair was painted in gilt, there was a pre-election running news conference. Miklós Haraszti, one of the best known of the former dissidents, was on the stage, fielding questions for the Free Democrats. We settled in.

We spent most of the weekend in Vera's company. There was dinner at an elegant restaurant on Friday evening, the party at her place the next night — her former husband, a psychologist, was among the guests — and then Sunday morning voting, followed by a press conference where we met reporters swapping "war stories" (there had been a recent violent incident between Hungarians and Romanians on the border), and finally, unhurriedly wandering through the old streets on the Buda side of the city, with frequent café stops. Vera seemed pleased to find that I was more interested in coffee and cigarettes and what she laughingly called the "national intellectual drink," an alcohol whose brand name was Unicom, than in trudging through three floors of paintings at the National Gallery.

Through it all, the most interesting theme was a sporadically told story of life during the later "soft" period of the Kádár regime, when intellectuals lived in its shadow in their own patchwork "civil society," as it was known — a creation of the unofficial opposition. Vera referred to the "charm" of the repression, as she described the semi-illegal lectures and large parties held in private apartments.

"We could define ourselves against the limits of the regime," she remarked, adding, "It was quite enjoyable in a way." Now there was more uncertainty: the weight of dealing with unstable jobs, money, existence itself, produced daily stress; people were suffering from "nervousness" in the midst of the country's democratic transformation. Vera conformed to my stereotype of the sophisticated, visually striking, approaching-middle-age European woman. She was instantly recognizable to me as someone from what I had begun to refer to, jokingly, as the Hermes Agency — a mythical international body that provided the people in your life who took you from one world to another.

The world Vera guided us into was that of Budapest. Every time we stepped out of a building, café, or shop, we seemed to encounter the sinuous Danube, spanned by its bridges, as it coursed through the city, dividing the two old towns. I tried to commit to memory the series of crossings, from north to south: Árpád, Margaret, Chain, Elizabeth, Freedom, Petőfi. And above the city was the church named for the fifteenth-century king Matthias Corvinus, the rococo embellishments of the Gellért Baths, the orange-gold lights that lent nighttime Budapest an air of faerie timelessness. Yet the city's beauty was not always epic in scale. The narrow streets and busy squares, the walkways along the riverside strip of luxury hotels and sidewalk cafés, the clanging trams, the nineteenth-century art nouveau buildings being sooted over and corroded by auto pollution, all had a feeling of being used, touched, trodden upon.

Budapest was more like a city encountered in dreams than any other I had experienced in Europe. Even in strolling along the twisting streets or entering the closed face of an apartment building, I had a sense of tunnelling, burrowing upwards to emerge in a courtyard. Coming out of the mouth of Ráday Street into Boráros Square, I felt as if I had surfaced on the banks of the Danube, as though the city were somehow underground, while the river represented ground level. And this underground city was itself composed of deeper historical strata. The innocent square whose traffic we now dodged had once been invaded by Russian tanks, beneath it were Petőfi and the 1848 Revolution, all the way down to the marauding Árpád.

⊰⊱

THE PRESS-CONFERENCE THEATRE, WHEN we got there, was packed to overflowing for the post-election briefing, as the leader of the Hungarian Democratic Forum party, a distinguished conservative named József Antall, responded to questions. The press corps had already determined him the winner, notwithstanding the electoral formalities still ahead. Yet the mood of the journalists was different from that of those who had covered the East German election with deadline excitement in Berlin a week ago. Here, the reporters were already bored with the Hungarian affair. Many papers, in fact, were using wire-service reports rather than sending their own correspondents. The electoral validation of the fall of Communism was already a foregone conclusion; the complicated distribution of voting percentages was reduced to a mention of "minor parties"; the phenomenon of the Fidesz youth party wasn't even noteworthy. The reporters, in short, had already packed their bags.

Tom had struck up a conversation with a young investment banker named Randall Dillard, and now he pulled me from the armchair-lined corridor and introduced me. The three of us went downstairs to a café. Dillard worked for a Japanese firm, Nomura, "the largest investment bank in the world," he quietly boasted. Contrary to whatever image I had of international bankers, he was casually dressed in jeans, white shirt, dark sports jacket. Although he was in his early thirties, he looked considerably younger. By the time I'd located a waiter and ordered coffee for us, Tom had begun a brisk journalistic interrogation.

"What's the labour cost look like in Eastern Europe compared to Japan or North America?"

"I can't say about Japan," Dillard replied, "but compared to Europe, you're getting one in five — it's one-fifth the cost. You can get it down to one-tenth, if you really want to go down to the bottom of the barrel, just labour-for-labour."

"So that's one of the appeals for investment," Tom suggested.

"Sure. Anything should be structured on the labour-intensive continuum."

"The Marxist theory of labour value strikes again," I said, half-jokingly.

Dillard missed the nuance. "Yeah," he replied, "the first thing you have to add is labour."

Tom noted that when he'd asked a woman we knew here — he must have meant Vera — about the changes taking place, she had replied, Yes, things have changed this year: we're much poorer.

"That's true," Dillard agreed, "now that the subsidies are gone. I mean, what the old government did was subsidize everything, and they would borrow to subsidize and give people an illusion of material comfort, and they were producing nothing." Dillard seemed appalled at the notion of producing nothing, although he had noted that Nomura didn't "produce" either, "we only arrange access to capital, we charge a fee for that; that's basically what we do." But "the IMF will not give aid unless they stop these subsidies, and everything's going to whack out, and that means they actually are going to be poorer in the short run. And the only thing that's going to stop that from being a complete freefall is new aid, and forgiveness of lump sums. Otherwise it's a total spiral."

Dillard was from Florida and had gone to Cambridge (on a Fulbright scholarship), where he'd acquired a Ph.D. in international law. He then clerked for the European Court of Justice, and eventually joined a big London law firm, doing debt rescheduling.

"I liked international law and banking, not because the ideas of international were so sophisticated, but I liked to travel, meet different people, and I thought, well, maybe I should try to focus on a lifestyle rather than technical interests, and you can't become international in America, so I moved over." He had done mergers and acquisitions through the rapacious 1980s, and that led to a stint with Merrill Lynch. "But they were just too erratic. So then I moved over to Nomura. Nomura — I probably shouldn't say this — they have very low technology, but a lot of money, and the interest. So I had the technology and Nomura had the time and money, and we found a good fit."

While the press scrum was trailing a potential prime minister upstairs, Tom and I were seeing the future of Central and Eastern

Europe. The bright-eyed advisers from the privileged West could order newly democratic governments to sell equity — "give it away if you have to, to get investment here, and get it off the budget deficit," Dillard urged — and at the same time innocently conceive of themselves as "focusing on a lifestyle," "finding a good fit." They were "intensifying coverage" of post-Communist Europe as naturally as Árpád's horsemen rode in from Transylvania.

Dillard told us about Tungsram, a Hungarian light bulb company that was one of the first sell-offs of state-owned enterprise. "Girozentrale, an Austrian bank, bought a majority stake in Tungsram and paid cash for it. They then went out and sold it to General Electric and immediately made, in six months, a forty per cent return. Now, one could argue that that's capitalism, that's the ugly face of it, but the Hungarians were shocked. I mean, they wanted companies like Tungsram to go into private ownership, but the idea that somebody would make money other than the government bothered them. To some extent, they're right."

Within a few months, back home, I would see a GE television commercial celebrating the purchase, complete with exploding fireworks over the illuminated Chain Bridge, and the faces of happy, freedom-loving, post-Communist Hungarians.

"The banality of evil" was a phrase coined by the philosopher Hannah Arendt to describe Adolf Eichmann's role in the Nazi extermination of the Jews. I doubted that genocide could be banal, but the banality of global capitalism in 1990 seemed to posit fewer problems of discernment. A popular novel had appeared in America a year or two before, in which aggressive Wall Street stockbrokers and bankers were referred to as "the masters of the universe." Randall Dillard didn't seem much like the restless, cocaine-snorting, luxury-car-driving, sexually predatory figures whose adventures adorned the bestseller lists. The real-life masters of this universe seemed well-mannered, educated, affable even. After all, why shouldn't they be? They were winning.

THE NEXT EVENING, SZABOLSC was waiting for me outside the Alfoldi restaurant when I arrived. It was a crowded student eatery with a brace of booths down the centre. Vera, who had recommended it, told me that the word "*alfoldi*" meant "the earth." But as soon as we were seated, I realized I had made a mistake. I had wanted to display my interest in Budapest by going to a restaurant with traditional Hungarian food, but Szabolsc was disdainful of the familiar, the local, irrespective of its earthy authenticity. He was attracted to the foreign, the new, the world beyond. From his point of view, we would have done better eating at the Budapest McDonald's. When I mentioned the thermal baths, one of Budapest's big attractions, it merely elicited an indifferent scowl. The baths were old-fashioned, too Hungarian. "I only go there to swim," he said.

Szabolsc was a conventional Westernized twenty-year-old, interested in cars, travel, and the music of R.E.M. When he said he had been to Greece with his family and I expressed some surprise, he lifted his sweatshirt to show me the T-shirt underneath as proof. The T-shirt had Greek calligraphy on it. They were the first lines of Homer's *Odyssey*:

Tell me, Muse, the story of the many-minded man
who was driven on far journeys, after he had sacked
    Troy's sacred citadel.
Many were they whose cities he saw, whose minds
    he learned of ...

After dinner, though Szabolsc might be the New European, he walked me through the streets of Old Europe, past the shops of Váci Street, along the corso by the Danube, across various squares with their statues of historical figures.

When we walked past the statue of Petőfi in the small park just north of the Elizabeth Bridge, he recalled that he'd been here in the environmentalists' demonstration a couple of years before, and that over there was where Fidesz had held an important rally. Across the river, the lighted castles high up on the Buda bluffs spilled their reflections into the water. On Váci Street, Szabolsc paused before a shuttered toy store, and remembered how important it had been to him to buy a particular model train there when he was fourteen. He also remembered the day at grammar school — he was twelve — when the students had been assembled for an important announcement.

"They said Brezhnev, the leader of the Soviet Union, had died that morning," Szabolsc said. "I was very frightened. What would happen, I wondered. Would there be a war?"

Through it all there was his always-shifting head, as he tracked reality without stereoscopic vision. I saw one eye, then the other — the brown one, deep and wild; the moonstone one, vacant and milky.

IF SZABOLSC WAS THE New European, the Last Communist was Peter Bihari, who lived out in a residential district of nearly identical rows of concrete buildings, not far from where the city had preserved a patch of woods. Bihari could see us between four and six in the afternoon, after which his wife would be coming home from the hospital with their newborn.

When we got there, Bihari was cleaning the freshly painted apartment in preparation for their arrival. His in-laws were taking care of their other child, a two-year-old, he explained. He was a lean man in his thirties, wearing a green polo shirt, prematurely balding, with a closely cropped black beard. He set aside the mop and pail, and seated us on brown corduroy-covered chairs around a low, glass-topped table.

I'd been shown a letter a few months before that Bihari had written to an economist friend of mine. The letter provided a Marxist analysis of political developments in Hungary.

"I got the impression from your letter," I began, "that it must be rather depressing to be a socialist in Hungary these days."

"Yes. Yes it is. It's a very strange situation," he said. Bihari had a quiet voice that I had to lean forward to hear, but which nonetheless precisely articulated his words in English. "I said in this letter that the left is dead in Hungary, but things have changed a bit since then.

Of course, no one on the left will be in power once the elections are over. The future government will be antisocialist," he conceded.

"On the other hand, the economy cannot change that quickly. Privatization is a dear idea for many, but it is not very easy to do." Conditions for privatization, he said, such as purchasing power or savings, didn't really exist. "Hungary is not an attractive place to invest," he pointed out, ticking off the reasons. "It is not cheap — it is more expensive than East Asia, for example; infrastructure is underdeveloped; union rights are strong. So I don't really see quick privatization. And if this doesn't happen, it will mean that the economic power and the political power will have some contradiction. That's my forecast."

"So, democratic poverty rather than authoritarian poverty," I suggested.

"Mmm, yes," he said, and then, as if the flippancy of my remark had stirred a thought, he added, "My other feeling is that this democracy ... first of all, it's very fragile, and of course these days there's no return to the former system, Stalin's or — well, I don't buy this description of Hungarian society as a neo-Stalinist system. I don't think it was a dictatorship in the ordinary sense of the word."

"Not a dictatorship of the *nomenklature*?" I asked, referring to the formerly privileged ranks of the Communist Party.

"No," he decided after a pause.

"How would you describe it?" Tom asked.

"I don't have a good description," he admitted. "I'm trying to find the terms. 'Distorted socialism' or ... or 'underdeveloped socialism.' I don't deny that the *nomenklatura* had too much power, and it was all over-centralized, and there were limitations on individual freedom. I don't deny this. My problem is that I'm not sure we've really moved from whatever it was to democracy. Formally speaking, it's democracy in the Western sense, which means everyone can form a party, join a party —"

"Which was prevented previously," I interrupted. In the back of my mind I registered a sense of unease about the way he had slid over "limitations on individual freedom" so casually.

"Yes, which was prevented previously," he agreed. "But my problem is that the current situation includes a very strong moral intimidation of people. I don't know if this word exists, I'm inventing a word —"

I missed it. It sounded like "radicalization."

"Ridiculization," he repeated.

Tom and I laughed, getting the point of his neologism. But then he offered a curious example. "I wrote this article for, it used to be the official newspaper of the Communist Party, now it is called *The Socialist Daily*, on a proposal made by a representative of Fidesz. Their position was to remove all Lenin statues from public squares and to establish a special park and to put all these statues in the park —"

I burst out laughing as I pictured the park.

"— and build a big fence around this park, and all those who are friends or followers of Lenin, they say, could go into this park and have their meditations."

Yes, it was an example of "ridiculization," but as my ill-suppressed laughter revealed, it hardly seemed commensurate with the humiliations the Party had visited upon Hungarians. Our whole conversation seemed coloured by a similar emotional dissonance, arguably of my own making. Bihari was a serious, quiet, thoughtful man, though capable of humour. When I asked at one point, "Where is Marxism left?" he replied laconically that, "Well, Marxism is left ... behind." He wasn't a political hack; he had been critical of the Communists, as he was of the post-Communist socialists, while remaining faithful to his own understanding of Marxian socialism. "I would make a very sharp distinction," he insisted, "between Marxism, what I mean by it, at least, and the system or politicians who continuously referred to Marxism."

Yet I was irked by what I took to be his complacency about the enormity of Communism's failures, as if it were a matter of a few technical adjustments, an avoidable miscalculation, and not a moral bankruptcy of historic proportions. Even his repeated reference to "the previous system," his resistance to characterizing it as a dictatorship, struck me as an evasive euphemism. Still, ours was an argument between colleagues, not opponents.

Though we talked about economics, Marxist theory, the causes of the fall of Communism ("the Party miscalculated the depths of the crisis," he said), it was, oddly, not the broad ideology but Bihari's insistence on local, specific details that reminded me of his seriousness. His remarks criticizing those who now mocked the ideas he believed in reflected not merely the petty, self-interested complaints of someone who had something to lose, but a profound intellectual distaste for distortions of objective reality — the very criticism I was making of him.

Near the end, he returned to the question of the Young Democrats. "The Fidesz people are very clever. I happen to be the teacher, at the university, of some of them." I laughed at the inadvertent implication, which Bihari hastened to correct. "This is not the reason they are intelligent, but I mean I personally know they are intelligent."

In the best known of the Fidesz campaign posters — we were talking about the semiotics of the political campaign — there was an arresting split image. The top half of the poster showed one of those classic Communist leadership bussings, Brezhnev kissing the former East German Party chief, Honecker, while the bottom half counterposed a photo of a young, attractive couple in the midst of a passionate kiss. The message was obvious: Why put up with that (the ugly old guys) when you can have this (the young and beautiful)? When Bihari cited this image, I allowed as how it was no doubt a bit simplistic, even childish.

"No, I don't object because it's childish," Bihari insisted, "but because it is a lie. The alternative is not this, either we young people are kissing each other, or we are going to get that. You don't have to overthrow the system to get rid of Brezhnev and Honecker, especially in Hungary. This is false propaganda, a manipulation."

We stood in the crowded doorway, shaking hands — simultaneous greetings and goodbyes — with Bihari's wife, new child in arm, and the relatives who had brought her home. In the procession of generations, a new, undefined one had arrived.

Tom and I reached Ráday Street just in time to get Vera's phone call. We had hoped to have a farewell dinner with her, but a domestic disaster had intervened. Her twelve-year-old son had locked himself in the house, gone to sleep, didn't respond to her frantic pounding on the door. It was a tale comprehensible to a fellow parent like Tom, who commiserated and said he would check in with her by phone the next morning to get her assurance that all was well.

I'D RESOLVED NOT TO make the same mistake again. When Szabolsc got off the tram at Boráros Square around noon the next day, I suggested that perhaps we could have lunch at a Chinese restaurant I'd noticed along the Dunacorso.

"It's very expensive," he at first demurred, though I saw that he liked the idea.

"Not at the rate of exchange we tourists get for our Deutschmarks," I said.

"And I'm not dressed for ..." He was in a denim jacket, white T-shirt, and jeans, carrying a mathematics text and a three-ring binder on which he had pasted a sticker bearing the Nike slogan, "Just do it."

At the Szechuan restaurant, I instructed Szabolsc in the mysteries of using chopsticks (he took them with him as a souvenir of his first Chinese restaurant). After lunch we took a walk. He was to meet his math teacher at four, but was ill-prepared, he admitted.

"Why didn't you study?"

"I talked too long to my girlfriend on the phone," he laughed.

We walked across the Chain Bridge to the Buda side of the river. On the shore, workmen were laying turf in preparation for spring. A passerby on the bridge carried a sprig of lilac. A hydrofoil bearing a boatload of tourists churned up the Danube beneath us. We made our way up the narrow streets to the castle, stopped at a café for a soda, and by the time we wandered back to the bus stop it was mid-afternoon. He rode back with me to the Dunacorso. On the crowded bus, I noticed a small boy, with the unselfconscious frankness of children, staring in wonderment at Szabolsc's glazed eye.

When Tom returned to the apartment, he reported on the interview he had done with an anarchist; I could listen to the tape later. Vera had phoned to say she had gotten back into her house, all was well with her child, and she sent me her farewells. And finally, Tom had learned that an hour before our train to Bucharest there was to be a Fidesz-sponsored demonstration at the Russian embassy to protest the Soviet treatment of independence-seeking Lithuania. We'd have time for a coffee before the taxi arrived to take us to the demo.

Outside the Soviet embassy, a crowd of several hundred people, and a cordon of police beyond them, gathered around a flatbed sound truck to listen to Istvan Hegedűs and another Fidesz representative deliver brief speeches, no doubt "ridiculizing" their former overseers. Bouquets of Hungarian and Lithuanian flags flourished among the demonstrators. At the end, there was a coordinated burst of chants in Hungarian. "Russians go home," the young Hungarians insisted, as had their fathers and mothers before them.

Berlin and the Angel of History

The most memorable image in the writings of Walter Benjamin is the angel of history. It appears in his "Theses on the Concept of History," a late schematic essay written in 1940, a few months before he committed suicide while fleeing the Nazis. It's an oft-quoted passage, but it bears repeating. Benjamin portrays the angel as a witness to the ongoing disaster of history:

> His face is turned toward the past. Where we perceive a chain of events, he sees one single catastrophe which keeps piling wreckage upon wreckage and hurls it at his feet. The angel would like to stay, awaken the dead, and make whole what has been smashed. But a storm is blowing from Paradise; it has got caught in his wings with such violence that the angel can longer close them. The storm irresistibly propels him into the future to which his back is turned, while the pile of debris before him grows skyward. The storm is what we call progress.

If any city can claim to be under the gaze of the angel of history, it must be Berlin. Nowhere has the wreckage of the past been piled higher — sometimes literally, as in the mountainous accretion of World War II rubble known as Devil's Mountain, or *Teufelsberg*, heaped up and greened over in the Grunewald forest at the south-western edge of Berlin. Nowhere has the storm of progress blown more ferociously.

The chain of events that we perceive, which the angel sees as one single catastrophe, and which qualifies Berlin for the angel's attention, is historically fairly recent. It was only with national unification in 1871 that Berlin became Germany's capital; previously, it had been a sleepy barracks town of the Prussian regime. But from 1880 to 1914, Berlin witnessed the most rapid and savage industrialization and population explosion in Europe. Then, in 1918, after four years of battlefield deaths and home-front immiseration, came the collapse of the German Empire, followed by a shooting revolution in its streets, right-wing coup attempts, and the creation of the social democratic Weimar Republic. In the 1920s, economic disaster struck, marked by an ultra-inflationary spiral in which a loaf of bread cost a billion Deutschmarks.

The cultural period where I become interested in Berlin, the city, is sometimes called "Berlin *noir*" for its challenge to more sedate artistic and moral boundaries. That was dissolved in the Nazi rise to power in 1933. The twelve-year Nazi Reich brought on World War II, and the Holocaust that slaughtered six million Jews. During the war, Berlin was carpet-bombed by the Allies and subjected to a war-ending Soviet ground assault that reduced much of the city to rubble. In postwar Berlin, the armies of four nations formally occupied the city, succeeded by the division of the city for forty years between West Berlin and East Berlin, capital of the Communist German Democratic Republic, during which time the unprecedented wall around West Berlin was built. As for West Berlin, in addition to being used as a showcase city for the West during the Cold War, it experienced, from the 1960s to well into the 1980s, two stormy decades of political strife featuring the "autonomous movement"; squatters; and green, gay, and feminist politics. With the fall of the Wall, followed by one of the more enormous building booms in European history after the reunification of the city in 1989, Berlin makes for a credible civic candidate for the angel of history's steady gaze.

The fall of the Berlin Wall on November 9, 1989, was emblematic of the alleged dissolution of a host of long-standing international divisions and hostilities. It marked, symbolically, the end of the Cold War between the West and the soon-to- collapse Soviet Union. It was the end of Communism, the twentieth century's major attempt at creating a political and economic alternative to democratic capitalism and undemocratic autocracies. And when the material Wall fell, the corresponding phantasmal metaphor of the Iron Curtain dissolved with it. For Germans, it was the moment when the four-decade-long division of their country into West and East Germany that followed the debacle of Nazi Germany seemed to become a wound that could be healed by reunification. For Berliners, it was the end of one of the strangest and most painful physical alienations in political history.

What was unprecedented, and frequently unnoted, about the Berlin Wall was that it was not built by its inhabitants in order to protect the city from enemies. Rather, it was a structure built by East Germany to prevent its citizens — East Germans and especially East Berliners — from entering a magical, apparently free city whose inhabitants enjoyed freedom of speech and assembly, multi-party democratic self-government, an uncensored culture, and economically prosperous lives. As in all phantasmal constructions, these mutually projected images of freedom and oppression were a mix of partial truths and purposeful distortions. Nations and cities had built walls throughout human history, invariably for self-protection. The purpose of the Berlin Wall was unique in its intentions and its effects.

There is a story of post-Communism in Berlin, especially the former East Berlin, bits of which I encountered casually or heard about over the years, but did not systematically follow. It is partially told in movies (Wolfgang Becker's *Good Bye Lenin!*, 2003), a few works of literature (among them, Thomas Brussig's *Heroes Like Us*, 1995), and much conversation. For East Berliners, it was in part a story of sudden disorienting freedoms and staggering economic adjustments, which resulted in increased immiseration for many of them. It was also a story of the dismissal and loss of virtues that were alive even in a formally oppressive Communist society, and a cruel kind of humiliation heaped upon the "backward" easterners by their countrymen from West Germany.

Within a few years of the fall of the Wall, when its remnants had been turned into tourist sites and souvenirs, people began to speak about "the Wall in the head," referring to the enduring differences of values, rhythms, and meanings between west and east Germany, which disadvantaged the easterners in terms of employment, equal wages, and even a sense of self-respect. At the same time, the differences shouldn't be exaggerated. Germany, after all, was a country linguistically united despite its political separation, and if certain forms of social solidarity were being lost with the dissolution of a closed and surveillance-dominated society in the east, the other Germany into which the former Communist Germany was being enfolded was what it purported to be: a country with broadly social democratic values and a functioning welfare state.

Yet there is something more to the city of Berlin than a particular set of political, social, and economic events and separations — the latest storm of progress under the angel of history's gaze. This is also true of the other cities where I had, in fact, more systematically explored the aftermath of the fall of Communism. I'm a confessed "cosmopolitan," a term that's often used derogatorily in the form "rootless cosmopolitanism," and my patriotism is reserved for the values embodied in democratic constitutions, the more universal the better, and tends to fly in the face of tribal or nationalist identities. Given this perspective, each of the great conglomerations of humans and structures that we call cities — from the ancient Mesopotamian city of Uruk ruled by Gilgamesh 5,000 year ago, to the cities of the present, including Berlin — develop and display a distinctive character that provides a context for interpreting the historical events that play out there. For its inhabitants, each city contextualizes specific memories and meanings.

As I've been thinking about the twenty-fifth anniversary of the fall of the Berlin Wall and the other European upheavals that toppled Communism, the recurring phrase I find myself turning over in my mind is "more and other." Despite my commitment to the human story told by history, there is something "more and other" than simply a linear record of human events. This something more and other often goes under the headings of "metaphysics," "art," and "culture," in the sense of "ways of living." Such ways are not preordained, eternal, or necessary, but are accretions of custom and thought that establish what I call contexts: patterns and clusters of ideas, habits, and meanings that shape experience, interpretation, and understanding of the events of history.

Using Walter Benjamin, the Berlin thinker of the 1920s and '30s, as my guide, I want to write about that more and other Berlin, before returning to the political character of the city that was the site of the fall of the Berlin Wall, the emblematic historical event of the latter part of the twentieth century.

"NOW I WANT TO recall those who introduced me to the city," is the way Benjamin begins "A Berlin Chronicle" (1932). "For although the child, in his solitary games, grows up in closest proximity to the city," Benjamin continues, "he needs and seeks guides to its wider expanses ..." As did I, a stranger to the city, and so I, also, will invoke my initiating guides.

The first of my guides to Berlin was the Canadian painter Michael Morris. It was a mid-March afternoon in 1990, a few months after the fall of the Berlin Wall, and just a day or so before the first post-Communist election in what was then still East Germany. Michael was waiting at a bus stop on the Ku'damm, the tree-lined main boulevard of West Berlin, when Tom Sandborn and I piled off a city bus with our heap of luggage. We had just ridden in from Tegel Airport after the long flight from Vancouver, at the beginning of a six-week tour of the capitals of Central and Eastern Europe in the wake of the fall of Communism.

From a bus window, Berlin is hardly a conventionally beautiful city. Half or more of it was destroyed during the bombings of World War II. In West Berlin, the rubble was gradually cleared away in the following decades and the gaps between surviving buildings filled in with brown and grey five-storey stucco dwellings through a civic construction program funded by the state. I noticed, once I became familiar with the city, that each new building was marked by a tiny metal shield bearing the image of Berlin's official emblem, a black bear rampant. The stucco apartment buildings were often incongruous neighbours to the ornate nineteenth-century edifices that survived the war. East Berlin's rebuilding program was comparable in scope, but favoured massive, often desolate, Soviet-style apartment-tower complexes.

In the luxurious Charlottenburg neighbourhood where Michael met us, dozens of art-nouveau or, to use the German term, *Jugendstil*, buildings from the turn of the twentieth century had survived. That period, circa 1880 to 1910, is when newly consolidated bourgeois wealth was displayed in elegant five-storey apartment buildings, with deep loge-like balconies held up by sculptured caryatids and atlantids; elaborate roof façades; and bas-reliefs of women with flowing tresses draped over ornate doorways. These buildings exuded their owners' sense of the satisfactory place they held in the social structure, promising an eternity of bourgeois prosperity. As Benjamin says, there "reigned a species of thing that, no matter how compliantly it bowed to the minor whims of fashion, was in the main so wholly convinced of itself and its permanence that it took no account of wear, inheritance or moves, remaining forever equally near to and far from its ending, which seemed the ending of all things." It was an eternity that would last barely half a century.

On that first day in Berlin, Tom and I dragged our suitcases along Mommsenstrasse, following our portly guide, who chatted away in the faint accent that he'd retained from his boyhood in England, until we arrived at the building in which he'd lived since the beginning of the 1980s. Michael had landed this upscale address thanks to a German cultural exchange program that was anxious, as part of Cold War cultural policy, to bring foreign artists to West Berlin — one more sign of the vibrant openness of the Free World (as contrasted to the closed world on the other side of the Berlin Wall). After his grant year, Michael, like other guest artists, had been given the option to stay on in Berlin in one of the rent-subsidized apartments that the cultural exchange organization controlled in some of the posher neighbourhoods of the city.

Beyond the building's main entrance and foyer, a second set of doors opened onto a courtyard (in German, a *Hof*) at the centre of which was a four-storey high chestnut tree. On the far side of the *Hof*, a turret staircase led to Michael's third-floor apartment and studio. Once inside, we dropped our bags and settled around the kitchen table, having reached that moment of safety for which all travellers long, while Michael lit the stove and put on a kettle of water for tea. The kitchen window offered a view of the bare branches of the chestnut tree in the courtyard, giving the whole place something of the feeling of a children's tree house. The walls of the kitchen were crowded with various paintings, both Michael's and those of artist friends. Tom and I had emerged from the sealed world of long-distance air travel into the "free air" of Berlin, as the city billed both senses of its atmosphere.

Now in 2014, after a quarter century of living part of my life in Berlin, that long-ago moment of entry has a magical double quality. From one point of view it simply "happens," as if I'd released the pause button on some digital recording device, and watched the mundane events of arrival. Michael bustles around the kitchen, keeps up a steady reassuring patter that, being the skillful host he is, he knows will help orient us. He disappears for a moment and then returns to bring us a photo album with which we can amuse ourselves while he prepares the tea. I'm looking at snapshots of the people Michael knows in Berlin, people I might conceivably meet, while Michael tells us anecdotes about them in a style I'll come to think of as his "illustrated conversations."

The next morning, Tom and I made our way to East Berlin, passing through a checkpoint of the remnants of the Wall, where gates clanged shut and border personnel still stamped the passports of foreigners — all these once-forbidding protocols would disappear with the formal reunification of Germany six months hence — until we eventually emerged into the desolate open space of Alexander-platz, the main square of East Berlin, and turned ourselves into unofficial observers of the first post-Berlin Wall, post-Communist, East German election.

But in its other aspect, I see the moment of my entry into Berlin as destiny. It's a freeze-frame sequence that, taken together, offers a panorama of my future. Though "destiny" is too grand a word for the accretion of such accidents of autobiography, it's the moment when, unconsciously, I decided that I would return to Berlin — again and again, as it turned out. It is the moment when I decided that the next phase of my life (I was about fifty) would unfold in Berlin, with its nightmarish resonances of the Holocaust and its then-uncertain prospects as the centre of an enlarged and shakily unified Germany. I didn't know any of that at the time — all I had at the exact moment was the tangy, sweet smell of a cup of hot tea rising into my nostrils, mixed with mentholated cigarette smoke, Michael's English accent, the pictures in the photo album that suggested a settled life in this legendary city, the tree-house-like feel of his apartment as I sat behind the table next to the window looking out on the chestnut tree. In my mind was the thought that, Hmm, maybe I could do something like what Michael is doing, and even that was gone by the next exchange of conversation. People who know that I live part-time in Berlin often ask, "Why Berlin?" The answer isn't simple. It includes elements of biographical accident, a preference for big (European) cities, a romantic idea of how to live my life, my erotic tastes, the famous Kultur of Berlin, and a sense of history and irony (what's a Jew doing in Berlin?).

So, yes, why not? Destiny — as both obedience to an injunction and the choice of free will.

"I HAVE LONG, INDEED for years, played with the idea of setting out the sphere of life — *bios* — graphically on a map," Benjamin says. "I have evolved a system of signs, and on the grey background of such they would make a colourful show if I clearly marked the houses of my friends and girlfriends, the assembly halls of various collectives … the hotel and brothel rooms I knew for one night, the decisive benches in the Tiergarten, the ways to different schools and the graves that I saw filled, the sites of prestigious cafés whose long forgotten names daily crossed our lips …"

My Berlin is equally built of such personal sites, routes, routines. My private map of the city isn't wholly constructed from the historical events of the past quarter century: the demolition of the Wall, the unification of the former East and West Berlins, the return of the German capital from Bonn to Berlin, or the intense decades-long building projects in the wasteland that was occupied by the Berlin Wall for nearly thirty years. Rather, it is a labyrinth of the city's different ways — like the "ways" in Proust's *Swann's Way* — to walk from my apartment near Charlottenburg Castle, say, to Savignyplatz, just north of Michael Morris's former studio on Mommsenstrasse.

Savignyplatz is an oasis of urban green with bowers, lawns, garden, and trees, divided by busy Kantstrasse and bordered on the south end by the urban railway, the S-Bahn. At its north end, where three streets converge on the traffic circle, there is a sculpture by August Kraus, done in 1930, of two nude boys tugging at recalcitrant goats, their pedestals facing each other under large shade trees. Savigny-platz was one of the first neighbourhoods in the city with which I became familiar when I returned to Berlin after my initial visit in 1990, one of the first places from which I contemplated the city.

One of the three streets emptying into Savignyplatz, Carmerstrasse, is where Benjamin lived as a child. Each weekday in the first decade of the 1900s he crossed Savignyplatz, fearful of being late, on his way to the "sad, spinsterish primness" of Kaiser Friedrich School, a red brick Gothic building still located in nearby Bleibtreustrasse, within sight of the elevated tracks of the S-Bahn.

Today, the square is surrounded by sidewalk restaurants and cafés. Among them, also on the north side and with a view of the goatboys, is the Zwiebelfisch, where, for a while, I used to drink coffee and read the first pages of some book I had just bought at the nearby Marga Schoeller bookstore, located down the street. The Zwiebelfisch is a café opened in the 1960s, and mockingly posted over the front door is Dante's line taken from the entrance to the Inferno, "Abandon all hope, ye who enter here." Many of the clientele there look like they've taken that injunction literally, and give off the air of the now-fading "generation of '68ers," as they're known, caught in the time-warp of outmoded hairstyles, clothes, and ideas.

DURING THE SPRING AND summer in 1991, when I returned to Berlin, I took Michael as my guide consciously, more so than in the previous year when he had been accidentally and briefly pressed into service. It was not so much the physical present-day post-Communist Berlin to which Michael now led me, although there was inevitably that too, but rather to the historical "mind" of a culture. The process was casual, and sometimes didn't require me to leave the large high-ceilinged room in his apartment in which he'd installed me.

The day of that first return to Berlin, I was plunked down in the room in a modernist chair of tubular steel and suspended black leather seat and back, located next to a desk illuminated by a table lamp with a milky-white cupola and a base of green glass. Michael handed me an oversized coffee-table book. It was a volume of the pictures of Herbert List, a photographer of the 1920s Weimar period who had grown up in Hamburg, an hour or two north of Berlin by train. With his characteristic discretion, Michael left me to my own travel-dazed thoughts, and went off to attend to domestic chores of his own. My eyes slowly settled into List's homoerotic images, and I fell into a meditation on the now long-dead or long-lost objects of the photographer's attention.

Hours passed while I looked at those photos that afternoon, and in those hours I began to locate myself in a Berlin composed of fragmented strata of intellectual currents. The room in which I sat, I began to understand, was filled with treasures. The chair and the lamp, I learned from Michael, were Bauhaus designs of the 1920s. Before long, I was no longer merely sitting in a chair that had somehow retained its sleek modernity some three-quarters of a century after its creation, but a "Marcel Breuer chair" (named for its designer); the cozy lighting fixture was a "Wagenfeld" lamp.

The chair and lamp were connected to a larger world of architecture, design, and ideas about domestic life, examples of which I would find scattered elsewhere throughout Berlin, so that I began to understand, in a more textured sense, where I was, a reassuring counter to the frequent sense I have that I don't really know where I am because of my sheer ignorance of much of the context in which I find myself. When I expressed an interest in these textures, Michael produced an illustrated history of the Bauhaus by Hans Wingler. A small library soon piled up on the desk. Each object or idea — photos, furniture, paintings, historical references, gossip about people in the picture albums — contributed to a portrait of an exfoliating larger realm, parts of which I absorbed, via Michael, and then joined to my own experiences of Berlin. "My Berlin" began to grow and evolve.

One evening that summer, Michael took me on a flaneur's stroll down the Ku'damm. It was the same Ku'damm I'd previously seen, and it was an ordinary enough after-dinner walk past the expensive shops with their well-known names, lighted display cases of costly goods set in the middle of the sidewalk, shadowy trees that lined the median of the boulevard, public toilets, and well-lit cafés (the Möhring, Kempinski's Corner, Kranzler's) whose crowds spilled out onto the sidewalk tables. But it was already, also, a thoroughfare transformed from my previous idea of it, one that was dense with intimations of a city I was about to discover.

I dwell on the subtlety and generosity of Michael's guidance because "the guide" is a persistently recurrent figure in my experience of the world. This figure ranges from my father, my teachers and mentors, both while I was young and as an adult, to the seamiest representatives of various *demimondes*. Even the stranger on a street corner from whom I receive directions to the next street is among their ranks. Individually and together, I imagine them as Hermes from classical mythology, the messenger who leads you from one world to the next and, in doing so, reveals to you the multiplicity of worlds.

❋

MY BERLIN NOW INCLUDES the numerous castles and parks around the outskirts of the city, spaces mostly designed by the nineteenth-century landscape architect Peter Lenné. They're the sites of regular Sunday walks with Mark Johnson, the second of my guides to Berlin. We met in a bar in the early 1990s, and soon this computer programmer — middle aged, with salt-and-pepper hair and a conservative, wry sense of humour and politics — was showing me the places, known to Berliners but mostly hidden from strangers, where one could stroll on summer days, arguing about current events or falling into a meditative state of mind that, to me, is inseparable from my idea of writing. I, too, came to know the places Benjamin recalls: "The orchard at Glienicke, the broad ceremonious promenade of Schloss Babelsberg ... the shadowy ways through the foliage leading down to Lake Griebnitz at the places where there were jetties."

Despite Berlin's bucolic core, it is possible to barely notice, as one observant writer, Anton Gill, puts it, "the wooded parks which cover half the city's acreage and which are, with the lakes," and the serpentine Spree River, "the reason for the city's good air." In the often obtuse descriptions that historians and travel writers offer of the city, there's too rarely an account of those moments in which the observer merely sits at the lakeside café next to Köpenick Castle in the southeast corner of Berlin or finds the "beer-meadow" across the water from Babelsberg park at the city's western edge. Even in the city proper, most passers-through don't have time to watch the swans floating in the Lietzensee lake on a summer afternoon, or dawdle at one of Benjamin's "decisive benches" in the central Tiergarten park or any of a dozen other places in the middle of a booming *Grossstadt* of four million people. I've learned to pay attention to those modest historians, like Gill, who notice that "the grey city alone on its plain has a necklace of countryside and parkland."

My Berlin also takes in Benjamin's "hotels and brothels I knew for one night" in his "Berlin Chronicle," various geographic zones of desire, beginning with the intersection of Eisenacher and Fuggerstrasse, just off Nollendorfplatz, southeast of the Ku'damm. That's where gay bars and other homosexually oriented businesses have been clustered for more than three-quarters of a century. Though stretches of Eisenacher Strasse were reduced to heaps of rubble during World War II (I'd seen postwar photos of the street by another German photographer, Herbert Tobias), the end-of-the-nineteenth-century patch of elegant buildings at the corner of Fuggerstrasse survived.

On the ground floor of one of them is a small bar named Pinocchio's. On a summer afternoon, I can sit at one of the tables outside the bar and watch the street traffic, chat inconsequentially with one of the regular customers or the bartender, or simply gaze at the pale blue stone walls of the apartment buildings across the street and the flowerboxes on their deep balconies spilling over with the fierce brightness of geraniums. At the corner there's a small, scruffy, fenced-in playground that contains a soccer cage, some trees and benches, and a stone ping-pong table where I often see some of the young men who hang around the bar play table tennis. I like the way a patina of the utterly mundane overlays the erotic currents, and the empty mirror of eternity and the immediacy of desire merge.

From the first time I walked down Fuggerstrasse in 1991, I sensed the countless stories that its bars, restaurants, and buildings held, stories of love affairs, disasters of the heart, even the casual encounters that merely raised the participants' heart-rates for a few moments. This was a history other and older than Communism, its consequences, and its end. One night, in Pinocchio's, its few barstools and half-dozen tables crowded with both the grotesque and the beautiful of human-kind, someone I knew, sitting at a corner table and playing a dice game with some of his pals, hailed me as I made my way through the mob, and then made a place for me to squeeze in on a stool next to someone he knew I was interested in.

At that moment, absorbing the flow of information circulating throughout the bar and at the same time the specificity of the person against whom I was pressed, I had the sense of being "inside." It was a half-formulated thought that, oddly, didn't have much to do with sex, although there were certainly enough currents of sexuality in the air. Similar thoughts have occurred to me in places other than erotic sites. It was an idea that felt distinct from the nominal sense in which, wherever I am, I'm "inside," whether it's a city, a building, a room, a relationship. At the same time, I'm also "outside," outside of a culture, a history, or even a group of people, "on the outside / lookin' in" as an old song has it. No, this was about a brief instant in which I felt free of a persistent sense of alienation from the world. At that moment, in a tiny bar that I imagined was a galley sailing through the nighttime sky, I felt the opposite of alienation, namely, an instant of integration: inside Pinocchio's, inside Berlin, inside the imaginary and real city.

BENJAMIN RECALLS "AN AFTERNOON ... to which I owe insights into my life that came in a flash, with the force of an illumination. It was on this very afternoon that my biographical relationships to people, my friendships and comradeships, were revealed to me in their most vivid and hidden intertwinings." At that moment he attempted to make a diagram of his life on a sheet of paper that was subsequently, to his chagrin, lost. But in remembering the labyrinth it sketched out, Benjamin says, "I am concerned not with what is installed in the chamber at its enigmatic centre, ego or fate, but all the more with the many entrances leading into the interior ... entrances I call 'primal acquaintances' ... So many primal relationships, so many entrances to the maze."

The entrances to Schlossstrasse, the street I like best in Berlin, are similar. Thomas Marquard and Ilonka Opitz, who were then married, are the third of my guides to the city. They were among my first friends in Berlin as well as upstairs neighbours in the building where I now live. Thomas taught Latin at a north Berlin academic high school, and played the violin. He was a lithe man with quick physical energy and a curious and open mind. He rather resembled a Hermes figure, a modern version with a brush cut. Ilonka had a master's degree in art history and was working in an upscale bookstore. Like Thomas, she was lean and energetic, and possessed a temperament that enabled her to be a radical political activist without the censoriousness that robs so many activists of the capacity to savour life's pleasures.

They were the ones who first led me to Schlossstrasse one summer evening in the mid-1990s, while we were out walking their golden retriever, Kimba. The "secret way," as Thomas once called it, to Schlossstrasse leads from my building on busy Kaiser-Friedrich-Strasse, past the Little Europe pub where various neighbourhood characters hang out, and past an always-failing café at the corner that in a later incarnation became a storefront daycare centre, down a little side street to where Haubachstrasse and Hebbelstrasse make a V-shaped intersection. Nearby, there is an obscure entrance path into a sunken rectangle of green lawn, with a few trees, park benches among the border of bushes, and cobbled paths, lit at night by imitation gas lamps.

The first evening I was led into Schustehrus Park, which pushes up against the nineteenth-century Oppenheimer Villa on the far side of the lawn, I had the sense not only of entering the maze, but of stepping into the previous century, its gaslight illumination marking out the dark anthropomorphic shapes of bushes and trees, a faint mist hovering over the grassy field. Emerging from the far end of the park, it is a brief walk along Schustehrus street to the corner of Schlossstrasse, where the bower garden of the Bohemian restaurant is located (the restaurant's name and owners have changed over a couple of decades, so the only constant is the garden). Thomas, Ilonka, and I occasionally stopped there for a drink beneath its tangle of vines. For me, all the names of streets and sites of cafés and restaurants, either taken for granted by long-time residents or merely exotic words in a foreign language for most strangers, have a particular resonance. They literally mark the place and, once entered into a vocabulary of memory, function like hypertext links that instantly call up particular stretches of urban landscape.

The street is partially paved with traffic-slowing brick, and divided by a parkway. The edges of the median are bordered by linden trees, and in the centre is a broad, sandy pathway, where local people gather to play boules, the small metal orbs clicking against each other as they collide. The pathway, several blocks in length, leads to the gates of Charlottenburg Castle, whose aqua-coloured cupola is illuminated at night, rising over the low, French-style early eighteenth-century building, once a summer stopover for Prussian royalty on their way between Köpenick Schloss in the east and Frederick the Great's San Souci Palace in Potsdam.

Schlossstrasse itself is lined with sombre bourgeois villas, now transformed into apartment buildings, a couple of museums, with some ground-floor cafés. Its cobbled sidewalks, shaded by lindens, become sticky in the summer from aphids' secretions. On the far side of the street, toward its south end, is my neighbourhood café, the Kastanie, where I go to drink coffee and read in the afternoons at a table in the back of the café. The only thing that has changed over the years is that my paper-and-ink books are occasionally replaced by my digital reader.

And the point of this description, this landscape? If I don't know *this*, or something the equivalent of it, all the rest — including the fall of the Berlin Wall, the end of Communism in Europe, and much more — will be leeched of meaning. Knowing this alters my understanding of the rest. Not knowing, I think, reduces knowledge to unprocessed and unintegrated information, the intellectual bane of our time. As Benjamin says, "So many entrances to the maze."

THERE WAS A MOMENT in 1995 that epitomizes my sense of post-Communist Berlin, both its confusions and occasional clarities. The year coincided with the commemoration of the fiftieth anniversary of the end of World War II. Film footage of the war had flooded North American television screens just before I left for Berlin in May. In the wake of military marches, formal ceremonies, and the inevitable media saturation, German television, my friends Thomas and Ilonka told me, had shown a grim, recently recovered film of Auschwitz, which was all the more shocking for being in colour. I had the sense that this was not simply a historical commemoration but the true end of World War II. It was only now, in 1995, a half-century after the fact, that the war was finally over as a matter of living memory.

Why? Most of the participants in the war who marked the fiftieth anniversary of its end wouldn't be alive when it was formally recalled twenty-five or fifty years hence. Conversely, the student-aged Germans I knew had been born to parents who were themselves born after 1945. When I thought carefully about the sensibilities of Thomas and Ilonka and the others I'd met in Berlin since the fall of Communism, it was no longer possible to think of Germany in terms of half-century-old stereotypes of Nazis.

One event that summer served as a sort of hinge between the pleasures of my private Berlin and the city's new public role in the world. The artist known as Christo and his partner Jeanne-Claude, whose specialty involved large-scale spectacular art events, had persuaded the German Parliament to let them wrap the Berlin Reichstag building in a rope-secured cloth covering.

For weeks, this absurdist project had been relentlessly hyped; not only were images of the about-to-be-wrapped historic building hawked everywhere, but the idea had been taken up by advertisers, so that pictures of wrapped commodities — especially giant beer glasses — peered out from every billboard, bus stop, and advertising kiosk. To make matters worse, the local government had decided to link the spectacle to its own architectural plans for the city, which were already being realized at dozens of construction sites (whole neighbourhoods of east Berlin seemed to be behind fences and under giant building cranes). A series of tented rotundas were strategically placed near the Reichstag, each containing photos, models, and three-storey painted panoramas of "Berlin 2000." Mark dragged me along one Saturday afternoon to join the crowds lined up to view the imaginary future. Once inside, the architectural exhibit struck me more as civic boosterism than a persuasive plan.

The fall of Communism and its aftermath, briefly a matter of interest for North Americans, had already begun, by 1995, to subside into an ahistorical past (even for Europeans). Ironically, the end of Communism, at first hailed as the epochal triumph of capitalist democracy, had yielded, just five years later, a period of sourness, and a series of governments headed by former Communists in Poland, Hungary, Russia, and elsewhere. The alternative to this unpredicted return of ex-Communists-without-Communism was a string of bloody ethnic nationalisms, ablaze throughout various former Soviet Republics, but more immediately within the ethnic enclaves of the former Yugoslavia. Christo and Jeanne Claude's wrapped Reichstag seemed a whimsically accurate, if enigmatic, comment on all that had happened, suggesting a widespread sense that we were in the middle of historical events whose dimensions — and implications — were opaque.

The oversold event had left me bored, convinced that we were being subjected to one more instance of kitsch in the name of art. When Mark came back to the bar from an earlier viewing of the wrapped Reichstag, improbably enthused by this artistic phenomenon, I put it down to ignorant populism. But then I got a series of calls from artist friends, one of whom reported that it was like standing next to a glacier and another that it was as if a cloud had been tied down to the earth. Thomas and Ilonka biked there one morning; when they returned, Thomas said, referring to the long history of the Reichstag building, "They've used it, burned it, abandoned it, renovated it, and none of it worked. Wrapping it *works*."

So, one morning a couple of weeks later, I walked up the vast lawn in front of the Reichstag with Mark and hundreds of others to gaze at the shrouded outlines of the old building, wrapped in a thick, silvery, shimmering industrial material, held in place by pale blue cording, the whole thing slightly fluttering in a late-June breeze. The preceding weeks of earnest TV and culture-page pondering over such questions as "Is it Art or ...?" instantly dissolved in the monumentality of what Christo and Jeanne-Claude had done.

The secret of its success, I saw — and one could only understand by seeing it in person, up close — was its size, the huge *objectness* revealed by wrapping it. In photographs it simply looked like a piece of household furniture with a sheet thrown over it. But its physical scale, commensurate to the size of the city that was its context, was crucial to its magic; for a moment, this Berlin fantasia relieved us of the burden of being in history. In the morning sunshine, it pro-claimed that beauty could be both comic and autonomous — and that the future was waiting to be unwrapped.

MY UNDERSTANDING OF BERLIN is governed by three main themes. The first is Benjamin's "angel of history," who watches over the successive cataclysms that shape the story of the city of Berlin: industrialization, war, revolution, war again, the fall of the Berlin Wall, and post-Communist reunification. It regards the catastrophes that have hit Berlin as irreparable, as permanent damage. Berlin is a city where history is repeatedly broken. The rubble may fade but it is never wholly transformed.

Second, I have the notion that the cultural history of Berlin should be read as a collective if fractious intelligence. If one takes up the metaphor of an imaginary human embodiment of the city, then there's a natural corollary in seeing its cultural history as the mind of that embodiment. The mind of Berlin consists of everything written, painted, danced, built, composed, and thought in Berlin over a period of about two centuries. That mind is specific rather than unique, as it is in all the great cities. From its popular cabaret traditions to its avant-garde experiments, Berlin's cultural history is not simply a linear accumulation of what occurs in Berlin but is integral to the city, *is* Berlin. In this way of understanding it, Berlin is a city of ideas, a city with something on its mind.

A third and final thematic, one that stands out for me, is that Berlin is a left-wing city. Its political character explains some of its behaviour during the post-Communist era, and the ability it has had to integrate the disparate values of the divided city. The historical evidence of that character is massive, consistent, and, to me, incontrovertible. Berlin was the centre of the naissance of the German Social Democratic movement — led by August Bebel in the 1870s and '80s — the political formation instrumental in creating the image of "Red Berlin" by the turn of the century. The city provided the thinker's study for Eduard Bernstein, an underappreciated social democratic theorist at the beginning of the twentieth century who envisaged the possibility of an "evolutionary socialism," and was a precursor of contemporary European centre-left thinking. Berlin was the site of, simultaneously, a civil war and a bloody internecine struggle among leftist parties in the era of the Russian Revolution and the end of World War I, as well as the place where a workers' general strike defeated an attempted right-wing coup, the Kapp Putsch of 1920.

The striking, often-ignored cipher of Berlin's relationship to the Nazis is that the city never voted for Hitler's party. From the tragic failure of the Weimar Republic of the 1920s through the rise of Nazism, Berlin's right-wing vote was always proportionally less than in Germany as a whole, and even in the various elections of the 1930s, at the time of and after Hitler's ascension to the chancellorship, the Nazi vote in Berlin never amounted to more than slightly over a third of the city's electorate, while more than a fifty per cent majority supported left-wing parties. After the Nazi debacle and the division of the country, West Germany opted for the Christian Democratic regime of Konrad Adenauer, but the city of West Berlin elected a postwar socialist mayor, Ernst Reuter. In the late 1950s, Berlin provided the base for the political career of Willy Brandt, one of Germany's most interesting left-wing civic and federal icons.

One is hard pressed to make sense of the various anarchist, "autonomous," student radical, "squatter," and green political activities of the 1960s through to the 1980s without placing them in the context of the history of Berlin as a left-wing city. In East Germany's first free election in 1990, while the newly post-Communist East Germans elected a Christian Democratic Union government (lured by the economic prospects offered by Chancellor Helmut Kohl's West German CDU regime), East Berlin gave fully two-thirds of its vote to the Social Democrats, the Party of Democratic Socialism (the leftist successor party to East Germany's Communists), and other left-of-centre formations.

Finally, twenty-first century Berlin voted into office (and then re-elected) a "Red-Red" coalition government of the Social Democrats and the Democratic Socialists, headed by a social democratic mayor who, shortly before the election, casually announced that, by the way, he was gay, "and that's okay, too." In the European Parliamentary elections of May 2014, much of Europe voted for extreme-right-wing, even proto-Fascist, parties in a backlash of popular dissatisfaction with the European Union. But both Germany and Berlin remained remarkably stable in their political expression. Germany as a whole voted, as it had in the past, for a majority of Christian Democrats, the party of the long-time chancellor of the country, Angela Merkel, and Social Democrats. The four leading mainstream parties, CDU, Social Democrats, Greens, and the Left took about eighty per cent of the vote, leaving little for the anti-EU fringe parties, unlike the results in France and the UK. In Berlin, the majority of votes were won by left-of-centre parties: the Social Democrats, Greens, and the Left Party.

The reason I point to this in detail is because of the historian's problem with the difficulty of locating the voice of the imaginary persona that is a city. If anything stands out in trying to determine what "Berlin thinks," it is the behaviour of its citizens at the polls across more than a century. One could argue that the support for the left is merely a sort of rhetorical posturing rather than a reflection of a civic mentality, but I think that's a hard case to make. While voting is hardly the only measure of what a city thinks, the strikingly consistent pattern of Berlin's voting, and its contrast to the national pattern, certainly makes it one of the foundations upon which to build the narrative of the city's history.

FINALLY, THERE'S WALTER BENJAMIN, my primary guide in this account of Berlin, and a man who authored portraits of other cities: Moscow, Paris, Naples, and Marseilles. In 2000, while visiting Chicago, I met Lisa Fittko, then 89 years old, the woman who had led Benjamin through the Pyrenees Mountains on his fatal flight from Hitler in 1940. For her, Benjamin was but another of the many left-wing Jewish refugees who appeared at her door in Port Vendres in southern France, seeking assistance from the small Jewish resistance group she led. "I took him over the mountains, not because he was the famous philosopher he became after his death," she told me, "but just because he was one of us."

In Fittko's own writings, she recalls the morning Benjamin appeared. "My dear lady," he said to her, "please forgive the intrusion — I hope this is not an inopportune time." Fittko adds, "The world is falling to pieces, I thought, but Benjamin's courtesy is unshakeable." Thanks to Fittko, Benjamin safely arrived in the coastal town of Portbou, Spain, hoping to make his way across that country to neutral Portugal, from which he planned to travel to the United States. But in Portbou, the fascist government of Francisco Franco cancelled all transit visas and ordered the police to return refugees like Benjamin to France. Fearing repatriation to Nazi Germany, Benjamin killed himself with an overdose of morphine tablets on September 25, 1940.

Sitting in Fittko's apartment on Chicago's South Side between the University of Chicago and Lake Michigan, and gazing at this elderly heroic woman, I experienced a strange sensation. Her sight, she told me, had grown fainter with the years, which caused me to glance up at her and realize that I was looking into eyes that had seen both Benjamin and Hitler. For an instant she was the embodiment of the angel of history whose empathic gaze falls on Berlin.

City without Citizens
(Budapest, 1993)

> *Dissidents, who have led this exodus, this desertion of the City, now find themselves in the wilderness ... We cannot describe it, since the public words, capable of speaking of things that are not personal, were exiled, together with all of us, when we left the City, all together.*
>
> GASPAR TAMAS, "THE LEGACY OF DISSENT" (1993)

> *... not infrequently our views can be read "between the the lines" ... Observers might well imagine that here is long-awaited proof that art is an adversary of the establishment.*
>
> MIKLÓS HARASZTI, *THE VELVET PRISON* (1987)

I returned to Budapest in June 1993. Apart from wanting to enjoy the city once more by walking its alternately beautiful and frantic streets again, I wanted to measure the political and cultural changes in Hungary since 1990.

A few weeks before I arrived, I'd read a lucid, bitterly self-critical, classically conservative essay by Gaspar Tamas, "The Legacy of Dissent: How Civil Society Has Been Seduced by the Cult of Privacy." Tamas was a philosopher and opposition member of the Hungarian

Parliament. Accompanying his article in the pages of the *Times Literary Supplement* (May 14, 1993) was a 1988 photo of him being arrested in Budapest and led away by the Hungarian police.

"In today's Eastern Europe, the dissidence of the 1970s and '80s is not popular," the essay briskly began. "In the Hungarian Parliament, any mention of dissidence is greeted with laughter, catcalls and jeers from the government benches," Tamas continued, pointing out that the former anti-Communist activists were increasingly marginalized in the political arena, often derided, however ironically, as Communist themselves. The very existence of dissidence as a historical fact was not only belittled, but sometimes even denied by the right-of-centre nationalist ruling party, the Hungarian Democratic Forum.

Tamas understood some of the backlash. "The attempt to create a respectable pedigree and the embarrassment felt by the present democratic leaders, who nearly without exception have been collaborationists, former Communist Party officials or at best pusillanimous 'sleepers' (having spent the last fifty years saying nothing), are understandable," he sneered, then added, "Nevertheless, the general antipathy felt towards dissidents calls for some explanation."

If anyone could explain what had gone wrong in Hungary, Tamas appeared to be the man. It proved easy enough to get a telephone number in Budapest for him. He was at home when I called, my unfeigned enthusiasm for his essay appeared to please him, and he invited me to visit him when I got to Budapest.

That something *had* gone wrong in the years immediately after the Central and Eastern European revolutions of the late 1980s was not in question. While parts of the new Europe were painfully transforming themselves into capitalist democracies (more painfully than expected, particularly in Hungary), elsewhere the end of Communism had produced chaos, kleptocracy, and horror.

The Soviet Union had ceased to exist, collapsing into its component ethnic parts, and was daily threatened with further splintering wherever a local militia could assemble enough men and weapons to raise a flag for a new "Absurdistan," as such entities were sarcastically dubbed by the international media. The former Yugoslavia had been turned into a multi-ethnic pit of terror. At the less extreme margins, ex-Communist and post-Communist socialist parties had, for the moment, wrested electoral power from the nationalists in now-independent Lithuania, and would soon do likewise in Poland. Whether former Communists had taken control of the governments of Romania and Bulgaria was a matter of dispute. Even in otherwise pacific Germany, neo-Nazi violence was on the rise, a reaction to the great waves of emigration under way across Europe, and the costs of German reunification had proved to be vastly more expensive than promised, even as the country struggled with economic recession and unemployment, particularly in the former East Germany. Now people spoke of the process of change requiring a generation, rather than a mere, if bumpy, two or three years. It was the matter-of-factness rather than the prospect of further suffering that was notable.

CHRISTOPH, THE PROPRIETOR OF the apartment on Leo Frankel Street in Budapest where I was staying, was an impoverished but enthusiastic composer. The flat had been leased as a studio to a painter named Ursula, who was off to Vienna for a week with her kids and her husband, an airlines executive, before making a quick stop back in Budapest (I'd get to meet her then) prior to taking off for a family holiday in Florida.

Ursula was a friend of my painter friend in Berlin, Michael Morris, who had made the arrangements for my stay. When I talked to her on the phone, she explained that she was in the process of giving up the lease but that I'd be looked after by the apartment's owner. Christoph lived at the top of the building in a half-finished garret. There he wrote his scores while wealthier artists provided some sublet income. It would be easy, she said, to fit me into the loose network of acquaintances and collegial relationships that wove through the flat on Leo Frankel Street.

At seven in the morning the stone floor of the apartment's balcony was cool to my bare feet as I took a cup of fresh coffee out to a wicker table where I could pile my morning reading. The front rooms of the apartment, protected from the summer heat by slatted wooden shades, overlooked the tram tracks running down Frankel Street, and looked out over the river a block or so beyond. The balcony faced west into a leafy courtyard and other apartments, beyond which were the rising green hills of Buda. The cloudless sky was a purer and deeper blue than any I had seen in several months in cloudy Berlin.

"Dissent was an anomaly," Gaspar Tamas wrote in the essay that I was reading for a third time. "The minority within the body politic which was aware of 'dissident activities,' as they were called, felt ambivalent about them. This was because the dissidents ... questioned the tacit assumption that all resistance was so dangerous it was impossible, thus challenging the moral stance of those who had been silently opposed to the Communist regime, but did not dare to do anything about it."

The guilty "sleepers" were the ones most prejudiced against the dissidents afterwards. "According to them," Tamas wrote, "dissidents were not so much telling the leaders of the regime to 'Go to hell!' as saying 'Shame on you!' to the majority of bystanders." Tamas admitted that he had been so frequently accused of this that he'd begun to entertain some doubts about what his motives had been. More important, and "in reality, 'dissident activities' also challenged another common East European assumption, namely that all politics are dirty, *civisme* does not exist, the law is only for the strong; it therefore followed that anyone who was prepared to make visible sacrifices for their political beliefs must be mad."

I studied the photograph of Tamas positioned in the centre of the TLS page. He was a man with a thick black beard and what appeared to be glasses that had been knocked askew (I couldn't see the detail in the photo's graininess), dressed in a short-sleeved white shirt and suspenders for his jeans, being frog-marched across a patch of open asphalt, one arm twisted behind his back by one of two uniformed cops.

Tamas offered a mocking portrait of himself and the other dissidents who'd resisted the Communists but had since been marginalized. Still, "at a time when 'thaw' and détente made Soviet systems seem almost acceptable, the lonely voice of dissenters from behind the Iron Curtain had some impact. Feeble voices, of course, but they proved, simply by having spoken, that the quest for liberty and justice remained universal, that state socialism was not a permanent fixture rooted in the ineffable traditions of the East, that the dilemmas of mankind were at least interrelated."

I had the tail end of the weekend to wander about the city in what was intense early summer heat. Beyond the Margaret Bridge, I made my way along the river for a while, then started up the hill on which the Matthias Church stood, following its hairpin turns until I found a shaded sidewalk café for a cool drink. For the rest of the afternoon I seemed to be traversing the bridges that spanned the Danube, crossing the Chain Bridge to the Pest side and, later, the long Margaret Bridge back to Buda. A few hundred metres past the apartment was a quiet square, where I had a solitary traveller's dinner in an almost empty neighbourhood restaurant called the Melodia.

When I got back to the apartment, Christoph was in the kitchen, having a late supper of buttered bread, pickles, and sausage. He was a thin, pale, strangely intense man in his early thirties, wearing round rimless glasses. We did a little French-style fencing over politeness — each apologizing for disturbing the other, although neither of us was actually disturbed, and anyway, the kitchen and bathroom facilities in his attic, which he was installing himself, were not yet functioning.

"Is this the apartment where you grew up?" I asked.

I didn't catch all the details, but the question led naturally to an account of the tangled history of his family, which included a sister, now married and the mother of children, who would soon claim the apartment for her expanding brood (something that Christoph felt he could hardly deny her). But the major event of his youth had centred on his brothers.

"I have two older brothers," he explained.

"Do they live in Budapest too?"

"Oh no, they've been in America for many years."

If it was many years, that meant they left during the Communist period.

"It was in 1975," he said. "They waited until the death of our mother. The next year, they fled to Italy, just like that."

"Do you mean you didn't know they were going?"

"They didn't say a word," Christoph said.

"You must have felt rather abandoned."

"I was sixteen," he said. "Well, of course there was my father and sister." There was also, as a consequence, the police, since the state had the right to seize the property of those who chose exile. "The police came and inventoried the furniture, even though it belonged to my father." They also, he noted, imposed a five-year ban on passport privileges for remaining family members.

Christoph hadn't seen his brothers again until last year, when he travelled to America. One of his brothers lived in San Francisco, where there was a music publisher to whom Christoph had sold some of his songs.

"Well, that must have been something," I said, somewhat neutrally, vaguely sensing emotions that weren't yet fully apparent.

"Not really. We're very different. They're interested in material things, cars, business, and I'm, well, more spiritual, I suppose. I felt estranged."

"Yes, of course."

"And then, all those years," he went on, "even though they were doing well, they sent nothing back to us." His mouth tightened. I grunted sympathetically. "When I arrived, I think he thought I simply wanted something. That I was, you know, a poor, primitive Hungarian."

"Well, at least there was the success with your music," I said, awkwardly trying to dispel the memory of familial bitterness I had inadvertently called up. "What sort of works do you write?"

"Oh, you must come up and hear it," Christoph offered, brightening a bit. "It's a new kind of music, very different." I missed the term he applied to it.

"Like the Renaissance. A reflowering. I call it 'Refulgence,'" Christoph said, repeating the word. He launched into an explanation

I was unable to follow, about fifths, sevenths, various chords. He was a seemingly shy man, his emotions kept carefully in check, but when he spoke of his compositions there was a childlike burst of delight mixed with fierce absorption.

"Well, once I hear it," I said.

"Yes, you must," he urged.

TOWARD THE END OF his book *The Velvet Prison* — in Hungarian it had the more pointed title *The Aesthetics of Censorship* — Miklós Haraszti discussed "the space between the lines."

I'd first heard of Haraszti in the 1970s, when an English edition of a book he'd written had been published under the title *A Worker in a Worker's State*. It was an autobiographical account of working in a Hungarian factory for a year, in which, in elegant and pungent prose, he disabused his readers of any illusions they might have of the "dignity of labour" under socialism, or the notion that the "workers' state" represented the workers who worked in it. It had affected my thinking about Communism, fuelling my doubts that it offered any solution to our problems. Its publication had also caused a small international fuss, since its author had been detained by the authorities and put on trial, occasioning petitions of protest from intellectuals in many countries. Then, as often happened with the dissidents of Eastern Europe, Haraszti slipped from view.

In the mid-1980s a second book by Haraszti, *The Velvet Prison*, appeared in the West. Though I had initially looked forward to reading it, I was, for some reason since forgotten, inattentive to it. I missed whatever its dark point was, and put it aside.

At the time of the Hungarian elections in 1990, I'd seen Haraszti briefly, then one of the dissidents-turned-parliamentary-candidates, at a press conference for the centre-left Free Democrats. Afterwards I'd gone up and introduced myself, making an appointment to interview him the following day, but something had come up that demanded his presence and the interview hadn't been done.

This time I'd brought along my copy of *The Velvet Prison* to read on the plane. As I noted on the copyright page, it had sailed under several flags. The French called it *The State Artist*, the English version had been given a typically catchy American title, but the original Hungarian name, *The Aesthetics of Censorship*, forced you to consider that "censorship," which we in the West thought of as brutal suppression, might have its own aesthetic — that it might be a system of art. In my reading of it this time, in the airspace between Berlin and Budapest, I grasped its point.

Haraszti accused readers in the West of taking pride in "reading between the lines." We scanned the pale parables that the censors had permitted to appear in print, he said, and imagined ourselves as co-conspirators with the daring authors who had inserted subversive messages.

"Observers might well imagine," wrote Haraszti, "that here is the long-awaited proof that art is an adversary of the establishment, even in its period of abject servility. What else would one find between the lines other than restrained protest, signs of cautious independence? The fact that one can read protest between the lines is, it is said, a concession of censorship that will all but defeat it … state culture's decay, in this view, becomes unstoppable the moment that art achieves the freedom of diverse interpretations — even if only between the lines."

If there was collusion in all this, he argued, it was not between authors and readers, as we had, with a touch of vanity, assumed, but between state artists and censors. "Censorship is no longer a matter of simple state intervention. A new aesthetic culture has emerged in which censors and artists alike are entangled in a mutual embrace. Nor is it as distasteful as traditional critics of censorship imagine … it is not that one does not encounter state meddling in the arts, rather, such meddling is no longer used to silence opposition to the state but to ensure that intellectuals will perform their proper role."

If we thought that Eastern European artists had regarded this velvet censorship as onerous, all we had to do was eavesdrop on their conversations at any of the "country villas reserved for intellectuals, or on the chitchat of high-ranking functionary artists after an official conference. One would be surprised to hear the satisfaction with which they tell each other about their 'misadventures' with the state. For censorship is the final glaze that the state applies to the work of art before approving its release to the public ... The artist and the censor — the two faces of official culture — diligently and cheerfully cultivate the garden of art together."

Haraszti declared that "many will prefer to believe that the poet will write a poem that he does not like because of the threat of imprisonment instead of accepting the much simpler truth: art is not wedded to freedom forever and always."

That was the heresy at the heart of his thesis, which made it not just a clarification of a fallen past, but a challenge to the post-Communist present, and it was as unsettling in its way as the philosophical proposal at its root that we might be living in a world that must do without truth, universality, reason.

"Rumour has it that freedom is an essential condition of art," but in fact, he reminded us, "these notions are actually quite recent. Only since the middle of the nineteenth century has art been seen as synonymous with anti-authoritarianism ... That artistic autonomy could be an end in itself was part of the promise of bourgeois civilization." We had, he argued, only to think of the ancient state artists of Greece or Egypt, or the visible lack of freedom in the art of medieval Christendom.

In any case, "the figure of the independent artist is now to be found only in the waxworks museum, alongside that of the organized worker," Haraszti declared. "Independent art is impossible because there is no independent audience."

That got me thinking. If there is no independent audience for independent art in the regimes that had recently been dissolved, I wondered, how independent was the audience outside the late state socialism that Haraszti pilloried? How free was our free-market art? Most people in the societies of North America no longer, if they ever had, found art relevant to their lives. Could we still describe as art those products whose final glaze was applied by "entertainment" rather than censorship?

Haraszti's message was not only a bleak admonition to his compatriots of a decade ago, but one that also resonated across the post-Communist present. The one taboo of state-directed art was the exclusion of any art "that might suggest that reality is, or sometimes is, nonaligned, indifferent, aimless, absurd, intangible, deaf, dumb or blind ... State art neither hates nor worships reality: it merely denies reality the chance to be mysterious."

THE PHOTOGRAPH ON THE cover of *The Velvet Prison* showed a prematurely balding man with a moustache and straggly beard lying back, half-exhausted, in a chair. Even his shirt seemed to sag against his torso. The lively, clean-shaven man with dark eyes and black hair before me bore no resemblance to that photo.

In an office several floors up in a white marble-sheeted building — it had been the Communist Party headquarters, but now it was at the disposal of members of Parliament — I showed Miklós Haraszti the cover of the English edition of his book.

"Who is that?" I asked about the man in the photograph, a person readers might assume was Haraszti himself since the edition carried no author's photo on the back.

Haraszti, who had seen it before, said, "I don't know. It must be the designer's idea. I think the designer thought that this was a typical East European intellectual."

We both began laughing.

"He looks like he's just suffered a complete intellectual collapse," I said.

"Yes, exactly," Haraszti chortled. "And look here," he said, pointing to a blur where the man's wrist met the arm of the chair, "the faint suggestion of a handcuff. Do you see it?"

"Yes!"

"As if his being handcuffed to the chair should be felt in your subconscious," Haraszti joked.

We talked for an hour or more. Haraszti was now a parliamentarian preoccupied with party politics, and hadn't written any books since the one about the aesthetics of censorship. "Predictably, I got the criticism that I exaggerated," he said, "that it wasn't that deep a mental slavery, it wasn't that unconscious."

Mostly, we talked about the theory of "civil society" that the dissidents in Hungary, Poland, and elsewhere had evolved, the notion that a self-generated parallel culture would gradually force the Communist regimes to accept the compromise of a social contract. He regarded the theory as a failure, or at best, moot: by the time the regimes were prepared for such a contract, "they were already so weak that it wasn't needed anymore." For the past three years he had been embroiled in a debate over the independence of radio and television. By his account, it was a losing battle for independence.

Before the arrival of democracy, his dissident politics and literary engagements meshed; they were, as he said, "a good solution to my schizophrenia." Now his life was "a mélange of useful engagement, personal discontent, and, well, some personal satisfaction too." But no, there weren't any new books.

WHEN I GOT BACK TO the apartment on Frankel Street that afternoon, Christoph was on the balcony outside the apartment with a well-dressed woman and two children. The woman was Ursula, the occupant of the apartment, just back from Austria and leaving for Florida the next morning. She'd brought a bucket of raspberries from the countryside, and a bottle of champagne, which we consumed while she showed us photographs of her American relatives.

After Ursula and her children departed, I followed Christoph up to his attic, under the eaves of the building. The half-finished kitchenette and toilet were a tangle of rough plaster and gypsum board, and the space's single room was more than half-occupied by a black baby grand piano. I wondered how he'd been able to winch it up and into his tiny nest.

When he sat before it and played, Christoph was transformed from the shy, emotionally careful person he presented in other circumstances. As he struck the keys, there was a power in his forearms that I hadn't noticed before, a set to his jaw; his eyes gleamed. The music was without any of the dissonance that the twentieth century had explored. It was a mixture of nineteenth-century melodies and the ethereal tones of what was known as "New Age" music, a brew of mysticism, fabricated ancient voices, and reincarnational determinism. I liked some of it, but I was more impressed by his skill at the piano, and by the sensory pleasure of "live" music.

Even the slightest encouragement, more politeness than enthusiasm on my part, was sufficient to launch Christoph into what was both a technical discussion — he played passages of Beethoven's late piano sonatas to show me how he resolved certain problems of chords in his own work — and a messianic announcement of the "Refulgence" movement. The music sought a metaphysical balance between the technical and the spiritual: he imagined a new Golden Age unfolding within it.

His madness seemed inoffensive enough that I invited him to dinner at the nearby Melodia. On the way back, he took me into a neighbourhood basement wine bar that I had passed several times without noticing. Its low ceiling was held up by rough-barked timbers, the Riesling on offer was decanted into tureen-sized metal containers.

After dinner, walking home in the dark, Christoph again stopped to show me something else I would otherwise have missed. It was an apartment building, set back from the tram stop in the square but not particularly different in appearance from its neighbours. An ornate metal grill gate opened into the courtyard, around which rose several floors of apartments. There were lights here and there, laundry hanging to dry, bits of sound, the normal life of a block of flats. But in the centre of the courtyard, instead of a tree or patch of cement, there was a squat, round building.

"What is it?" I asked.

Its window frames of crumbling cement held a Star of David motif, as did its locked entrance.

"A synagogue," he said.

"Really?" I was surprised. "Do they still use it?"

"Yes, I think so."

In the darkness, we walked halfway around it. Again I had the
sense of encountering a depth of Budapest I couldn't possibly come
to know. Old Jewish neighbourhoods, crumbling remnants of a long-
past community life, bitter histories, all of this glimpsed for a few
moments in the night.

MY RETURN TO BUDAPEST, ostensibly intended to survey the progress
of a fledgling post-Communist democracy, had taken a rather different turn. I'd ascertained that its parliamentary government was,
if unloved, sound enough (there were preparations for future elections as the first four-year term wound down). I had some idea of its
standard of living: impoverished compared to Western Europe —
precarious even — but not in utter ruin, as was the case with several
of the republics that had emerged from the former Soviet Union. And
there was sufficient pluralism that a zany composer could imagine
that his melodies might inspire a social movement.

Yet the story whose spoor I followed seemed to be that of the fate of
a certain kind of *thought*. What had happened to the ideas of the dissidents, to the theory of civil society? This story was discursive despite
its brief moments of "action" — a drink in a bar, the playing of a
piano. It hinged on stitched-together passages of exposition, reflections on the unexpected outcome of the fall of Communism that I
kept losing my grip on in my aimless, almost dreamy perambulations
through the streets and over the bridges of Budapest in the hot sun.

On Molnar Street, a block back from the Danube, I arrived in my
overheated state at Gaspar Tamas's apartment. He led me into a study
lined with books from floor to ceiling. Not only were the shelves
full, but piles of books and journals occupied every available surface,
spilling onto tables, chairs, and a small daybed against the wall. I
mopped my forehead with a handkerchief.

"Here, let me," he said, hauling away a tottering heap of books
to make a space for me to sit down. Tamas was thinner than in
his dissident days, his once bushy beard now carefully trimmed, his
fluent English still tinged with the accents of an Oxford don.

I had spoken with Haraszti about the dissidents' notion of "civil society," and he had dismissed it in a single, backward glance. Tamas was not content with that. After all, the notion that there could be a civil society had informed the resistance to dictatorship not only in Hungary but throughout Eastern Europe, from Poland, where Adam Michnik had expounded its tenets, to Václav Havel's Czech Republic, which had been peacefully severed from Slovakia at the beginning of 1993 — the "Velvet Divorce," as it was called in the press.

Tamas's essay about the legacy of dissent may have begun with an inquiry into the post-Communist "general antipathy felt toward dissidents," but his deeper interest was in the dissidents' own understandings and misunderstandings about a number of central ideas: civil society, democracy, and the resistance to the Communists that Hungarian writer György Konrád had dubbed "anti-politics." What Tamas found profoundly disturbed him.

The idea of a civil society held by the Eastern European opposition had been inherited, Tamas noted, from the Enlightenment liberalism in the West. The classic problem of Western liberal society, where the power of the state was weak compared to the absolutist monarchies that preceded it, had been to fashion a civil society in which the initiative necessary for self-government could be sustained through the activity of citizens in voluntary associations. "In other words," Tamas put the question, "how were they to hold society together in the absence of a preordained hierarchy?"

The problem faced by Eastern European opponents of the Communist regimes was entirely different. If Western theorists had to figure out how to "persuade the autonomous individual in a free society to be a citizen ... my generation in Eastern Europe had to counter the crushing preponderance, the all-pervasive omnipresence of the police state. Our fear was not ... that individuals would become 'atomized,' disoriented, amoral, oblivious to duty. We were afraid that without diversified, pluralistic voluntary associations the dutiful citizens of the totalitarian state would become *automata*."

The Eastern European idea of civil society, Tamas argued, therefore had to be pitched *against* the state. If the Western idea of civil society was political, "the East European dissident idea was anti-political. The East European idea was, as can be seen from the works of Havel and Konrád, to avoid politics altogether with the aid of a straightforward morality which would stress the beauty of everyday life, integrity in small matters ... and above all, *authenticity*." Havel had called it "living in truth." The result was a deep suspicion of institutions, particularly those established and controlled by the state. Tamas thought that such anti-political disdain for "institutional discourse, the imposition of codes of behaviour, ideas of justice, and an abstract universal language" were contributory factors to the present disarray.

Given such a view of society and state, it is not surprising that dissidents focused on a campaign for individual human rights. The campaign had been successful, to a point. Since Communist states had signed international human rights accords, they had to face the dissidents' question: Why can't people say what they believe to be the truth?

The human rights for which Tamas and others had fought, he now believed, had been selected "so as to be anti-political," to interfere little with the existing structures of power. Perhaps this was understandable, given the overbearing and violent reality of Soviet power and Western acquiescence to the status quo of a world divided by the Iron Curtain. But it also reflected the view that for most dissenters, "civic community, the state, the law were all suspect. Freedom resided in individual moral action. In Eastern Europe, dissenters believed, human rights would leave action to a very small state manned by administrators."

In the end, those rights would "nullify any conceivable claim of the City on its citizens: the exodus of the citizen from the City would be completed. Dissidents, who have led the exodus, the desertion of the City, now find themselves in the wilderness. They find themselves faced with a body of opinion which fails to recognize any institutional authority, any civic duty, any political obligation, any idea of the common good, while at the same time impatient with disorder and squalor."

It was a withering critique, I thought, and one that also applied to the societies of the West, where the retreat from politics was as widespread as Tamas claimed it to be in post-Communist society. The sources of disaffection might be different — consumerism, entertainment, trivia, a media-driven disdain for the "City" — but the results were similar.

"It seems to me that this is a very lacerating self-criticism," I said about his essay, once I had settled myself into the crowded study.

"Well, that's what it is, yes," Tamas agreed, as he wedged a window open to stir the sticky, warm air of the room.

I was curious to know how he had made the journey from the dissident insistence on individuals "living in truth" to views that seemed to sail within sight of Plato's *The Republic*. Tamas had begun as something of a libertarian, and now he was a parliamentary representative of a centrist party, even a left-centrist party. Yet his thinking had brought him to an ancient conservatism.

"Well, we went through this period of self-admiration," he began. Then, as if impatiently brushing it away, added, "And we've had quite enough of all that. It was time to find out what had happened to us, and what happened to this country, to establish the part of responsibility we share for what I see as a flop of these Eastern European democracies."

He underscored the word "flop." "We shouted on the streets of Budapest, 'We want democracy!' Not rule of law, not liberty, not justice, but democracy." And now one could see what the idea of democracy had amounted to, simply by looking at what people presently considered anti-democratic. "Imposition of political will by an elite — law — is anti-democratic. Coercion used to elicit uniform behaviour — public order — is also anti-democratic." And the list continued through representative government and the redistribution of wealth through public taxation — all were seen as anti-democratic. What was left but "an overwhelming desire for the obliteration of the public realm"? In his essay, Tamas invoked a passage from Hannah Arendt's *The Human Condition*, which admonished us that "this enlargement of the private, the enchantment, as it were, of a whole people, does not make it public, does not constitute a public realm, but, on the contrary, means only that the public realm has almost completely receded."

Tamas looked back on it ruefully. "We were all part of the great web, weren't we; the heroic times, thank God, are over, a new world begins, a world of creative disorder," he said, ironic to the end. But despairing also. "We cannot describe it, since the public words capable of speaking of things that are not personal, were exiled together with all of us, when we left the City, all together," he had written.

It was late when we left the stifling study and walked through the dark, empty streets, past the closed courtyards of apartment buildings that lined the neighbourhood streets.

Tamas had been raised in the Transylvanian city of Cluj, a member of the Hungarian ethnic minority in Romania. His father, a descendant of the petty nobility, had been the manager of the local provincial theatre there. His mother was Jewish. Tamas described the city of his youth as a place frozen in the past.

"I did things in childhood like Austrian children did in the nineteenth century," he remembered, as we walked toward a nearby restaurant. "Sunday afternoon visits where children were seen and not heard. My father came home every night in a hansom cab. This was in the 1960s, mind you."

"You mean, with a horse?" I asked, trying to imagine the backwater from which this thoroughly cosmopolitan philosopher had emerged.

"Yes, of course. It wasn't for tourists, it was the real thing. It was creaky and old and it smelled." Tamas wrinkled his nose. He had studied philosophy in Cluj, and managed to get in trouble with the Romanian authorities for "refusing to conform, rather than doing anything in particular. So I just had to go." He had immigrated to Hungary when he was thirty.

But it was not his student days that were on Tamas's mind so much as the views of his students at the institute where he now taught. "I see the new generation of students," he said, "and their perception of the democratic changes and mine are diametrically opposed to each other. What do they say? They say that the present-day democracy is an abdication. They think that there was a socialist dream, which was beautiful, but human nature is so depraved that we just cannot live up to that vision, and so we have to face the prose of everyday life, the sinful nature of man."

"My students say the same thing," I commiserated.

"And they're bored," Tamas added.

The restaurant was an expensive, splendidly-appointed basement establishment. Tamas was known to the management, who fussed over him. Across the crisp linen, we shared a bottle of rosé wine through a procession of dishes. When the brandy arrived at the end, we were still engrossed in the image of the endangered City.

"There's a shyness and taboo everywhere when it comes to thinking about the state," Tamas insisted. He cited as examples the current bloodbath in Bosnia, and the lawlessness of Russia. "The warriors in Bosnia don't say that it's their right. They don't say that their culture is superior. They say, 'If you don't give way, I'll shoot you.' That's all they say. An inarticulate, personal, individualistic idea which has nothing to do with the state, with institutions. And this is compounded by the demise of the state itself," he went on. "Look at Russia — the problem with Russia is not that Russia has a state which has failings of this or that kind; Russia doesn't have a state — the state has simply disappeared, sucked into the black hole. Are the Russians free? I very much doubt it."

"Essentially you're saying that, insofar as you had an influence, you created a city without citizens," I said.

"So it unfortunately seems," he concurred. "My fear is that there will be no city. No city can survive for long without citizens."

At midnight, we emerged from the underground eatery. The air was still warm. The streets were deserted, but shadows flitted along the arcades of the silent buildings. We had come to the surface of a city that seemed, for the moment, to be emptied of a citizenry. It was not the Ancient City, but our own. If Gaspar Tamas was right, then the ruins of the abandoned city would not only be found in Budapest.

❦

I WALKED ACROSS THE Margaret Bridge one more time on my last evening in Budapest. Though I was uneasy with heights, a fear compounded when the heights were situated over water, for days I had trudged back and forth over bridges. I averted my eyes from the water far below, fixing my gaze either on the tram tracks that ran down the centre of the bridge or on the ornate Parliament Buildings along the shore. At the end there was a pedestrian tunnel that dipped under the road, emerging either at the tram stop in the busy centre of the avenue, or on the walks to either side of it.

We had agreed to meet at nine, but he hadn't arrived. I watched each of the trams unloading, looking for him. The light was going, the day's heat still lingered. I dodged through the traffic and stood across from the tram stop by a flower seller's kiosk. After about fifteen minutes of scanning the faces of people descending from the trams, I began to think that either I'd gotten the meeting place wrong, or he had stood me up.

The first time he passed, at a distance, we missed each other. Then he spotted me, and crossed over from the tram island to where I was standing.

"I'm sorry to be late," he apologized, shaking my hand and shifting a small knapsack from one shoulder to another.

"Szabolsc," I said. I hadn't quite reconciled the young man I'd briefly met three years ago with the one before me now. We had exchanged letters and a couple of phone calls in the interval. When I got to Budapest I phoned his house and his father gave me his number at work. "Well, let's get a drink," I said.

"Yes, of course, but I'm afraid that I can't stay very long," he answered. "I have to be on the other side of town by ten thirty."

It was only after we found a basement pub and were seated on stools, having a beer, that I began to see him. His hair was drawn back severely and tied in back. His green shirt bore a design of black arrowheads. Facing him, I saw both eyes at once, the dark sighted one and the blank, milky one.

"Well, what's happened to you since we last saw each other?" I wanted to know. "What's the place you're working at?"

"It's an advertising agency," he said. I missed the name, a set of initials.

"What do you do there?"

"I'm in charge of the computer system," he explained.

"Computers," I said.

"It's quite a big place," he said. "Over thirty people work there. The directors are two women. They're really nice, it's very non-hierarchical."

It must pay pretty well, I thought.

"Well, I'm working long hours, but the pay is good. It's about $500 a month. In fact, I'm a little embarrassed because I'm making more money in three years than my father, who's worked at his place for twenty years."

And was there a girlfriend?

"She's an American. She was teaching English here in Budapest a couple of years ago, but now she's back in America. I've visited her there a couple of times."

He had been to New England. He was impressed by its unspoiled nature, and the cleanliness, but he didn't think he could live there. "The cultural differences, I think, are too great for me. I'm hoping she'll come here."

"It sounds like love," I joked.

"Yes, perhaps," he allowed.

"So it's all worked out for you pretty well," I said. "What about Fidesz, is that still your political party?"

"I think it's still the best party, yes," he said, and recited the most recent opinion poll figures.

He related one or two anecdotes about the hectic pace of work, then glanced at his watch. "We have this ten thirty dinner meeting with some Austrian clients. They've come from Vienna. It's about a new software accounting program."

"Well, it's been good to see you again," I said, as he lifted his backpack onto his shoulder. I walked him back to the main street, where he could catch a cab to his dinner meeting. It was dark, and the avenue was now bustling with traffic.

"Do you remember," I asked him, just before we parted, "when you told me three years ago how frightened you had been as a boy the day they announced Brezhnev's death?"

The memory made him laugh.

"That was a long time ago," he said, perhaps referring not only to the death of a former leader of a former empire, but to three years ago as well. The cab took him away, quickly swallowed by the surge of traffic as it disappeared into the city. I turned back toward the bridge.

The Springtime of Nations

In 1989 I read the phrase "the springtime of nations" in a piece by the British historian and journalist Timothy Garton Ash. The phrase originally referred to the European revolutions of 1848, which had challenged the absolutist state. But in the magical year of 1989, Garton Ash applied it to the mixture of reform from above and non-violent uprisings in the streets that was then underway across Europe. Poland and Hungary were the first to experience these "refolutions," as Garton Ash dubbed them, and then within months, a seeming chain reaction brought down the Berlin Wall, transformed Czechoslovakia and Romania, and sent a shudder of impending change through Europe from the Baltic to the Balkans.

A couple of springtimes had come and gone, and it was now 1993. The ebullient seasons of the early 1990s had given way to warier, wearier ones as the mid-1990s approached. One might still refer to the end of Communism, as one commentator did, as a "historical event comparable in importance to the fall of the Roman Empire," but increasingly I found myself thinking of other empires, other tyrannies — the Hapsburgs, the five-hundred-year Ottoman Empire — which had become dim memories. Maybe the fall of Soviet Communism would assume a similar, much diminished place in the historical record. Communism (or at least *that* Communism, so as not to foreclose the possibility of future ones) had, although predicated on an idea of human freedom and economic equality, irreparably ruined the lives of three generations between 1917 and 1989.

As early as mid-1991, Václav Havel wrote in *Summer Meditations*: "The return of freedom to a society that was morally unhinged has produced something ... which has turned out to be far more serious than anyone could have predicted: an enormous and dazzling explosion of every imaginable human vice." The former intellectual dissident who had sounded the alarm during the Communist era was once more issuing cautionary admonitions as the president of post-Communist Czech society.

"Thus we are witnesses to a bizarre state of affairs: society has freed itself, true, but in some ways, it behaves worse than when it was in chains," said Havel, echoing Rousseau's celebrated paradox in *The Social Contract* ("Man is born free, yet everywhere he is in chains."). "Criminality has grown rapidly," Havel continued, "and the familiar sewage that in times of historical reversal always wells up from the nether regions of the collective psyche has overflowed into the mass media. But there are other, more serious and dangerous symptoms: hatred among nationalities, suspicion, racism, even signs of fascism; politicking, an unrestrained ambition, fanaticisms of every conceivable kind, the rise of different mafias; and a prevailing lack of tolerance, understanding, taste, moderation, and reason." It was an extensive enumeration of ills.

"Demagogy is rife," Havel said, "and even something as important as the natural longing of people for autonomy is exploited in power plays, as rivals compete in lying to the public. Many members of the Party elite, the so-called *nomenklatura* who, until very recently, were faking concern about social justice and the working class, have cast aside their masks and, almost overnight, openly become speculators and thieves. Many a once-feared Communist is now an unscrupulous capitalist ..."

Despite that litany of woes, Havel insisted, "As ridiculous or quixotic as it may sound these days, one thing seems certain to me: that it is my responsibility to emphasize, again and again, the moral origin of all genuine politics, to stress the significance of moral values and standards in all spheres of social life, including economics, and to explain that if we don't try, within ourselves, to discover or rediscover or cultivate what I call 'higher responsibility,' things will turn out very badly indeed."

Zagreb (1993)

I WENT TO ZAGREB, Croatia, in 1993, to see the writer Slavenka Drakulić, and — I don't know how to put this other than awkwardly — to get closer to the war. Not to get *into* the war, mind you. I'm not given to heroics, nor was I tempted by the tales told by reporters in Berlin about donning flak jackets to wander through the various shooting galleries. I simply wanted to get to an edge of it where I might be able to appreciate, second hand, what had befallen the former Yugoslavia.

Two years after the collapse of Communism in most Soviet-satellite countries, the Balkan mosaic of ethnicities that had become Communist Yugoslavia after World War II fell into division and war. What became known as the Yugoslav Wars, largely national and ethnic conflicts that began in 1991, quickly led to the breakup of the country and to deadly residual battles ostensibly over the issue of ethnic minorities. The wars, fuelled by nationalism, particularly of the Serbian government of Slobodan Milošević, but also that of Croatia, were the deadliest European conflict since World War II, and eventually became infamous for war crimes, including "ethnic cleansing," crimes against humanity, and extensive and sometimes systematic rape of women — crimes formally described as "genocidal" by the United Nations. Worse, much of Europe seemed intellectually indifferent, and emotionally frozen in its failure to respond to the catastrophe. One of the few clear voices that could be heard came from the former Yugoslavia itself.

Drakulić had written, in a book called *Balkan Express*, of the mis-understandings and indifference of Western outsiders, of their refusal to regard the present barbarities as a war in Europe. "Astonishment gives way to anger at the way Europe perceives this war," she wrote,

"— 'ethnic conflict,' 'ancient legacy of hatred and bloodshed.' In this way the West tells us, 'You are not Europeans, not even Eastern Europeans. You are Balkans, mythological, wild, dangerous Balkans. Kill yourselves, if that is your pleasure. We don't understand what is going on there ...'"

The assumption some former Yugoslavs had of belonging to European civilization was badly eroded. "We have been left alone with our newly won independence, our new states, new symbols, new autocratic leaders, but with no democracy at all. We are left standing on a soil slippery with blood, engulfed in a war that will go on for God knows how long," Drakulić lamented. "The accumulating deaths make the wall dividing us from Europe and the world even higher and more formidable, placing us not only on the other side of the border but on the other side of reason too." (Slavenka Drakulić, *Balkan Express*, 1993.)

When I asked the telephone operator in Berlin to connect me to Zagreb, she said, in a concerned and un-operator-like voice (but one that confirmed Drakulić's claim of European confusion), "Isn't there a war going on there?"

"I hope not," I said.

The next night, when I had to phone Drakulić again in Zagreb, I happened to get the same operator.

"Didn't I talk to you last night?"

"Yes, that's right."

"Well, I found out that there isn't a war going on in Zagreb," she said, relieved for both of us.

Zagreb was an unexpectedly beautiful city, but also cold and bitterly windy for the end of March. I don't know why I found its beauty unexpected. In fact, I don't know what I was expecting — perhaps that it would be like one of those architecturally patchwork neighbourhoods in Berlin.

That spring I was living in a small, coal-heated, whitewashed studio in the back of a run-down four-storey walkup in Berlin's Schöneberg district. It was a busy commercial neighbourhood of Turks and Germans, where the local red-brick Gothic church (St. Paul the

Apostle) was across the street from the Forum of Unknown Authors Café, and nineteenth-century *Jugendstil* edifices were jumbled amid copy shops, ethnic restaurants, and dilapidated heaps of plaster-faced apartment buildings.

Zagreb, by contrast, presented a certain grandeur, and it was laid out with a clarity that immediately alleviated the irrational minor panic I always feel on confronting the maze of an unknown city. The airport was south of the city, and the bus that took us to town passed through Zagreb's outer precincts, with the commercial modernist architecture that increasingly seemed to be a feature of cities everywhere.

But once we reached the imposing nineteenth-century railway station at the south end of the city centre, it became clear that we were in an elegant metropolis of the last century, with a grid street plan, spacious parks, and solid public buildings decorated with loggia-like balconies, art-nouveau goddesses embedded in corner alcoves, and muscular caryatids bearing the weight of tiled mansard roofs. The northern edge of downtown was occupied by Ban Jelačić Square, a large expanse of stone and marble where the tramlines all converged, tangles of embedded rails carrying the blue- and cream-coloured streetcars in various directions.

Behind the square, above an open vegetable market, narrow streets wound upwards and through twin medieval hill towns on the Medvenica uplands, where the present city of more than a million people took root over nine hundred years before. Above the city the dual spires of St. Stephen's Church were wrapped in construction nets and scaffolding for repair.

In Ban Jelačić Square, in addition to the crowds waiting huddled for trams in the late afternoon, knots of people gathered in conversation despite the wind — among them the occasional unarmed soldier in neatly pressed camouflage fatigues, the only sign that we might be near a war zone. Fronting the square were large coffee-houses. To escape the battering wind, I ducked into the Gradska Kavana, a cavernous room with plentiful tables and a broad, red-carpeted staircase leading up to a mezzanine. Once the hot milky foam of a cappuccino touched my chilled lips, I felt safer — and my "fool's errand" of coming to Zagreb to see a writer for an hour or two seemed slightly less ludicrous.

Slavenka Drakulić was, to my mind at least, one of those writers who had addressed the most difficult subject matter possible at the time. Although she thought of herself primarily as a novelist, Drakulić had written two remarkable works of literary non-fiction since 1989: *How We Survived Communism and Even Laughed*, and *Balkan Express*. In a later edition of the first book, after the Yugoslavian wars had broken out, she conceded that the title was all wrong. "We have not yet survived communism," she amended, "and there is nothing to laugh about." Other than that, nothing in either book had been superseded by subsequent events. The two books were, in effect, a single piece of work — consisting of, as she herself described it, "short half-stories, half-essays," dispatches from a shifting and interiorized "front" — which, as I'd seen from further newspaper publications, was ongoing. A few years later, she would complete this trilogy with *Café Europa: Life After Communism* (1996). I had been sufficiently moved by both the pain and the beauty of her writing to want to seek her out.

I reached her by phone from my room in the Hotel Dubrovnik. "Zagreb is surprisingly beautiful," I announced, as if she had specially arranged it for me.

"Well, why not?" Drakulić said in greeting. She couldn't see me until the following day. "There's a birthday party for a friend of mine that I have to go to. She's forty."

"Forty," I repeated.

"So, what will you do tonight?" she wondered.

"I haven't thought about it yet."

"Well, the movies are in English," she suggested.

"Maybe I'll wander up the street off the square with all the bars," I said noncommittally, although the cold, slate-grey sky didn't make outdoor wandering seem very inviting. She said the name of the winding lane I had seen on a map but couldn't pronounce. I was thinking that the logical place to be was at the birthday party.

"Perhaps the thing would be for you to come to the party," she said.

"Yes," I agreed.

"Well, I have to call Verna — it's her birthday — to see if it's all right to invite you. If it is, I'll call right back." Then she thought of the other possibility. "But if it isn't, then I won't call back because, well, I'll be too embarrassed."

A minute later the phone rang. "Verna says that anybody who has come all the way from Berlin to Zagreb to see me deserves to be invited," Drakulić reported. She gave me instructions for finding my way there.

At night, the dark empty streets I was walking through were forbidding. The wind blew down their length without letup. At the east end of Ban Jelačić Square there was a fork in the road, where one tram track curved to the south while another went straight ahead. I bore to the left, as I'd been instructed. I tried to shrink inside my jacket, but the wind chapped my face. At a major intersection, where a stoplight swayed in the gusts, I found the diagonal Rackoga Avenue that Drakulić had told me to look for. The instructions contained one odd bit that somehow humanized their functionality, a detail one wouldn't invent for a story: when I found the name on the doorbell — I had to take out my cigarette lighter and hold it in a cupped hand tosee the names on the listings tablet — I was to stick a pen tip into the hole where the button had broken off in order to ring the buzzer.

A man in a bow tie and tuxedo jacket greeted me at the door.

"You're the one who's come to see Slavenka," he said in English. He was the husband of the woman whose fortieth birthday it was. Suddenly I was inside, safe in the warmth and light of a large apartment.

The man led me down the entrance hallway to a black-gowned woman whose wrists were decorated with gold-coloured bangles. Drakulić and I shook hands. She was a strong, friendly, elegant woman in her mid-forties; a wave of her long, dark hair swept down over an eyebrow onto her shoulder. "So, you'll see a little bit of Zagreb intellectual life," she said, immediately taking me into the living room and introducing me to her friend Verna, to whom I offered birthday greetings. In a larger room beyond, a buffet — ham, salads, cheese, breads — had been laid out on a long table. Verna's husband brought me a whisky and soda. I was presented to a succession of people — a woman from a foundation, an engineer, a bearded historian, a young visiting Englishman who taught political science — their names going by me like the night wind. Slavenka and I agreed to meet at the Gradska the next afternoon.

I settled on the hefty, bearded, cigarette-smoking, whiskey-drinking historian, who had wedged his bulk into a space at the end of the hallway, at a juncture between the living room and kitchen through which the partygoers continually passed. We shared an over-full ashtray perched on the ledge of a set of shelves.

"Can you give me some idea of how things are?" I asked.

His body lifted in a gloomy shrug. His name was Zoren and he was associated with the opposition party. He made a point of assuring me that no one here was one of those Croatian nationalists who monopolized the news accounts I had no doubt read.

When the precarious federation of states that had made up Communist Yugoslavia under Josip Broz Tito from World War II to the latter's death in 1980 was finally swept aside in the wake of the events of 1989, the northwestern republics of Slovenia and Croatia quickly declared their independence, and succeeded in securing recognition throughout Europe, notwithstanding the opposition of Serbia, the dominant state in what remained of Yugoslavia. The elections in newly independent Croatia, however, had not produced democracy but a right-wing, populist, authoritarian government under Franjo Tuđman, one of Tito's former generals.

When the Serbian tanks, under the flag of the Yugoslav Federal Army, rolled across first Slovenia and then Croatia in response to their withdrawal from Yugoslavia, nationalism in the new republics became even more extreme than it had been. For more than a year now there had been a ceasefire between the Croats and the Serbs, with the latter occupying a third of the country, separated from Croat forces only by a United Nations buffer contingent. Croatian towns had been bombed — some reduced to rubble — and many people had been killed, but Zagreb had only been threatened with air raids, never hit. The war, in a more savage form, had moved south to Bosnia.

"So how is it here now?" I asked. We had been joined by the visiting British political scientist.

"It's neither not-war, nor is it not not-war," was the way Zoren formulated it, in a raspy voice that he soothed with Jim Beam bourbon.

The youthful Brit suggested to Zoren that the best way to understand the present situation was to study the period of 1900 to 1914, just before World War I exploded in the same area.

"Yes, we've always been in history," Zoren sighed on behalf of the Balkans, then added, "I wish we could have a five-minute break from history." He tossed back another Jim Beam.

Later, as I was leaving, I stepped into the kitchen to say goodnight. Slavenka, Verna, and the woman from the foundation were engaged in a bitter argument. Their necks were stiff with barely contained rage, but they had slightly hunched over to lower their voices. Slavenka broke off for a minute to see me out. "It's a local thing," she murmured, "about who will control a radio station we applied for." Behind her, in the kitchen, Verna and the other woman pursued the argument.

SLAVENKA APPEARED JUST AFTER noon in the Gradska Kavana. It was crowded and noisy downstairs, so we went up the grand staircase and found a secluded table on the mezzanine. While I waited for her, I'd glanced at one of the local tabloid newspapers lying on a table. There was a photo of a United Nations truck convoy bogged down in the snow somewhere to the south, in the Bosnian mountains, where it was still winter.

When I asked Slavenka what had happened since I'd read her latest words (the introduction to *Balkan Express* was dated some six months before), she too referred to the bogged-down nearby war.

"The situation has continued to be almost the same," she said. "In Croatia, we live in some kind of limbo. At one moment it seems as if there is a war going on, at another it seems as if it's not going on."

A waiter came up to take our order. I asked for a cappuccino, and Slavenka wanted a glass of cherry juice. As she ordered, I again noticed her physical vigour, in contrast to the weariness with which she spoke of the war. She was wearing a black turtleneck sweater, a long skirt, and leather boots. Her thick hair, striated with several dark tints, cascaded onto the turtleneck.

"I mean, here in Zagreb, you don't feel it. You can sit here in the café and see your friends as if nothing is happening. But only fifty kilometres from here is the front line, you know."

"Fifty kilometres?"

"Fifty kilometres," she repeated, "just about forty minutes' drive, nothing. So you are aware, constantly aware, that Zagreb could be hit at any minute. We learn to live with this kind of parallel reality. On one side feeling that you could practically die at any moment, and on the other side just pretending this is normality, keeping up with the normal kind of life as if nothing is going on. Because I think it's very important to live like this, to have music, to have flowers, to go visit friends, because it keeps the sanity of your mind."

We talked about the meaning of the war, which I had some idea of from her book. Its subject was how something unimaginable came upon you, closer and closer, until it was inside you. At one point "war was a distant rumour, something one managed to obscure or ignore — something happening to other people, to people on the outskirts of the republic, but never to us in the centre, in Zagreb," she wrote. "We were busy with our private lives, with love, careers, a new car. War was threatening us, but not directly, as if we were somehow protected by the flickering TV screen which gave us a feeling of detachment — we might just as well have been in Paris or Budapest. For a long time we have been able to fend off the ghost of war."

But even while you tried to live your own life, the war seeped in, in intimate and poignant ways. "As my daughter pauses a little before packing her suitcase for a holiday in Canada, 'Shall I take only summer things? Perhaps some light autumn clothes, too?' she asks me, as if not sure how long it will be before she comes back," Drakulić writes in *Balkan Express*, a book dedicated to her then-teenaged daughter, Rujana. "In her question, I recognize war creeping in between us, because the real question behind her words is: am I coming back?"

Finally, the war arrived in Zagreb as Slavenka and a friend were sitting down to lunch. "I prepared *pasta al bianco*, opened a bottle of red cabernet and just as we were about to eat, we heard the strange, unnerving sound," Drakulić recounted in *Balkan Express*. "I remember looking at my fork half way down to the plate, holding it there for a long moment as if something, some unknown force, was stopping me from putting it down. Only then did we hear the air-raid alarm — a long howling sound that until that moment we only knew from TV reports. I knew what we were supposed to do — run to the nearest shelter and hide." Instead, they both remained at the kitchen table listening to the roar of fighter jets flying low overhead. "It was not fear that I felt, or panic," Drakulić wrote. "There was no trace of emotion in me. Instead, I felt an empty space opening up like a hole in my chest, and with each passing moment my legs grew heavier and heavier, as if they were turning into stone ... The war was in my mind, in my legs, on the table, in the plate of pasta getting cold." Fortunately, no bombs had fallen on Zagreb.

In Slavenka's conversation, as in her book, her daughter was a frequent presence. When Slavenka referred to the future — "We have lost the future twice," she said, meaning once under Communism and again now — she seemed to be thinking of Rujana, a college student who had transferred to a university in Vienna. "I'm more or less old enough not to have any illusions any longer, but you have these young people and when you talk to them you have this feeling that they're not planning anything, they're not ... you know, it's very difficult to live when the future has been taken away from you."

Later, when we were talking about whether there was any point in writing during a war — Slavenka had cited the proverb, "While there is a war, the Muses are silent" — she again referred to her daughter. "I know that words are very weak weapons, but I don't have any others. I'm too weak physically to go and fight. I would never fight unless I was absolutely forced to, in self-defence, because I think

I would be capable of killing in self-defence or in defence of — I don't know — the person I loved, or something, like my daughter. I would be absolutely capable. So I am not one of those persons who think they are saints and say, I can't. I would fight for my life and the life of my daughter and my friends."

The great horror for her had been a recognition of the human capacity for war. "Part of us, as human beings, is that we are capable of these kinds of things." She recalled the Nuremberg trials at the end of World War II, which had seemed to proclaim an end to barbarism. "But when the first pictures appeared last year of Bosnian concentration camps here on TV, everybody was astonished. Did we learn anything from history? No, we didn't. Are we doing the same things? Yes, we are doing the same things." It was as though she was reciting a catechism. "Why are we doing the same things? Are we stupid? No, no, we are not stupid, we are just human beings, and human beings are really cursed in a way." The Enlightenment vision of human perfectibility had collapsed. "We are capable of everything. I think that I myself am capable of everything."

Her books had not been published in Croatia, though they had been translated into the languages of the world. One of her novels, *Marble Skin*, about a mother and daughter, was about to appear in English. "I am considered a *persona non grata* because I have criticized the government in the foreign press for not being democratic." Drakulić and some other dissident women writers and intellectuals had been collectively dubbed "the witches of Zagreb." The magazine for which she had written for several years, *Danas*, had been gutted by the regime, and the journalists removed. "In the media here there is some kind of picture of me as a dissident. They say I'm a traitor, that I'm not a good Croat, that I'm Yugo-nostalgic, and so on."

"Yugo-nostalgic?" I asked. She explained that, in the mood of nationalist fervour, the Yugoslavian past had become unmentionable.

"What they mean is that nobody has the right to write the way our memories are, to reconstruct our past. Forty years of our past has been wrong and bad. That's not true, you know," she insisted. "I had a normal decent life for the last forty years, and I don't want to forget it. I want to keep the memory, I have a right to keep the memories of my past, and I have a right to speak about that. What I don't like is the erasing of the past."

The square outside the coffee house where we were meeting offered an instance of history's zigzags. It had been named for a hero of the 1848 revolutions, but when Tito triumphed they redubbed it Republic Square, as it still was called on the old street map I had. The new nationalist government had restored the old name, and had installed a replica of the equestrian statue of Duke Jelačić, which now gleamed in the windy afternoon.

But it was not only the historic noble who had reappeared in independent post-Communist Croatia, Drakulić said. Names of figures from Fascist Croatia — the one previous era in the country when it had been independent — were now adorning renamed streets.

"Anti-fascism is something we should be proud of," said Drakulić, who was neither a Communist before nor a nationalist now. "I'm not saying Yugoslavia was good or bad, I'm saying this is part of my life and I have a right to remember it. So don't force me to forget it."

SLAVENKA WENT OFF TO a late lunch after our conversation, and I wandered the streets. The wind had dropped some, but as I traced the medieval streets of the upper town, the chill was still in the air. The winding lane behind the main square was spelled Tkalčićeva and lined with cafés, but the fenced-in café patios were empty and the big shade umbrellas for the outdoor tables were folded. I retreated to the hotel. In the evening I went out again, and walked as far south as the railway station and the nearby Hotel Esplanade, wandering aimlessly, admiring buildings and the darkness of the parks. I passed through the Hard Rock Cafe, the Zagreb branch of the international chain of bars, filled with people in their twenties chatting, colourful drinks set before them, enjoying an evening out in the "not not-war." But I didn't stay.

I phoned Slavenka in the evening, she put me in touch with Verna, and when I explained that I'd like to talk to someone from the university, maybe from the philosophy department, she gave me the number for Gvozden Flego. He was at home when I called.

"What hotel are you staying at?" he asked. After I told him, he suggested, "Then why don't I come by to get you tomorrow afternoon, about five?"

Gvozden was a lean, tall man in his forties, whose reserved manner I immediately liked. We crossed the square and went into the Gradska, where we found a free table near the windows that looked out toward the mounted duke, who brandished a scimitar above his head.

I sought the reassurance of shoptalk. "What's the mood of your students?"

"Well, I see them as withdrawn, apathetic; they're not very interested in discussing politics," Gvozden told me.

Gvozden had been a member of the renowned Praxis group, a circle of Yugoslavian neo-Marxist thinkers whose works were read in the West. The war had broken it up. The split between the groups in Zagreb and Belgrade had been bitter, exacerbated when the leading Serbian member of Praxis began spouting nationalist dogma with increasing vehemence.

Gvozden didn't identify with the distasteful rhetoric. He was an admitted "cosmopolitan." Again the phrase "Yugo-nostalgia" cropped up; he, too, had been subjected to it as an accusation of insufficient enthusiasm for the newly popular nationalism. As Drakulić had written, "Before this war started, there was perhaps a chance for Croats to become persons and citizens first, then afterwards Croats ... right now, in the new state of Croatia, no one is allowed not to be a Croat."

Increasingly, I was coming to think that "Yugo-nostalgia" was justified. The Yugoslav idea — flickering into life during the nineteenth century, when the Balkan lands were mere pawns in the ongoing contest of the Great Powers, and then briefly realized between the First and Second World Wars — had been intended to solve the intractable geopolitical problems of the Slovene, Croat, and Serbian peoples. They were a linguistically- and ethnically-related population divided for centuries between the Ottoman, Russian, and Hapsburg empires, then further divided by religious differences and bitter history — and by the Roman and Cyrillic alphabets. For all its faults, socialist Yugoslavia, with its emphasis on ethnic equality and federalism, and its hope for the lessening of national ambitions through improved economic circumstances, struck me as both the most rational and the most intellectually advanced solution to the Balkan problem to date.

Furthermore, Yugoslavian socialism had been at least a partial success, despite the anti-democratic rule of a one-party state and the suppression of dissent. By the time Yugoslavia began to founder economically in the mid-1970s — partly through internal sclerosis, but also partly due to the developments of globalized capitalism — it had produced a relatively high standard of living for eastern Europe, had spawned some interesting and lively alternatives to standard models of socialist production (thanks in part to the Praxis group), and had even won the allegiance of a significant proportion of a younger generation that saw itself as Yugoslav rather than Croatian, Serbian, or whatever.

As Gvozden verified for me, the standard of living, which had been at least three times that of most other eastern European states, had in the last three years collapsed to about one-eighth of pre-independence standards. "We're working for half a loaf of bread an hour, if that," he said.

The early evening was coming on. Our cups of coffee had been replaced with fresh brew, and the conversation had ranged from the details of everyday life to philosophy (Gvozden was writing the preface to the Croation edition of Richard Rorty's *Contingency, Irony, and Solidarity*). We had even, for a moment, found ourselves arguing about the twelfth-century craftsmen of Gradec, one of the two hillside villages that had been the precursors of Zagreb, whose hills we could see from the windows of the Gradska.

Shortly before we left, there was an unforgettable anecdote. I'd asked something about the period when Zagreb was under threat of attack. Gvozden remarked that he hadn't experienced any particular fear during the air-raid warnings, then added, almost as an afterthought, that he'd noticed that others were affected. "I was at home in my study, writing a paper that I was supposed to deliver at a conference in Strasbourg," he recalled. "My son — he's six and a half — was also there, playing or watching me." Then the air-raid warning sounded. "As usual, we went to the basement. When the all-clear was sounded, I immediately went back to my desk and continued writing. Then something strange happened."

The boy had just begun school. Although there had been air-raid warnings before, the child hadn't evidenced any reactions to the war situation that were noticeable to Gvozden. "He came to my desk and said to me, 'Daddy, will you teach me to write?' I was surprised. I asked him why he wanted to learn to write."

"If I was writing, I wouldn't be so afraid," the boy had said, learning, prematurely, the secret most of us come upon only much later.

THE NEXT DAY, MY last in Zagreb before returning to Berlin, spring arrived, at least temporarily. The sun was out and the beach umbrellas blossomed along Tkalčićeva — by now I'd learned that it was pronounced "T'kal-chee-chay-va" — as the café patios suddenly filled with customers, mostly young people. I sat outside and drank a pleasantly strong coffee. Then I walked back through the city, stopping at the Mimara museum, which I'd noticed recommended in a guidebook.

Until then, I'd come across none of the secondary effects of "not not-war" other than in my conversations with Drakulić and the other people I'd met, or in the figure of an occasional soldier. I hadn't sought out the refugee camps where thousands of displaced persons from Bosnia were living, nor had I interviewed, as I habitually did in other places, politicians and newspaper editors.

The museum was open but almost empty. I walked across the deserted foyer, up marble staircases, and through empty galleries, before I found an attendant who explained to me that the collection had been put in storage for the duration of the war. In a couple of gallery rooms, there was an exhibition of children's drawings of Vukovar, a Croatian city that had been destroyed by the Serb invasion. The war was crayoned bursts of fire and drifting black smoke.

I crossed a boulevard and in the afternoon sunshine walked through a park. At the end of it I found another, smaller museum, the Strosseman Gallery, named for a local bishop who had collected European masters and donated the paintings to the city in the 1880s. Again, everything was gone. As I was leaving, with a vague sense of being unable to penetrate to some interior aspect of Zagreb that I intuited was just beyond my reach, a woman approached me.

"Everything's been put away, you know," she said.

"Yes, I can see."

"But I'm the librarian here. Why don't you come along and I'll show you a book with the paintings in the collection," she suggested. "At least you'll have an idea."

I followed her through a door off the foyer into a small library. She seated me at a long work table and in a minute reappeared with the volume. I thumbed slowly through the colour-plate reproductions of the museum's holdings.

I turned a page and my gaze was suddenly arrested by an eighteenth-century painting by a Croatian artist, Federiko Benković. It was a portrayal of Abraham about to sacrifice his son Isaac as proof of his faith in God.

The knife-wielding old man — white-haired, hawk-nosed — was poised in an attitude of anguish as he testified to his belief. Isaac was sensuous, naked except for a gauzy bit of cloth floating across his genitals. I was amused by the libidinous Isaac, which gave the painting a touch of eighteenth-century camp. At the same time, I experienced the conventional meaning of the scene. In that test of faith, the angel of God has intervened to stay the father's hand, satisfied by his piety. Here, in the former Yugoslavia, the fathers had sacrificed everyone — children, spouses, themselves, and espe- cially their sons — in a test of loyalty. Yet here also, I remembered, mothers had dedicated books to their daughters.

Sofia (1993)

ONE OF MY STUDENTS at the college where I taught just outside Vancouver was a Bulgarian named Plamen. Through one of those bizarre
itineraries that were the lot of many enterprising Eastern Europeans,
he had managed to get out of Bulgaria in the late 1980s, and had
zigzagged his way from the Arab emirates through Europe until
he finally landed in a Canadian classroom where I happened to be
rambling on, in a course called Environmental Ethics, about the
thoughts of dogs and the possible rights of trees.

Plamen was in his late twenties, dark-haired with a perpetual five
o'clock shadow and a mouth that curved downward in what might
be read either as a frown or smirk. He was eccentric, energetic, and
intelligent, and quickly developed a passion for the fate of British
Columbia's forests and aboriginal peoples. When he learned that I
would be in Berlin once the spring semester was over, he proposed
that we meet in Sofia, since he was returning for a visit in spring
1993 for the first time since the political changes of the late eighties.
We could meet Blaga Dimitrova there, he said. Dimitrova was a poet
and novelist, some of whose essays I'd read in the *New York Review of
Books* and then quoted in class. In the first post-Communist elections,
she'd become the country's vice-president on the opposition United
Democratic Front ticket.

Though Plamen had promised to meet me at the Sofia airport, I was
pleasantly surprised, since he was one of those people who always
had a dozen appointments to get to and still more things on his
mind, to see him waving from the other side of the passport control
booth. He was with a large, reddish-blonde-haired woman his own age
named Diana, who turned out to be the daughter of the family where
we were to stay. We'd barely piled into the car he'd somehow com-
mandeered before Plamen began relating an adventure on the border
between Bulgaria and Macedonia from which he'd just returned.

"I've arranged for you to meet with the leader of the Macedonian
opposition," he announced. "I just have to phone them tonight to
confirm."

"Macedonia," I moaned. "Plamen, I've just gotten to Sofia."

He plunged into an account of the complexities of Macedonian, Yugoslavian, and Bulgarian politics. I hardly had a chance to see the city whose streets we were weaving through, and now I had to conjure up a mental map on which to locate Macedonia. We passed an onion-shaped church dome, a defaced Russian war memorial in a park, statues of two scholarly brothers eternally seated on either side of the entrance to the university they had founded, the white marble mausoleum that had displayed the preserved remains of a famous Bulgarian Communist, Georgi Dimitrov, until the "mummy" was removed and cremated in the upheaval of 1989.

"Macedonia must be at least six hours away by car," I calculated, "and six hours back. Anyway, I don't have a visa."

"We can make it in four," he assured me. I snorted, imagining the kind of drive it might be. "And we'll get through the border without papers."

"We'll wind up in a Bulgarian jail. Anyway, I thought we were going to meet Dimitrova."

"We are, tomorrow afternoon."

Plamen pulled halfway onto the sidewalk to squeeze into a parking space on a narrow street in downtown Sofia. We were soon crammed into a small sitting room with a round table, armchairs, and a cabinet full of cut crystal and china, to meet Diana's parents. Her father was a retired doctor, a pale man with a grey brush cut who entered the room trailed by a small dog of indeterminate breed. Diana's mother was a slim, energetic woman who was called Lilly Pepa. She put on a pot of coffee in a small kitchen that had a balcony where wash was drying.

The five of us, plus the dog, would be sleeping in their tiny apartment. Diana's parents slept in the front room, where the couch converted into a bed; there was apparently also a place for Diana, who was staying over because her own apartment was being reno-vated; and finally, in a crowded storage space off the sitting room area, there were head-to-head single-beds to billet Plamen and me. It was going to be a tight fit.

"Look, we can't go to Macedonia," I said to Plamen, after he'd come back from a quick shower to wash off the dust of several days on the road, and an electric-razor shave that hadn't made much of a dent in his stubble. "But how did you happen to go there?" I asked.

Diana brought in a coffee pot for the three of us.

"I went to see Vanga about my mother," Plamen began.

"Vanga?"

"You've never heard of Vanga?" He pretended to be surprised, since one of the teacher-student games he played with me was that I was supposed to know everything. Plamen went through the frosted glass door into our sleeping quarters to rummage around in his backpack, returning with a paperback book. Vanga, according to Plamen, was an eighty-year-old blind seer with powers of extrasensory perception.

"Come on, you're kidding."

"No, no, look," he said, showing me the book about Vanga, which was in a language and an alphabet I couldn't read.

"What's wrong with your mother?"

Plamen's parent lived in the mountain village where he'd grown up. He ascribed his mother's illness to "nerves." It was while he was consulting the renowned Vanga that he met a Macedonian woman who aroused his interest in her country's politics. In the middle of the convoluted tale, there was a brush with the law that he'd wiggled out of, and finally there were the wonderful Macedonian opposition-ists, anxious to get their story out to the world.

"You'd really like them," he concluded, trying to keep the possibility of going to Macedonia alive.

Coffee and conversation about the Bulgarian political situation continued through a dinner that emerged from Lilly Pepa's kitchen. Lilly, an activist in the opposition, outlined the chronology of recent events. Plamen translated her Bulgarian for me; Diana and I communicated in fractured French.

Todor Zhivkov, the longest-reigning and last of the country's Communist rulers, had been ousted a day after the fall of the Berlin Wall. In the West the news had been swallowed up, sandwiched between the events in divided Germany and the Velvet Revolution in Czechoslovakia that followed on its heels.

The Communists became the Bulgarian Socialist Party and a few months later, in mid-1990, won an election for a constitutional parliament. But the following year, new parliamentary elections produced a split between the former Communists and the opposition, each of them taking an indecisive third of the vote, while a spectrum of lesser parties received the rest. In the presidential elections of 1992, Zheliu Zhelev, a scholarly oppositionist who had authored a suppressed book, *Fascism*, became president, and Blaga Dimitrova succeeded to the vice-presidency.

Now, another springtime later, the situation was again unclear. Governments had fallen. Zhelev appeared to be leaning toward the former Communists. The question of returning farmland to private owners was being acrimoniously debated, as was the issue of whether to dismantle the Russian war memorial. The former Communists had struck a deal with the party representing the country's Turkish minority. Since neither of the main parties had a parliamentary majority, it was difficult to determine who was actually running the country.

After dark, Plamen and Diana took me on a long, leisurely walk through Sofia. Cities always surprise me. Here, the urban geography remained somehow beyond my ken, though I doggedly traced the streets on the maps I had, trying to decipher their names. Instead, in the warmth of the night, it was specific buildings that emerged from my mental fog. The onion-shaped dome of the Alexander Nevsky church, built early in the century, loomed above us, commanding a vast square. Plamen was excited by the appearance of cafés, bars, late-night little stores, which had replaced the silence of the well-ordered but dull streets he remembered from his adolescence. Abutting the city's central park, which contained the disputed Russian war memorial, was the sprawling palace of culture, a multilevel modernist concoction of copper-coloured glass and suspended white concrete pillars.

While Plamen and Diana gossiped about mutual friends, I gave in to my bemusement about the "land of Orpheus," as one guidebook referred to Bulgaria. The Romans had marched here, dividing the country on either side of a range of mountains. Slavonic tribes had absorbed the peaceful farmers in the mid-sixth century CE. A Turkic-speaking tribe, the Bulgars, had appeared in 679, founding a kingdom that lasted until the horrible moment in 1014 when the Byzantine emperor Basil II defeated the Bulgarians under Samuil, captured his 15,000 soldiers, and ordered them blinded, leaving one man in every hundred one-eyed to lead the rest.

Seeing the sentence in a history book, you shuddered and passed by, shaking yourself. When you returned to it, you were forced to imagine not an abstract number, an impersonal atrocity, but one man after another being blinded — but where? In an open battlefield? And how? What was the gruesome eleventh-century technology of it?

Dimitrova had a poem that began:

> They go on and on, Samuil's blinded men
> Even as we doze on summer's shore,
> divested of our history, memory washed
> of bloodstains in the sea, manacles rusted
> shadows in the deep, even as we utterly forget
> the where and whether of our coming
> 　　　　　　　　　　... They go on
> endlessly ...
> to make us see through these dark holes ...

In the underground levels of the culture palace there was a café, a sub-basement disco whose thumping bass rose to the surface, and a late-night bookseller's table. Plamen stopped to see if it had anything by Dimitrova.

When he returned to where Diana and I were standing he'd learned that Zhelev's daughter had committed suicide.

"Who?" I asked.

"The daughter of President Zhelev. Her name was Jordanka," Plamen said. The bookseller hadn't known any details.

We emerged from the underground into the large park. The nighttime amble was beginning to feel like a forced march.

"It's time for a drink," I pleaded, and Plamen assured me that our next destination was a jazz café.

THE NEXT MORNING EVERYONE moved around the small apartment with the gingerly solicitude of strangers in a crowded train compartment. Lilly Pepa and her husband tiptoed between the front room, the kitchen, and the bathroom. A radio was on in the next room broadcasting the news. Plamen was still asleep behind the frosted glass door. Diana brought me coffee at the sitting-room table, and received my thanks in halting French before heading off to her morning wash-up. I read some Dimitrova I'd brought along, and thumbed through a volume on Bulgarian politics. Successive scenes of horrible history — no worse than anywhere else, I suppose — tramped through the Thracian mountains in bloodstained boots. Byzantines, Ottomans, nineteenth-century Russians, twentieth-century Red Army liberators, a draconian forty-year Communist regime.

We had to dash to make a 10 a.m. meeting with Edwin Sugarov, the editor of *Democracy* newspaper, the opposition daily. Plamen's sense of timing was contrived to turn everything into an imperative. He'd slept late, but as soon as he had a cup of coffee in hand he began working a recalcitrant phone, lining up a roster of appointments that quickly diminished the possibility of seeing the monastery at Rila, much less the Macedonian border. Diana came in carrying a jar of water in which a bright-red comb was half-submerged. While Plamen held the phone to his ear with a raised shoulder, meanwhile balancing a notebook stuffed with bits of paper and documents, all of which periodically spilled out onto the floor, Diana draped his shoulders in a towel, and gave him a haircut. Lilly Pepa made us breakfast. The trip to Sugarov's — Plamen behind the wheel — was a last-minute scramble, and I reminded him that he'd always turned up for class fifteen minutes late. "We have plenty of time," he laughed, remembering that I had often noted his arrivals in the classroom with a loud announcement of "Now we can begin."

"How have you handled the coverage of the suicide of the president's daughter," I asked Sugarov.

"Jordanka," he said pensively, handing me a copy of that morning's edition of his paper. Sugarov was a tall, bald-headed man with a shaggy grey-tinged beard, wearing a grey suit and a striped tie. His fourth-floor office looked down onto red-tiled roofs of nearby buildings, which gleamed in the morning sun.

"We've been quite restrained in our comments. We've tried to avoid the wild speculations of some other newspapers." He paused to answer a phone. When he picked up the thread again, it led not to the daughter but to her father. "Mr. Zhelev was nominated by the United Democratic Front, but afterward changed his course against the UDF. He did everything possible for the fall of the UDF government."

"Will the death of his daughter affect his political course?" There had been talk that the suicide might have been something other than a personal matter, that perhaps it was partially a response to the political turmoil.

"Last night, on the TV, it said that there is an investigation," Sugarov replied, "so we've chosen restraint until we hear the results." But then he added, "There was a very sharp reaction, a reaction from the people in the democratic forces who believe in Zhelev. The reaction is very passionate." Bitterness seeped from his sentences. "Our national history is full of betrayals," Sugarov said, "and our people don't have any respect for traitors."

It was clear that Sugarov was aggrieved by this unexpected political split with an old friend, or at least a close colleague, whom he had helped to attain the leadership of the country.

DIMITROVA WAS STILL AT the funeral, Plamen and I were told by a thin, white-haired emissary who met us on the ground floor of the government building. He didn't know if she'd be able to keep her appointment with us but, if we wanted to, we could wait. We rode the elevator to the third floor and followed him down a length of red plush carpet to a pair of armchairs outside her office. He produced some coffee and orange juice, and then disappeared into an outer office from which we could hear a television blaring.

Time passed. I watched the red carpet narrow out to a horizon, and sank into one of those moments in a journey where you feel you'd be content to never move again while you figured out how to fit one disparate bit — landscape, history, human beings — into the uncooperatively ragged jigsaw edge of another. Even the whirling dervish of Plamen's soul subsided for a moment, as if sensing the difficulty.

Dimitrova appeared at the far end of the corridor after about half an hour, a heavy-set, elegant woman with short blonde hair that curled down onto her forehead in bangs. She was wearing a dark dress and a plain coat, and approached us with the heavy tread of someone grieved. Two younger women flanked her. We stood up and shook hands through a round of introductions.

"I've just come back from the funeral," she explained, inviting us into her office. We sat down around a large oak conference table. The tall windows behind her were draped in brown velvet, with lace inner curtains through which there was a view of the square below. On a side table, in a glossy red vase, was a bouquet of orange marigolds.

The two young women, her assistants, both in suit jackets and with their hair similarly and severely drawn back, sat alongside Dimitrova. The poet and vice-president was, according to the biographical preface to a book of her poems, a woman of seventy, although she seemed much younger, closer to my age.

"Mrs. Dimitrova is too upset," said the woman next to her, "for an interview today."

"Yes, I understand completely," I replied, glancing over at Plamen before he unpacked the gear he had loaded himself down with — cameras, books, documents, a camcorder with a tripod.

"Perhaps we could do it tomorrow afternoon," Dimitrova suggested.

"That would be fine," I said.

"But we can have coffee, yes?" she asked. One of her aides went to the outer office.

Plamen reached into one of his zippered carryalls and produced a coffee-table book of coloured photos of the Amazon region that he'd brought as a gift; the rescue of the Brazilian rainforest was one of the environmental issues in which he'd become engaged. Dimitrova turned the pages of the book, gradually becoming absorbed in the lush green photos, as she and Plamen chatted in Bulgarian. The grey-haired attendant arrived with a tray of coffee and bottles of mineral water.

We slipped easily into a conversation about writers and writing. I mentioned that I'd recently visited Slavenka Drakulić in Zagreb. Dimitrova knew her work. I commented on the difficulties of being a writer in Croatia.

It was not dissimilar in Bulgaria, Dimitrova remarked. "It's a very dangerous moment. We're all on our — how do you say? — on our toes."

"But are those the toes of a tiger?" I joked. I was thinking of a poem of hers I'd read that morning that asked, "How did you allow that tongue of yours — / wild, unbroken, leaping / over the toothed fence — / to be tamed?" The poem said that the tongue licks "words / like a tiger licks its wounds / but in a locked cell."

"A tiger?" asked Dimitrova. "No. Of a cat."

"This isn't the tiger who leaps through the bars of the teeth in your poem?"

"Ah," she laughed, remembering. "Perhaps. We have already jumped over the bars of the zoo. The first bars."

"Does that put you in the jungle?"

"In the jungle of the free market," she quickly replied. "It's a test period now, if our culture will survive, whether it will be created by officials, bureaucrats, or by true creators, men and women of art."

Dimitrova had published an essay that I'd read called "The New Newspeak." Like Václav Havel, she'd noted that "the reality is more surprising than anyone had at first thought. The euphoria of the early days when we first gained the freedom to say aloud what had been forbidden" had largely faded away. "The old totalitarian attitudes and stereotypes are being thrown away and are being replaced, by what? By the same attitudes and stereotypes, only now turned in the opposite direction. Newspeak, version two, one might say." (Blaga Dimitrova, "The New Newspeak," *New York Review of Books*, March 5, 1992.)

I liked the detailed examples she provided of the new rhetoric about the old Communist regime. "The superlative 'most' is now conjoined with negative adjectives to describe yesterday's overpraised system: it was the 'most inhumane,' the 'most cruel,' the 'most criminal,' etc. In the city square you hear epithets that are not logically suited to superlatives: 'the most unparalleled tyranny in history,' the 'most pernicious methods,' the 'most unfathomable depths' ...

"The conditional mode is in any case out of fashion. Instead, there is the resort to the drastic imperative: 'No way back!', 'An end to Communism!', 'Total dismantling!' While the old mechanisms of power still remain largely untouched, we have a new language for giving orders."

Was that the way to Europe? she'd asked. Or was there a danger of "creating a new totalitarian speech? ... How can a different language, a human one, be created and cultivated, without lies, without fanaticism, without false promises of the future as a heavenly kingdom for the righteous, without hate?"

I wanted to know if the New Newspeak continued to drown out a more human language.

"We still haven't adapted ourselves to a new reality. All of us, we bear the traces, the scars of that period," Dimitrova said. "It's the last wall, the most difficult one to destroy. Long ago, before the recent events and changes came, I had written about the Chinese Wall."

"I imagined it at first sight, and it — me," she'd written, upon seeing the Great Wall of China.

> *I patted the stones intimately*
> *and spoke to it silently:*
> *You were embedded in my cells*
> *long before I was born.*

"It was a foreboding of what was going to happen to us," she said. "This wall, especially in Balkan minds, lasts a long time."

Although we'd put off the official interview, we talked for an hour and a half. I apologized for our prolonged cup of coffee.

"No, it was good for me. It took my mind off it," she said, referring to the death of Zhelev's daughter, as she walked us to the doorway where the red carpet began.

On the way home that afternoon, we stopped for a moment at the disputed war memorial. Wooden scaffolding surrounded the plinth of the Soviet Red Army memorial that supported a heroic sculpture. Some temporary fencing had been put up to prevent vandalism, and a police jeep was parked a discreet distance away. I moved closer to look at the bas-relief at the memorial's base. It portrayed a fearless platoon charging forward, flags waving, guns raised, and a small, wheeled howitzer being loaded. The monument's critics had carefully painted parts of the relief in fluorescent colours — the rifles were a glowing orange, the soldier's boots were daubed white and were labelled "Nike," a circle on a pike bore the international peace symbol in spray paint. The memorial had not only been defaced, but wittily desacralized. It was one answer to the kitsch of remembrance.

THERE WAS A PHONE call at Lilly Pepa's.

"I'd completely forgotten about her," Plamen said, as he hung up.

"Who?"

"It's an old friend of mine, Maya. She and her husband are artists, but I haven't seen them in five years. They're still very committed Communists. Would you like to meet them?"

"Yes, of course."

We arrived a little after eight in the evening at a tall concrete-slab apartment building set back from a broad boulevard, already darkening in the dusk. Inside, the building looked like an ordinary set of flats, the rough concrete walls decaying, the smell of cooking trapped in the corridors. Bogomil and Maya had a two-storey studio flat on the top floors, where they worked at sculpture and painting; they apparently lived elsewhere.

When we entered the spacious atelier — I immediately recognized it as one of the perks of officially approved state artists — a third person appeared, their sixteen-year-old son, Kalin. The boy was carrying in his arms a puppy no more than a few weeks old.

Maya, a woman in her late thirties with straggly blonde ringlets, was wearing a brown suit jacket with muted stripes. There was an enamel broach on the lapel and she wore a violet-coloured blouse beneath it. She quickly established herself as the most politically vociferous member of what I imagined as an official family portrait of the happy (but serious) ideal Communist Party household unit.

"The whole family have been and are members of the Party. I have always been a member," Maya said, and then, her voice rising slightly in exasperation, added, "and for me it's unusual that in a difficult moment like now people are leaving the Party. It's a betrayal of the principles of my father and grandfather, who devoted their lives to a great idea, unfortunately corrupted by other people."

It was a long conversation, lasting almost until midnight; they insisted graciously on answering all my questions. Bogomil was a slight, thin man, shaggily long-haired, bearded. His softer voice intermingled with Maya's quicker emotions as they jointly fashioned answers, correcting each other, adding details to one another's accounts, all of which Plamen translated through the sniffles of an oncoming cold.

But it was difficult to locate exactly those people who had "unfortunately corrupted" their great idea. I couldn't pierce the armour of the ideology in whose vocabulary Maya and Bogomil had been raised. There had been "mistakes," in the past, of course, but the Party had now adopted "two very important principles," Maya said. "That the party should function democratically, and that the market economy is the gradual way to solve the crisis, while maintaining social protection for everyone." It seemed to me a little late in the game for the discovery of such principles, but one could hardly dismiss their evident sincerity. Still, I noticed that they were more intent on discussing the shortcomings of the current opposition than those of the Communist Party's past.

"When we talked to Blaga Dimitrova ..." I began, and then glanced toward Plamen. "Was it yesterday or the day before?" When I looked back at Maya, I saw that the mention of the poet's name had had an effect.

"I don't want to talk about her, about Blaga," she said, using English for the first time.

"Because?"

"Because," she said, with a nervous laugh, and then switched back to her own language. Bogomil joined in. "She was one of those," Plamen translated, "who wrote poems for Zhelev at one time, and later changed her colours."

I let it drop, but later, toward the end of the evening, I remembered Dimitrova's essay about the "New Newspeak." "Have you read it?" I asked Maya.

"No," she said, followed by a short fiery outburst to which she appended a nervous laugh, as if startled by her own anger. "And I have no intention to."

Normally I tried to avoid being intentionally provocative in such interviews, especially if I had some sympathy, however distant, for the interviewees' views. But here I was frustrated by the bland, if unintentional, evasiveness. I started to outline the argument in Dimitrova's essay.

Maya couldn't contain herself. "She was one of them," she broke in. "She was one of them who did this, and she has never been suppressed, or been in jail. She has been one of them!"

DIANA BROUGHT ME MORNING coffee. She was wrapped in a blue house-coat, slightly hunched over, looking worried. I couldn't tell if she'd slept badly or if her troubled look was simply a style of solicitous concern. Still, if even the most ordinary domestic moments contained a hint of ineffable mystery, what was I to make of larger ambiguities? The allegedly duplicitous Dimitrova that Maya had inveighed against late into the night didn't seem to bear any resemblance to the elderly woman whose sensuous poems I read in the little sitting room that morning.

> *More and more I confide*
> *in the dead, because the living won't discuss*
> *what's most important.*

She added,

> *And the dead are not afraid of death —*
> *they're its interpreters, their voices*
> *soothing as my father's used to be ...*

And who was it — her mother? — who died "without any cry, or moan, or shiver" —?

> *Carefully, your hand*
> *grew cold in my hand*
> *and imperceptibly led me*
> *into that beyond to death*
> *just to introduce me.*

I felt at home with the dead who wandered through her texts, and with a "Self-portrait" that allowed

> *Loneliness when at the age of love,*
> *love when at the age*
> *of loneliness.*

Was Dimitrova the person she appeared to be in her poems — which my intuitions upon meeting her seemed to confirm — someone who'd remembered rather than forgotten "being"? Or was she one of the "traitors," as the Party sought to define her?

Plamen straggled into the sitting room, and Diana appeared with fresh coffee and a morning paper. Reluctantly, I disengaged myself from Dimitrova's poems.

"Zhelev Buries His Daughter," Plamen said, translating the head-line for me. "Doctors claim that Jordanka Zhelev hanged herself in the government hospital, but no official source has confirmed this. Dr. Nicolae Alexandrov, head of the military medical academy, said unequivocally that the case is a suicide. 'The reasons are deeply personal,' said Dr. Alexandrov, without specifying his source."

There were the predictably conflicting accounts. Jordanka, accord-ing to unconfirmed reports, had been undergoing treatment for depression in the hospital where she committed suicide. There were rumours of unhappy love, but close friends who had seen her at a weekend party denied this story.

"The president learned about the tragedy at Sofia airport from the head of security and the doctor's team sent to meet him ..."

DIMITROVA WAS IN A blue dress with tiny white polka dots. Her hands rested in her lap as she leaned slightly forward to talk to me. A photograph that Plamen took of us showed that I too leaned forward, a plump figure whose thinning hair unsuccessfully straggled across a mostly bald head. While the two women at Dimitrova's side trans-lated, I had long moments to gaze at her face.

Plamen had hoped to get Dimitrova to sign a petition on behalf of the Bulgarian government protesting the destruction of the Amazonian rainforest. The sag of his disappointed shoulders told me he hadn't gotten everything he wanted — but then, I suspected he'd be satisfied with nothing less than a threat to declare war. Dimitrova said she might, for the moment, be able to add her name as a private individual. Getting a government declaration would take considerably longer.

We talked very little about politics. She'd been a young woman at the beginning of Communism in Bulgaria, never a member of the Party, though she'd gone to Moscow and what was then Leningrad to study and write a thesis about Mayakovsky. I tried to locate a point at which disillusionment had turned to opposition. Instead, she remembered the sources of her stories.

She recalled the time she'd gone to the Rhodope Mountains in southern Bulgaria, in the late 1950s, to write a novel. There, she'd met a young engineer who had been assigned the job of building an extraction plant for a local mining operation.

"This engineer was given the task of finishing the construction," she said, "for some important holiday or anniversary — I think it was for the month of September, which was then the national holiday — and he argued that it was impossible because a container for the chemical tailings should be built. At the time, the word 'ecology' didn't exist. So he refused to undertake the project, but it was built anyway, by someone else."

The bureaucracy had its way, in other words. The requisite solemn ceremony was held on schedule, with the prime minister in attendance. "And all the contaminated waters went directly into the River Arta," Dimitrova said. "The river was famous for its trout, and the next day all the trout were floating dead in the river with their bellies up, poisoned.

"And I witnessed an extraordinary scene. The women on both banks of the river were lamenting — long lamentations — on the hills along the riverbank. There were groups of women who sang and the echoes from one group went to the next, and it just went along the banks of the river, the women mourning the fish."

I listened in silence to the story.

"I described that scene in a novel of mine, *A Journey to Oneself*, but the censorship wanted me to take out those scenes. Of course, I couldn't accept that because it was important, the culmination of my novelistic work. So the dilemma was in front of me, either to stop the novel, refusing to make the cuts, or to accept the cuts." She paused, with the second nature of a storyteller who knew where a moment of suspense was required, then added, "Chance helped me."

Chance took the form of the lawyer husband of a friend. It so happened that a similar incident of fish poisoning had occurred at the Bulgarian-Greek border, and the Greeks had formally protested. Dimitrova was telling her troubles about the book to her friend, also a writer, when the husband, whose specialty was international litigation, walked in and was caught up in both the story and the issue. "But this book must be published," he insisted, inspiring the novelist to fight for her book.

"So this is a story with a happy ending," I said.

"But the story doesn't stop there," Dimitrova replied.

Some twenty years later, when the book was due to be reprinted, it ran into another political storm. "This was in 1985, when the authorities were forcing the Turkish minority to add Slavic suffixes to their names," she explained. "They were very beautiful and colourful names, and those were the original names of the characters in my novel. Now the editors wanted me to change them. For example, I have a character named Raffina, and they wanted it to be Rafka. Of course I refused to change the names, and the second printing had to wait. So the adventures of just one of my books shows what we lived through."

Dimitrova had written another novel entitled *Face*. "It had an even more interesting fate, because it was imprisoned," she said. "Bulgaria is perhaps unique in the world because we had a book prison, a prison for books. Only for books."

"What do you mean?" I asked.

"What books were imprisoned there? The Bible, Dr. Zhelev's own book, *Fascism*, my novel." She named some other writers whose names I didn't recognize. "I'm proud that my novel was part of the group that was imprisoned, and stayed there for nine years."

"I don't understand," I said. "What do you mean, the novel was imprisoned?"

"The day the book was published, it was taken by trucks and distributed to bookstores, and whoever could, bought the book," she said. "But the same day there was another truck, a black truck without windows — the trucks that took prisoners to jail — and it made the same tour around the bookshops, confiscating the books. For a long time I didn't know what happened to the books, I thought maybe they were burned."

In fact, they hadn't been burned. Dimitrova paused to tell a story within the story. Once, when the regime had ordered a book burning, an updraft had swirled half-burnt pages through a chimney, scattering them through the surrounding neighbourhood. Her husband still had one of those singed pages in his possession. "Since then, less inflammatory measures have been adopted," she punned. "Instead, they established a special warehouse in the town of Slivan, a little way out of Sofia. That's where the books were taken."

It was a story with a little epilogue. "Afterwards, I wrote a poem on the imprisoned books. The books themselves — the Bible, Dr. Zhelev's *Fascism*, some others, and my novel — have a conversation among themselves as they sit in their prison."

AT THE END, MY mind again wrestled with that jigsaw puzzle of images as I made my way to the airport departure lounge, accompanied by Plamen and Diana. The images were of Dimitrova and her poems, of a girl named Jordanka whom I'd never seen, but whose hanged body I had to imagine, of people seething with suspicions of betrayal, but most of all of Plamen himself, with a dozen things on his mind, even as he was seeing me off on the flight that would take me back to Berlin. For me, Plamen was the emblem of this mysterious place as it emerged from the long dictatorship of Communism — his zany energy, wild plans, causes that would save the world — or at least make it more interesting — his sense of an important appointment that was just beyond the horizon. He waved from the other side of the glass wall that sealed off the departure lounge. "Macedonia," he mouthed, with a crooked smile.

The Dead at Vilnius (1993)

I went to Vilnius, Lithuania, because my father said he had been born there. Precisely when that was, or when he left Vilnius for Chicago, along with the order and birth dates of his three brothers and four sisters, were matters of endless family dispute whenever his side of the family gathered. Or I should say our side of the family, since I regarded most of my mother's family as unexplained strangers with whom my father and I had been accidentally and unfortunately linked by the fact of his loving my mother.

"Now, Morrie," his sister Emma insisted to my father, "you couldn't have been born in 1901 because ..." and then would follow a set of genealogical details and circumstances that a battalion of logic-chopping Jesuits couldn't have sorted out.

"It was 1901," my father said, attempting to hold his ground. "The old man" — Grandfather Jacob, that is — "was here for two years before he sent for us."

"Morrie, Emma is right," my Aunt Patty broke in, "because I was born in —" and then there was another date in that history of fertility. Uncle Harold supplied the historical background of Grandfather Jacob's odyssey, Uncle Gob had his say, Uncle Lew offered his own fanciful version. And on and on it went. That's how I first heard of Vilnius.

⟨❈⟩

ASTA MARKEVICIUTE WAS A tomboyish woman in her early twenties
who, through a number of phone calls between Berlin and Vilnius,
agreed to be my guide to the city of my father's birth. She was a
student at Vilnius University — an English major writing a graduating essay on Willa Cather's *My Ántonia*. She told me about school as
a cab took us from the airport along the shore of the Neris River, which
undulated through the city, into the Antakalnis Hills on the northeast
edge of town where a travel agent had booked lodgings for me.

When we arrived at the hotel, I felt uncomfortable. For one thing,
it was too far from the city centre, and it wasn't so much a hotel as
a sort of dormitory for visiting sports teams. As soon as I saw the
room — a rough-hewn space with a bed and bad lighting, no toilet
— I knew I had to get out of there. At that moment, two representatives from the local travel agency associated with my Berlin ticket
agent showed up. I recognized that they were holdovers from the old
regime, used to dealing with supervised tourist groups, but in the
now-privatized economy, where wandering loners brandished international credit cards, they were gamely attempting to adapt. No
problem, one of them told Asta, I could be relocated to a hotel downtown, and he would arrange for my luggage to be taken there. I
could check in later. At least they didn't try to tell me that everything
was full, as they would have in the old days. One even attempted a
friendly capitalist smile.

Asta and I took a long tram ride back to Cathedral Square. As
we stood between the white-columned neoclassical church and
a baroque bell tower, she gave me a choice of walking down
Gedimino Prospekt or venturing into the winding streets of the
Old Town. I chose Gedimino Prospekt, a long, wide boulevard that
ran northwest from the cathedral all the way to the Parliament
Buildings on the shore of the Neris. There was little vehicle traffic
apart from the occasional lopsided, crowded bus, and people casually crossed the uneven black paving stones without evident fear of
being run down.

The particular beauty of the street was derived from its linden trees, with their small, precisely serrated green leaves, which lined both sides of the street all the way to the horizon. They were planted in the middle of the sidewalk, and each one had its roots guarded by a wrought-iron metal grille that formed a small black square around the base of the tree.

We ambled along in the afternoon sunshine, partially protected from the heat by the intermittent shade of the lindens. Asta occasionally pointed out a public building, a café — the Literary Café at the top of the boulevard — or a theatre, where, above its marquee was a sculpture of three black-shrouded Fury-like women urgently pressing toward us. I knew, thanks to my assortment of guidebooks, that Gedimino was a street whose name, and even the languages in which it was named, had frequently changed. I'd brought with me three volumes of memoirs of Vilnius (or Wilno, Wilna, or Vilna, as it was variously called) by Tadeusz Konwicki, Lucy Dawidowicz, and Czesław Miłosz, all of whom had either grown up or lived here. Actually, there was a fourth interpreter, if you counted that part of Miłosz's book was a "Dialogue about Wilno with Tomas Venclova," a younger exiled poet with whom Miłosz had exchanged letters about the city of their youth.

The street was called Gedimino after the fourteenth-century nobleman who had allegedly founded Vilnius; the ruined ramparts of his castle towered above the city from a hill just behind Cathedral Square. According to Adam Mickiewicz, the nineteenth-century Polish poet who also lived in Vilnius, he had "Built Vilna city like a wolf that broods / Mid bears and boars and bisons in the woods."

But Czesław Miłosz, who had grown up here in the early decades of the twentieth century, recalled in *Beginning With My Streets* (1991) that "the street that was supposed to be the main street was definitely not cosmopolitan. It was officially named St. George Boulevard at first, then Mickiewicz Boulevard … when I was a schoolboy it was still called 'Georgie' for short."

Lucy Dawidowicz, who studied Yiddish history in Vilna in 1938, said in her memoir *From That Place and Time* (1989), "The most elegant street in Vilna and one of its longest (a little over a mile) was *ulica Adam Mickiewicz* ... an east-west boulevard densely lined with trees." She remembered the cafés, tea dances, the "rich and luscious" pastries. "I imagined that Paris must be like this," she wrote.

But Tomas Venclova, who grew up in Vilnius after World War II, reminded Miłosz that "the history of that street's name deserves a separate description. The Lithuanian authorities changed it to Gediminas Street but left the name of Mickiewicz on its extension. In 1950 or thereabouts, it was announced that, in deference to the pleas of the working class, the name of the street would be changed: it would become Comrade Stalin Boulevard. It bore that proud name until the Twentieth Party Congress [1956]. One of my acquaintances, a young graphic artist, wrote a petition to the authorities at that time proposing a return to the old name. He was immediately expelled from college ... In the end, of course, the street became Lenin Boulevard. My generation always called it Gediminke, however, and still does."

Asta and I passed a large park with red gravel paths that made an "X" through its centre. "The statue of Lenin used to be there," she said, nodding toward the now empty space where the diagonals intersected.

The blocky, rough-hewn stone fortress facing the park had housed the local branch of the secret police. "The former KGB headquarters," she noted.

When we reached the Parliament Buildings, a modernist affair with a large concrete plaza, Asta asked me if I wanted to go on across the river, where Gedimino became Mickiewicz. I simply put up my hands to indicate my sweat-dripping skull. She laughed. "We can get a drink in the Old Town."

Returning down Gedimino, I remembered that Asta had unself-consciously talked about the lesbian aspects of Willa Cather's *My Ántonia*.

"Is there a gay bar in Vilnius?" I asked her.

"It's right over there, the Akimirka," she said, pointing out a squat hotel across the street. There was a restaurant on one side of the entrance, and a bar on the other. "It's not really a gay bar, but it's where the gays go."

THAT AFTERNOON WE RETURNED to Cathedral Square, stopped along the way for mineral water in a basement bar where men were slugging back shots of vodka, and then had a look at Vilnius University, founded in 1579, where there were courtyards in its labyrinth, according to legend, where no human had ever set foot.

We went along University Street into the old town, where it turned into Gaona Street and the old Jewish quarter. Napoleon, hastily passing through Vilnius on his retreat from Russia in 1812, had dubbed the city "the Jerusalem of Lithuania." The Gaon of Vilna (1720–1797) was a Jewish scholar and an Enlightenment figure. The city's Jewish population from the seventeenth century to the middle of the twentieth had amounted to between thirty and fifty per cent of Vilnius, despite recurrent pogroms. We wandered the streets of the Jewish quarter. The oppression of Jews under the Russian czar had "set in motion a mass emigration between 1881 and 1914 when Jews in unprecedented numbers left Russia, among them Jews from Vilna as well," wrote Dawidowicz. The émigrés had included my grandparents and their young children.

I was dazed with the heat, and Asta promised that there was a nice shady bar in the nearby art centre. As we turned in that direction, I found myself gazing at a patch of grass, then a cobblestone on the path, asking myself if I felt anything while I walked through the Jewish quarter. My grandfather had walked these streets. The thought of him crossing these narrow lanes — possibly carrying my infant father — sated my desire for personal sources. But the truer story of the Jewish quarter was on a small plaque on one of the streets that said 11,000 Jews had been rounded up from this ghetto during World War II and transported to nearby Paneriai Forest, where they had been murdered.

MY NEW HOTEL WAS on Gedimino Prospekt, No. 12. I had a beautiful room in back, overlooking an untended grassy garden in which a statue of Hermes presided over puffy-headed dandelions beneath a maple tree. There was a good writing desk, a lamp, a round table and chairs, a comfortable box bed, and a bathroom.

After dinner with Asta, who would collect me in the morning for our round of interviews, I took a walk under the lindens on Gedimino to the Akimirka Hotel. Because of Vilnius's northerly location in Europe, there was still light after nine o'clock. Inside the foyer of the Akimirka, I turned left and entered the gloom of the Akimirka bar. Along the far wall there was a set of wooden booths occupied mostly by mixed couples, several of whom seemed well advanced toward a state of vodka-fuelled oblivion.

Immediately off the entrance there was a long bar that ran all the way to the back of the room. Various men sat on stools along its length. White muslin curtains shaded the windows that faced Gedimino, and contorted plastic extrusion lamps from the 1950s cast a faint glow down the bar.

I'd been sitting at the bar for a couple of minutes, waiting for the woman serving at the far end to notice me, when a man on my right, who had been talking to a friend, leaned over and said something to me. He was in his late twenties and had curly, slightly thinning hair.

"What did you say?" I asked.

"You have to go down there to order," he said in English.

When I came back with a coffee and brandy that I'd gotten by pointing at things, he introduced himself as Igor. His friend was named Vytas.

"Where are you from?" he asked.

"I've come from Berlin, where I'm staying, but I'm a Canadian. Are you from here?"

"Yes, I live in Vilnius. He's from Minsk." Minsk was the nearest major city across the border, in what was now nominally independent Belarus, formerly the Belorussian Republic of the Soviet Union.

"Your English is excellent," I said.

"Well, it's one of the subjects I teach at a grammar school here," Igor explained.

That led to a conversation about work and living standards.

"About 6,000 *talonas* a month," Igor said, in answer to my question about the average monthly wage. *Talonas*, a monetary coupon, were the temporary local currency; the government was having banknotes printed abroad, but there had been a screw-up of some sort. The going rate of exchange was three hundred *talonas* to a US dollar.

"But that's less than twenty dollars a month," I said. Igor nodded in unhappy confirmation.

"What does coffee cost?" I asked.

"Mmm, about eight hundred *talonas* for a small tin," he said.

"Then it's impossible."

"Very difficult," he amended.

"What's it like here for gays?"

"Well, you can see," Igor said, indicating the Akimirka. The repression of homosexuals, he claimed, had hardly been improved by the demise of Communism, the rise of nationalism, the fall of the first post-Communist conservative government, or the re-empowerment of the reformed Communists. But since the Akimirka was tolerated, it seemed that economic misery was higher on the list of difficulties than sexual harassment.

As I'd found in other places, checking on the status of gays and Jews was a shortcut to getting an idea of post-Communist Vilnius. Here, not only was it the case that homosexuality was barely tolerated, and simply treated as a category of vice, but the dire economic circumstances made gay life especially difficult. For one thing, limited economic opportunities meant that gay men were often living with their parents and it was difficult to find private space to pursue their sexual lives. The suppression of gay life here was blatantly obvious, and I didn't have to pursue every detail to get the picture.

Then we just gossiped, as people do in bars anywhere. I bought Igor and Vytas drinks, eager to do something sociable with my sudden comparative wealth. Vytas had to go off to his night watchman's job at a local restaurant and Igor had work in the morning, so we left the bar and headed in separate directions. I walked back to my hotel down the dark, dusky Gedimino Prospekt.

In my room, I stepped out onto the balcony for a minute to check whether the wing-footed, helmeted Hermes was still there. A spotlight from an adjoining building fell on his greenish, mildewed body. Through the leafy maple, a full moon rose.

AT A REASONABLE MID-MORNING hour the next day, Asta and I walked the length of Gedimino to the modernist Parliament Buildings with their windows of copper-coloured tinted glass.

The politicians were charming but elusive. We spoke with Laima Andrikienė, an agricultural economist and a member of Parliament from the centre-right National Union Party, an organization that had developed from the Lithuanian independence movement, Sajūdis. She wore a beautifully patterned black and brown dress, and had a vase of yellow tulips on her desk.

Her mother's family had been deported to Siberia during the Stalinist terror after World War II; her father had been sentenced to ten years. "They came back after Stalin's death in 1953, and sometime in 1964, 1965, my father was invited to KGB headquarters and they said, 'Forget everything, you were not guilty.' And he said, 'I will never forget, because I lost my best years in Siberia, working in the labour camps.'"

She had been present at the founding of Sajūdis five years ago, in 1988. The Lithuanian Communist Party declared itself independent from the Communist Party of the Soviet Union, but Sajūdis nonetheless won the election of 1990. Though Soviet tanks rolled through Vilnius at the beginning of the following year and unarmed civilians were killed by Soviet troops in their assault on the local television station, Lithuanian independence, which had been declared by Sajūdis in 1990, was confirmed by an eighty per cent referendum majority in February 1991. But the Sajūdis government ran into problems, and the standard of living precipitously declined.

A few years before, the economy had been part of the Soviet rouble system. The average wage had been about 250 roubles then, Andrikienė said. "It was enough to buy coffee, to pay rent, to buy gasoline, but it was not enough to buy a house." At the next election, in autumn 1992, the former Communists, reconfigured as the Lithuanian Democatic Labour Party, won a landslide victory over the bumbling Sajūdis government, and again returned to office in this country of four million people.

I wanted to know what the former Communists believed.

"I don't think that they are Communists, or that they have a vision of Communism," Andrikienė said. "Probably they joined the Communist Party for other reasons. They were thinking about their careers, their lives."

"Why did the Democratic Labour Party win?" I asked.

"I don't have an answer to this question," she said, and then laughed in helplessness. "You know, I can understand our people because they have a lot of problems, but I can't understand how the Labour Party was able to persuade them that they would solve all those problems, to give cheap milk, cheap meat, cheap everything, and do it all this year."

THE MAN REPUTED TO be the brains of the Labour Party, Gediminas Kirkilas, was available for an interview late that afternoon. He was proud to be a professional politician. He was the eldest of three brothers and four sisters, and while doing his military service in the Soviet navy an opportunity had arisen to join the Communist Party. He had joined in 1972 "because Lithuanians needed to be Party mem-bers to occupy positions in Lithuania." He had a taste for literature, wrote some journalism, and rose rapidly to become cultural commissar for Lithuania and a member of the Lithuanian Party's central committee.

"You make it sound like joining the Party was necessary to a successful life, but there must have been an ideological commitment too," I remarked.

"I have to admit that my reasons for joining the Party were career-oriented," Kirkilas confessed easily. "I think most Lithuanian Communists didn't deeply consider Communist ideology, or Leninist theory, or even Marxism. The question was simply whether to accept the rules of this game."

"Are you saying that you were a Communist without being a Marxist?"

"I read Marx," he allowed. "But I wouldn't consider myself a Marxist."

Rather, he was a practical politician. Kirkilas had masterminded the new party's successful campaign during the recent election, and he was more comfortable talking about political technique than ideology.

"There are articles in the press saying that on television I'm the master of spontaneity," Kirkilas noted. "But this is not true, because I never say anything on the spot. I'm always carefully prepared, because the camera is ruthless."

The former Communist lamented the state of the economy, as had the conservative Andrikienė, and pondered whether the intrusion of the mafia in the Lithuanian economy should be regarded as normal in the initial stages of capital accumulation. He didn't think it ironic that former Communists had proven to be the most adept at commanding capitalist enterprises and noted that it was actually the right who had turned out to be "collectivist," and not the former Communists. He described Andrikienė's National Union Party as "state socialist and national fundamentalist," whereas the left represented "social liberal thought." Asta and I smiled at his "dialectically" turned definitions.

When I trotted out my by now standard question about the price of coffee, Kirkilas agreed. "Of course this price for coffee is too much, it's overpriced." But once there was a stable currency, matters would improve, he assured us. The new currency would arrive in a couple of months, but couldn't yet be officially announced. "That's a state secret," he laughed.

Looking over my shoulder as we left, I saw that there was a vase of yellow tulips on his desk, as there had been on Andrikienė's. They seemed the most substantial cipher in a bewildering tableau in which conservatives were baffled by their ouster and former Communists had never been Marxists.

BETWEEN THE MORNING AND afternoon interviews with the parliamentarians, I met Ričardas Gavelis at the Writers' Union building. He had published an allegedly shocking bestseller a few years earlier entitled *Vilnius Poker*. Asta explained that the title referred to card rooms around town where poker players had gathered in the old days.

We entered the Writers' Union building through an unprepossessing wooden door on a hilly side street. But inside there was a grand black marble stairway whose metal grillwork was trimmed in gilt, as were the flanking lampstands and the details of the wooden ceiling. Gavelis, a slim man in his forties wearing faded jeans, a black T-shirt, and tinted glasses, led us up the staircase to a noisy antechamber where our conversation was punctuated by passers-by, the creaking of frequently opened doors, and the clicking of secretaries' heels on the parquet floor. I felt more comfortable with Gavelis than I had with the politicians.

Gavelis understood English but preferred to speak in Lithuanian, so Asta only had to translate his replies to my questions. *Vilnius Poker*, he said, was shocking not so much for its frank sexual scenes but for its "not really benevolent attitude towards what we call the Lithuanian national character." It had been a success. "As many copies of *Vilnius Poker* sold as the Bible," he said, "but all the money was eaten up by inflation, so again I'm a free artist without a cent in my pocket."

As for the book itself, "it's an attempt to describe the world in which we lived for many, many years. It's difficult to sort out where it's reality, where it's a vision, a dream, a fantasy."

He had begun as a physics student, but when it was time to write a doctoral thesis, he decided he wanted to write literature instead. He had gone on from Joyce and other modernists to read the Latin American magic realists, "literary monsters" like Jean Genet, and post-modern writing. He'd worked on *Vilnius Poker* semi-secretly through the 1980s. "Even my wife didn't know about the existence of the manuscript," Gavelis said. "I was afraid she might speak out about it unintentionally." The book was published in 1989; since then he had published another novel and a volume of short stories, and a new, related book, *Vilnius Jazz*, was due to appear shortly.

We talked briefly about politics and the economy. The successful new businessmen, he noted, were not only "the old Communist *nomenklatura*, but young flexible guys with an orientation toward crime and the mafia."

One thing I wanted to know was whether any of his writing was available in English.

"About thirty pages of the beginning of *Vilnius Poker* are translated, but I don't have it with me now," he said.

"That's what I want to read."

"Well, it's possible to borrow it," he offered.

That night, I stayed in my hotel room and read. I left the door to the balcony open; the Hermes waited below, spotlighted. During the day, someone had cut the grass and dandelions around the statue.

Vilnius Poker was, as Gavelis had said, a shifting, dark mixture of dreams, memories, horror, and the overarching spectral presence of the totalitarian "Them," interspersed with brief moments of mundane reality: "you open your eyes, and once again see your room, books on the shelves, clothes flung on a chair." Much of the rest was "the nightmare of history," as Joyce put it, from which we're trying to wake.

"It seemed Vilnius stopped sighing, pulled itself together and became quiet, waiting alertly. Waiting too, greyish monuments and grimy, smoke-eaten Vilnius lindens. Something had to happen. Both of us sensed it, standing lost in the gloom of old town, drenched by the fine city rain." The woman or phantasm that materialized before them "looked around as if she found herself here on this earth for the first time. Such a thing can only be encountered in dreams and in Vilnius at night: the street had been empty as far as the eye could see, but suddenly standing beside you is a dark-haired woman ..."

It was midnight when I finished, turned out the light of the desk lamp, closed the balcony door (the spotlight on the Hermes had been extinguished) and settled into bed, haunted by the ghostly dimension of Vilnius that seeped through Gavelis's pages.

THE LITHUANIAN STATE JEWISH Museum was located on a hillside street a couple of blocks above Gedimino, in a faded green wood building resembling a barracks. Its rooms were bright in midday sunlight that not only poured through the windows, but also crept under doorways and seemed to penetrate the worn walls themselves. A white-haired man in his sixties was our guide. He spoke only Russian but it was another of the languages Asta could translate.

These rooms contained the archives of the slaughtered Jews of Vilnius. During World War II, ninety-four per cent of Lithuania's 160,000 Jews had been exterminated, the highest rate in Europe. Some maps, photocopied documents, a few objects, and photographs were all that was left. It was an impoverished but straightforward display.

I stared at the faces of those long dead, as if I might recognize someone I knew. A Polish journalist, the Russian-speaking guide recounted, had lived in the vicinity of the forest. He had seen those who were to be executed marched past his cottage, and had recorded what he'd observed in his diary, a proof of the slaughter, if one was needed (and alas, it would be). Fearing for his own fate, he had put the diary pages in sealed bottles, and buried them in his garden. The journalist was indeed shot by the Nazis in 1944, but the evidence was dug up from the garden some years later. Photocopies of his journal pages were affixed to the museum wall. I was transfixed by his handwriting, as Asta read translated passages.

There were maps of the Vilnius ghetto, a few copies of letters, photographs of the dead that appeared to have been taken in the forest (by the Nazis?) at the time of the shootings. Had someone actually photographed the victims as they were toppling into the pit? Apparently, yes.

There was also a display documenting the resistance put up by Vilnius Jews. Not all of them had gone to the slaughter "like sheep," as it was sometimes put. Later, I saw a videotape of the resisters — old men who had been in the ghetto and in the woods, who had survived and lived to tell the tale, years after, mostly in Israel.

But it was not the resisters who haunted us a half-century later. We understood them, or thought we did. No, it was those who had died without crying out, whose silence echoed in these rooms.

The Polish writer Ryszard Kapuściński, in a magazine interview I'd recently read, recounted being in his hometown of Pinsk, in what is now Belarus, a place not all that far from Vilnius, and where he had, as a boy, witnessed some of what happened to Jews there during World War II. "There was nothing strange in the behaviour of those people," he said. "It was natural. Because if you don't see any hope, you are very passive ... Lack of hope paralyzes their will, paralyzes their brain, their movement."

Kapuściński had later interviewed people who had witnessed the liquidation of the Jewish ghetto in Pinsk. "When the moment of the Final Solution came, they were sent through the town, in columns. Rabbis marched at the head of each column. And in columns — one huge, long column — they walked to the place which is about ten kilometres out of town, in a small forest. There were many graves dug there, long graves, and on the opposite side of every grave was a Nazi soldier with a machine gun. And the Jewish people were taken to the verge of the grave and were shot. One row fell in the grave, and the next row came, was shot, fell down, and the next row ... All in silence," Kapuściński said.

Here too, in Vilnius, they had gone to their deaths with similar passivity. Here too there was a forest, mass graves, and these few scraps of testimony by which a visitor might remember.

On the hillside below the museum, Asta and I sat in a tree-protected space that seemed far from the streets. As tiny as the museum had been — a few rooms, financially poor — it was impossible to escape some sense of the horror. We sat on a bench smoking cigarettes under a flowering maple tree whose blossoms drifted onto our heads.

There was a little square plaza of paving stones where we were sitting and at the far end a two-metre tall sculpture of an abstracted human figure with his arms half raised, bearing on his head a watermelon-shaped wedge of pale red stone.

THE NEXT MORNING, I took my cup of coffee and walked into the back garden of the hotel where the statue of Hermes was. The day's heat had yet to descend as I strolled around the wing-footed figure whose bronze body had mildewed into a striated aquamarine.

Asta arrived at noon. We took a series of buses southwest through an industrial zone to a place about ten kilometres outside the city. At the end of the bus line, we walked from the edge of a suburban neighbourhood to the railroad yards. A high walkway had been built across the tracks. Below it was a small station. Dandelions spotted the grass between the rail lines. At the bottom of the stairway on the far side of the tracks, we turned right and walked along a road that ran parallel to the tracks, passing small farmhouses. A few brown hens wandered in and out of old picket fences.

The road rose slightly and ended in a paved parking area, but there were no cars, just an empty parking lot surrounded by trees. At the far end of the lot stood a large granite memorial stone more than two metres high that carried a Hebrew inscription for the 70,000 Jews killed and entombed in unmarked pits in the Paneriai woods beyond.

When I asked Asta earlier that day at the hotel if she would take me to Paneriai (or Ponary, as the Jews of Vilnius had called it), she had pleased me by not questioning my proposal, but only remarking, "I've never been there."

We entered the woods. The small cottage that housed a museum was closed for renovations, and a couple of workmen were the only people we saw. Inside the forest, winding footpaths led to two or three unimposing monuments. Behind one of them there was a broad swath of burned pine trees, and an abandoned, rusted-out bus. I wandered through the charred remains of the trees, understanding that what had happened in these woods had occurred long before this fire. There was, in that sense, nothing to be seen here. There was only the quiet, sunlit forest.

We walked back along the same road. It was possible that some of the older people still living in the farmhouses had also seen the Jews marching along this road on the way to their deaths. It was in one of these gardens, where hens now roamed, that the Polish journalist had buried his diaries.

Back in the city, as we were on our way to catch a bus at Cathedral Square — we had an appointment with an elderly Jewish writer — we passed the theatre on Gedimino where the sculpture of three shrouded women presided over the entrance. Outside there was a small handwritten placard on a tripod. It was only after we passed it that Asta mentioned that the sign announced a tulip show in the lobby.

When I hesititated, she asked, "Are you interested?"

"Will we have time to get to Kanowitsch?" He was the writer we were about to visit.

"Yes, I think so."

Inside every story, I had discovered, there were trails that led to other stories, often no more than digressions that had little connection to the story you thought you were following. But often enough they told you something about life that you hadn't expected, something worth knowing, and it was a good idea to pay attention to your intuitions about the stories-within-stories. "Sure," I said.

The theatre lobby was spacious, constructed of marble-like slabs of brown stone. In vases around the sunken central area there were nearly a hundred different varieties of tulips, as the sign had promised.

We wandered slowly around the display, stopping to admire particular tulips that caught our eye, pointing out ones we liked to each other, reading the labels alongside the vases. I stopped before a tulip called the Abu Hassan, with deep brown petals fringed in brilliant yellow. Though I had seen tulips on the desks of the politicians, and there would also be some at Kanowitsch's house, I had never really looked at a tulip carefully, never really seen one until this moment.

"WHAT DID VILNIUS LOOK like in 1945?" I asked Gregory Kanowitsch. He was a Jewish novelist in his mid-sixties. I didn't know his work. His parents had escaped Lithuania in 1940 to avoid the fate of the Jews and made their way to Soviet Kazakhstan. At the end of World War II, when Kanowitsch was sixteen, the family returned to Vilnius.

"It's in Kafka's novels," he replied, sitting on a sofa in the large living room of the apartment where he and his wife lived. He was wearing a short-sleeved shirt and a tie slightly askew. "Everyone, not just Jews — soldiers, Lithuanians, Polish — seemed uprooted, flying between the heavens and earth. That's why I remembered Kafka."

"When you returned, was the extent of the Holocaust apparent to you then?"

"It was shouting. It was shouting," he said, and repeated the phrase a third time. "From every window, from every basement, from every hole."

"When we were at Paneriai today, my colleague here," I said, nodding toward Asta, "asked me why they hated the Jews so much."

"Well," he began, sighing, "this is not a simple thing ..." He offered some conventional speculations about religious and ethnic differences, the particular history of Jews in Vilnius and anti-Semitism in Europe, questions of class and envy, and mentioned that he was planning to immigrate to Israel soon, thus reducing the minuscule Jewish population of Vilnius by one more. What I remembered most, though, was the sigh that accompanied his weary remark that this was "not a simple thing."

After we left Kanowitsch, Asta showed me the tram that would take me back to Gedimino; she was going home in the opposite direction. Standing toward the back of the streetcar, catching an occasional glimpse of the sun on the river, I experienced an instant in which I felt both the comfort of being alive — just to see the powdery substance of fallen maple and linden blossoms clogging the cracks between the black bricks of the street — and the melancholy of our losses. Who is the "our" in that phrase "our losses"? I mean all of us. Nothing returns the dead to us.

I WALKED UP GEDIMINO in the early evening. I thought of the various cities I had travelled to in order to try to understand the end of Communism. In its last years, Soviet Communism had not been as brutally tyrannical as in its middle phases from the 1930s to Stalin's death. It had fallen not because of its cruelty, but because of economic stagnation, its inability to compete with Western capitalism, its doctrinal bankruptcy and loss of legitimacy, its corruption and patronage — and the fortuitous appearance of Mikhail Gorbachev, whose belated attempts to reform it had hastened its demise.

What was to succeed the tyranny was still undetermined, and the spectrum of possibilities was broad, ranging from the integration of some societies into the system of democratic capitalism, to out-and-out social collapse and savagery. Capitalist democracy was triumphant for the moment, but the notion in the West that what followed would be simple had proved illusory.

Enough time had passed since the fall of the Berlin Wall to dispel the idea that democracy, like nature, abhorred a vacuum. Democracy did not necessarily rush in to fill the gap. What rushed in after Communism was largely dependent on the particular conditions, traditions, loves, and hatreds of a given country. In the former Yugoslavia, a nearly impossible country had splintered into nationalism and ethnicities baring their fangs. Here in Lithuania, an ancient nation that had barely become a state, the economy hardly provided subsistence. Yet in both places, and everywhere else I'd been, there were citizenly people, if not yet citizens; everywhere there were streets and buildings and landscapes whose magic required only imagination and memory. Democracy would require as much, maybe more.

DURING THE NIGHT, I remembered what I had imagined that afternoon in the Paneriai forest. Some of the dead were sitting in chairs, others were standing around the charred woods, coffee cups and saucers in hand, wearing their death clothes — dark jackets and trousers, white shirts with slightly frayed collars, black hats on their heads; the women were in plain black dresses, one or two of them absently smoothing wrinkles in the cloth. The dead children were farther off, playing among the trees.

They were not all Jews, though Jews were prominent among them. Their ranks included contemporary combatants and civilians from places whose unfamiliar names listeners had forgotten as soon as the nightly newscasters pronounced the names of the new cities under siege.

I was there with Asta and there were some of the other guides who had shown me the places they knew. The dead gazed at us, oddly but patiently, from the other side of a piece of time. They didn't speak among themselves, nor did we, the living. But I felt that both the living and the dead, separated by time, wanted to speak to each other. It seemed there was everything to say.

25 Years After the
Fall of the Berlin Wall (2014)

I.

In the globalized digital world of 2014, everything is simultaneously distant and near, real and virtual, under omni-surveillance and clouded by disinformation. So, maybe it's not so strange that I had a very odd thought during a horrific moment. It was the week in mid-February 2014, just after the crisis in Ukraine that has been simmering for more than a decade spilled over into the fatal shooting of dozens of demonstrators in Kiev's Independence Square — or the Maidan, as it's better known. While I was sitting in Berlin watching Qatar-based Al Jazeera's television footage of unidentified people running through the streets of Kiev to a soundtrack of equally ill-identified but lethal gunfire, I found myself entertaining the conceit that Vladimir Putin, Barack Obama, and I were all attentively reading Christopher Clark's *The Sleepwalkers: How Europe Went to War in 1914*.

Or maybe Russian president Putin and US president Obama were attentively reading Max Hastings's *Catastrophe: Europe Goes to War 1914* (2013), or Canadian historian Margaret MacMillan's *The War that Ended Peace: The Road to 1914* (2013), or any of a number of recent books commemorating the centennial of the outbreak of World War I by trying to understand it. Since I was sitting at my desk in Berlin, it occurred to me that it was even possible that German chancellor

Angela Merkel, the most recognized face of the European Union, was reading Jörn Leonhard's *Die Büchse der Pandora: Geschichte des Ersten Weltkriegs* (*Pandora's Box: The History of the First World War*, 2014), a recent, more-than-thousand-page German-language contribution to the century-old puzzle.

It was a fantasy, sure, but one firmly grounded in hope. I hoped they were reading *something* about how Europe stumbled into war a hundred years ago — a war that left ten million mostly young people dead — and just as fervently, I hoped they were wondering why it happened. World War I was the result of a political brew that included aggressive nationalisms born from tribal nostalgia, the ill-considered assertion of "big power" interests, and a host of contingent diplomatic miscalculations, all revved up by an enormous amount of mouldy rhetoric and a not-inconsiderable number of political crazies and administrative incompetents. I hoped those international leaders were reading about it because they and their colleagues seemed to be stumbling toward something very dangerous in Ukraine, too. The crisis there contained many of the elements that ignited the conflagration of World War I. The events of the present, as is frequently the case, are haunted by the spectre of history. If the events in Kiev spun completely out of control, Walter Benjamin's angel of history would once more be casting its gaze on the catastrophe that is history.

Until the shooting started in Kiev, I had paid only passing attention to events in Ukraine, a place to which I have never travelled. There was, as a result, a lot of catching up to do. For those who, like me, haven't followed Ukrainian affairs in detail, a rough timeline of the country's history will provide some context to understanding recent events.

- 1919–1991: After centuries of being mainly controlled by the Russian Empire, with Ukrainian-speaking territory divided among several other countries, there was, in the wake of the Russian Revolution of 1917, the establishment of the Ukrainian Soviet Socialist Republic. That entity lasted until 1991, although there was massive disruption and loss of life from the German invasion of 1941 through 1944.

- December 1, 1991: Ukraine becomes an independent country as the Soviet Union breaks up.
- 2004: disputed presidential election between Viktor Yushchenko and Russian-backed Viktor Yanukovych results in a popular uprising, known as the "Orange Revolution," that brings Yushenko to the presidency and Yulia Tymoshenko to the office of prime minister, as well as prospects for an improved Ukrainian democracy. The new regime fails to solve the nation's political and economic problems.
- 2010: Yanukovych elected president, defeating Yulia Tymoshenko, after a period of perceived widespread corruption, economic turmoil, and government ineffectiveness. Tymoshenko is subsequently jailed on corruption charges.
- 2012: parliamentary elections give Yanukovych's Party of Regions a plurality.
- November 2013: after months of negotiation, Yanukovych, at the last moment and under pressure from Russia, refuses to sign a major trade agreement with the European Union that will move Ukraine economically closer to the EU.
- November 2013: pro-European Union students occupy Kiev's Maidan (Independence Square) in protest, are attacked by police, and are subsequently joined by successive waves of the public of all political persuasions, including extreme-right-wing groups.
- January 2014: Yanukovych attempts to crack down on the Maidan movement by passing new "anti-protest" laws to limit free speech and right of assembly. This produces a further backlash against his government.
- February 2014: a leaked phone call between US State Department official Victoria Nuland and the US ambassador to Ukraine demonstrates the extensive degree of "imperialist" involvement in Ukrainian affairs by external powers.
- February 18–20, 2014: further armed crackdown on Maidan movement results in the shooting deaths of dozens of demonstrators and brings the crisis to a head.
- February 21, 2014: an internationally brokered agreement

between Yanukovych and opposition forces calls for early elections and constitutional changes, but the deal quickly falls apart. Yanukovych is ousted and flees to Russia, while the Ukrainian Parliament authorizes an interim government until a new presidential election can be held on May 25, 2014. The interim government includes several members of far-right political groups.

- February–May 2014: pro-Russian groups in Ukraine's Crimea stage a coup with Russian military support and hold a referendum for separation from Ukraine and reintegration into Russia. Russia reincorporates Crimea into Russia. Unrest develops in Ukraine's eastern Donbas region, as separatist groups seize control of various cities, but there is no further direct Russian intervention. The Ukrainian army's attempts to oust the separatists are ineffective. US and EU respond to Russian involvement in Crimean coup by imposing some economic sanctions; ratcheted-up rhetoric and Russian troop movements on Ukrainian borders raise fears of a broader international conflict.

- May 25, 2014: veteran Ukrainian politician Petro Poroshenko, an oligarch who made his fortune in the confectionary business, is elected president of Ukraine, with a fifty-five per cent majority of the vote, defeating Tymoshenko, who runs a distant second (thirteen per cent). Separatists remain in control of various eastern Ukrainian cities, but international tension eases as Russia indicates it is not seeking incorporation of the eastern Ukrainian provinces.

- June 27, 2014: Ukraine signs trade agreement with EU.

By mid-March 2014, after developments in Ukraine had been in the newspaper headlines, or the lead item on television news, or the subject of Facebook "news feed" links for weeks, an attentive reader or viewer could begin to identify at least the players in what was an unusually complicated situation. But penetrating deeper was difficult. A closer examination of a few of the timeline events above can explain some of the internal complexity of the Ukrainian situation, the machinations of international big powers, and especially the difficulty that interested observers and the general public have in trying to understand these events.

Ukraine, an economically poor eastern European country of 46 million people that borders Russia, Poland, Romania, and several smaller countries, had acquired a new interim government. That was clear enough, but exactly how that government had been selected, and by whom, was murky. It was evident that the new executive was cobbled together under pressure from the thousands of protesters who had been encamped in the Maidan for months, and who toppled the elected — if terminally corrupt — regime of Russian-backed President Viktor Yanukovych. But it was unclear exactly how the transformation had occurred and what role the use of violence by some of the protesters had played. The presence in the interim regime of several far-right-wing ministers suggested that the role of armed right-wing activists among the Maidan protesters had been significant. Further, the role the international community was playing, especially the US, remained opaque.

There was also, in the wake of the Maidan "revolution," another new provisional government, supported by Russian troops, in Ukraine's Crimea, the plump strawberry-shaped southern peninsula of the country that pokes into the Black Sea. If the Maidan was a form of revolution, the events in Crimea were an outright coup, or counter-revolutionary putsch, designed to restore an older historical relationship. Unlike the popular upheaval in Kiev, the Crimean counter-revolution was carried out by a small self-proclaimed armed group backed by the significant power of "foreign" troops already on the ground in Crimea, and considerable public support from Crimea's Russian-speaking majority. The Russian troops were present because the Russians held a lease from Ukraine that permitted a large Russian naval base in Crimea, along with the right to quarter 25,000 troops.

Crimea's new regime immediately announced — and then quickly held — a referendum to determine whether the two-million-person majority Russian-speaking Autonomous Republic within Ukraine would seek to separate and be reincorporated into Russia. It was announced that the hastily organized referendum had overwhelmingly passed, although it was difficult to get reliable information about the results or the conditions under which the referendum had been held.

In short order, Russia's president Vladimir Putin and the Russian Parliament recognized the referendum results and made the peninsula a part of Russia, as it had been in the past. The formalities of incorporation were carried out with almost reckless speed. As if the Crimean events weren't enough, in the eastern Ukrainian provinces known as the Donbas (or Donets Basin) region, which borders Russia and is also populated by a Russian-speaking majority, armed groups of Russophile activists seized and occupied government buildings in a number of cities, demanding separation from Ukraine.

While all this was unfolding, Russia, the United States, and the European Union, between conducting hasty diplomatic meetings in various capitals of Europe to defuse what was now recognized by all as a serious situation, were busily engaged in a public exchange of charges and counter-charges attempting to interpret, manipulate, and maybe even to resolve the crisis. This willingness of the big powers to ratchet up the rhetoric and to engage in sabre-rattling troop movements and bank-account-rattling economic sanctions was among my reasons for hoping that world leaders were reading up on the origins of World War I.

The various publics of the United States, Russia, and dozens of European countries can hardly be blamed for being thoroughly bewildered by what was going on in Ukraine and what it meant. The satirical US news website *The Onion* had more than an ironic point to make when it mock-reported an imaginary poll that found Americans were fiercely divided on the Ukraine question — between total ignorance and sheer apathy. As the fictitious pollster quoted by *The Onion* put it, "We're seeing local workplaces, friends, even families ripped in two by their desire to either ignore the whole thing completely or spout an inane, half-witted opinion on it like they're some geopolitical expert." As one shrewd reader of the send-up story put it, "I get the joke, but it's not funny"; that is, *The Onion* account was too close to the truth to inspire much mirth.

Many of the thousands of digital respondents to the Ukraine crisis trotted out the tired cliché that public confusion was being caused by the "bias of the media," especially the "mainstream" media (or "lamestream," as condescending right-wing critics like to call it). But this didn't seem to me to be a case where the media, main- or minor-stream, could be faulted for ignoring or underplaying the crucial details of the situation. Rather, this was a typical case of too much unprocessed information and specious — or simply inexpert — interpretation. Certainly there was no shortage of "inane half-witted" opinions, as *The Onion* put it, from self-anointed geopolitical experts. Few of the Internet comment threads seemed to consider the possibility that people were confused because the situation actually *was* confusing.

When I wasn't busy sorting through the internal politics of Serbia and the origins of World War I as described in Clark's book, I had the benefit of the opinions of every outlet on the media spectrum, from the comic relief *Onion* to the clomp-clomp rhetoric of the *Workers Weekly*, produced by a far-left groupuscule called the "Revolutionary Communist Party of Britain (Marxist-Leninist)"; from the liberal *New York Times* to the English-language on-the-ground *Kyiv Post*. I had one Facebook "friend" who posted a large number of "relevant" dispatches from *Russia Today TV*, *Voice of Russia*, and various American and European ultra-left think tanks to make sure the rest of us were up to speed on the views of the "other side." The task of extracting a more or less sensible interpretation from the salient facts and views wasn't and — more than halfway through 2014 — still isn't easy to do.

But I think the meaning of what is happening in Ukraine is eminently comprehensible. If the centenary of the beginning of World War I is the appropriate anniversary to call to the attention of the world powers directly or clandestinely involved in the Ukraine crisis, the appropriate event for the Ukrainians themselves is the twenty-fifth anniversary of the fall of the Berlin Wall and the other eastern European revolutions of 1989. By historical coincidence, the Ukrainian popular uprising of 2014 just happened to unfold twenty-five years after other former Communist societies rose up to achieve goals similar to those to which Ukrainians aspire: democracy, the rule of law, non-violence, the reduction of corruption, and decent economic lives.

II.

The first thing that needs to be done here is to sort out who's who in Ukraine. For starters, begin with "the people," especially the ones who made Ukraine's latest revolution. Timothy Snyder, a liberal professor of history at Yale University, and the author of the estimable *Bloodlands: Europe Between Hitler and Stalin* (2010), reminds us that the demonstrations in Ukraine began with students. "The students were the first to protest against the regime of President Viktor Yanukovych on the Maidan ... These were ... the young people who unreflectively thought of themselves as Europeans and who wished for themselves a life, and a Ukrainian homeland, that were European." (Timothy Snyder, "Fascism, Russia and Ukraine," *New York Review of Books*, March 20, 2014, and Snyder, "The Haze of Propaganda," *New York Review of Books* blog, March 1, 2014.)

The students were set off by the failure of the Yanukovych government to sign a major trade agreement with the European Union, in no small part due to pressure from Ukraine's neighbour, Russia. It was this failure to move Ukraine closer to Europe (and correspondingly further from Russia, the major power in the region) that brought the students to the square in a movement they often called "Euromaidan."

The leftist Slovenian political philosopher Slavoj Žižek confirms and deepens Snyder's point about the cause of the protests. "The massive protests that toppled Yanukovych and his gang should be understood as a defense against the dark legacy resuscitated by Putin," Zizek argues. He reiterates the point that the protests were triggered by Yanukovych's decision to "prioritize good relations with Russia over the integration of Ukraine into the European Union," and he directs his criticism against those who chided Ukrainian protesters for their naïveté about the EU. "Predictably, many anti-imperialist leftists reacted to the news by patronizing the Ukrainians: how deluded they are still to idealise Europe, not to be able to see that joining the EU would just make Ukraine an economic colony of Western Europe ... In fact, Ukrainians are far from blind about the reality of the EU ... Their message is simply that their own situation is much worse." (Slavoj Žižek, "Barbarism with a Human Face," *London Review of Books*, May 8, 2014.) Practically speaking, the border many Ukrainians (especially western Ukrainians) look across is the Polish one, where they see not only a democracy that seems enviable, but a country with a standard of living three times higher than their own.

The riot police, at the behest of the Yanukovych regime, attacked the students in the Maidan where they had camped out in late November 2013. At that point a new group, "men of middle age, former soldiers and officers of the Red Army" from previous decades when Ukraine was part of the Soviet Union, came to the square to support and protect the students. The occupation of the Maidan continued, and it grew larger. After the veterans, says Snyder, "many others, tens of thousands, then hundreds of thousands" came, "now not so much in favour of Europe, but in defense of decency." Among the masses of people who filled the Maidan through the Ukrainian winter, "a fraction of the protesters, some, but by no means all, representatives of the political right and far right, decided to take the fight to the police. Among them were members of the far-right party Svoboda and a new configuration of nationalists who call themselves the Right Sector."

But the reality, Snyder insisted, was that the protesters represented every group of Ukrainian citizens, both Ukrainian and Russian speakers, all religions including Muslims and Jews, feminist groups, and even gay activists, who staffed a hotline for missing persons. Snyder underscored the point that the goal of the people on the Maidan "began with the hope that Ukraine could one day join the European Union, an aspiration that for many Ukrainians means something like the rule of law, the absence of fear, the end of corruption, the social welfare state, and free markets without intimidation from syndicates controlled by the president."

In January, in response to the Maidan occupation, Yanukovych attempted to "put an end to Ukrainian civil society," Snyder claims. "A set of laws passed hastily and without following normal procedure did away with freedom of speech and assembly, and removed the few remaining checks on executive authority. This was intended to turn Ukraine into a dictatorship," he asserts. One result of the attempted legal crackdown was that "the protests, until then, entirely peaceful, became violent." Furthermore, Yanukovych began to lose support, even within his own political base.

The turning point was the incidents of February 18–20, 2014, in which, apparently, state-ordered police forces shot dozens of protesters in the Maidan, presumably at the orders of the embattled president. I write "apparently" because later critics of the new interim government claimed that the shootings may have been, in part or whole, a right-wing provocation, and the situation in Ukraine has remained sufficiently turbulent that a firm determination of what happened will have to await future investigation. Whatever the intentions of the perpetrators of the massacre, the event riveted world attention on Ukraine, and the Yanukovych regime began to unravel, with defections from its own parliamentary supporters as well as from the state's security forces. An attempt to reach a compromise, brokered by diplomats from Poland, Britain, and France (with the United States and Russia onsite and in the wings), yielded an emergency agreement in which Yanukovych agreed to early presidential elections, withdrawal of riot police, and constitutional changes that would reduce executive power. But by then the calls for his resignation were too loud, and within forty-eight hours, a new interim government was being crafted. Yanukovych fled into exile in Russia.

Again, a clear account of how the interim government was constructed will have to await investigation, but the notable result was that the temporary presidency and prime ministership were allotted to long-time parliamentary opposition figures associated with former prime minister Yulia Tymoshenko, who had been jailed by Yanukovych and was now released from prison (her release had been one of the demands of the protesters in the Maidan). Further, far-right-wing representatives received a quarter of the cabinet posts, a percentage disproportionate to their electoral strength (about ten per cent), and this fact would play a crucial role in the subsequent debate over the character of the uprising.

Another vital strand in the who's who of Ukraine is the 450-member Ukrainian Parliament (or *Verkhovna Rada*) elected in 2012, and the considerable state apparatus of bureaucracies, security police, and military forces that it nominally controls. It's a famously fractious institution that has seen everything from brawls in the aisles to the usual parliamentary skullduggery common to more sedate legislatures. Despite this, it has been, since the early 1990s, a significant institution engaged in post-Soviet developments in Ukraine. (Prior to the collapse of the Soviet Union in 1991, Ukraine had been one of the dozen-and-a-half nominally independent republics inside the USSR; as well, there were "satellite" Communist countries that, with the USSR republics, made up the Soviet Bloc. In reality, such countries were neither "independent" nor "republics" except in name.)

The leading party in Parliament after the 2012 election was the Party of Regions, the political vehicle of then-president Yanukovych, which commanded a plurality of some 200 seats in the 450-member body on the basis of 30 per cent of the parliamentary vote. (After the overthrow of Yanukovych, its numbers quickly shrank through voluntary defections to about 120.) The second party in the *Rada* is the Fatherland Party, with about 100 seats and 25.5 per cent of the vote. This is the party of former prime minister Yulia Tymoshenko, who had emerged as a central figure in the 2004 "Orange Revolution."

The Party of Regions and the Fatherland party are followed by former world heavyweight boxing champion Vitaly Klitschko's reformist UDAR party, which has 40 parliamentary seats and gained 14 per cent of the vote in its debut electoral run in 2012; then comes the Communist Party of Ukraine with 13 per cent of the vote and 32 seats; followed by the far-right Freedom Party, or Svoboda, which polled 10.5 per cent of the vote but secured 37 seats. The rest of the body is made up of unaffiliated MPs and representatives of a half-dozen lesser parties with minuscule percentages of the vote. To make matters more complicated, all the parties tend to be weak, their memberships and representatives very fluid, and their ideologies hard to discern other than the fact that we would describe most of the leading parties as conservative or centre-right. The next parliamentary elections, slated for 2017 (though there is current consideration of a proposal to bring them forward to autumn 2014) are likely to produce a substantially new configuration.

The fluidity of parliamentary loyalties proved important in the confusion that followed the slaughter of the Maidan demonstrators. After Yanukovych's sudden flight, it was that legally-elected Parliament that formally removed him from office, with more than 300 deputies voting for his ouster, including members and former MPs from his own Regions Party.

Two other groups must be mentioned to round out the account of who's who in Ukraine, although I can't provide much depth here. The first is the group of extraordinarily wealthy businessmen in Ukraine known as "oligarchs." The history of their acquisition of wealth and power, in the wake of Ukrainian independence and the consequent privatization of production, is obscure, and in many instances there is plausible suspicion of linkage to criminal and/or mafia activities. The oligarchs not only control enormous wealth, but also hold various government offices.

While the oligarchs are by definition a small group of people (though they may control large "security" forces), a larger, worrisome aggregate is the spectrum of right-wing forces that are organized both as political parties and armed militia groups. What's more, they claim a historical connection to Ukrainian nationalist forces led during World War II by Stepan Bandera (1909–1959). As Snyder puts it, "Bandera aimed to make of Ukraine a one-party fascist dictatorship without national minorities. During World War II, his followers killed many Poles and Jews ... Bandera, who spent years in Polish and Nazi confinement, and died at the hands of the Soviet KGB, is for some Ukrainians a symbol of the struggle for independence during the twentieth century." Many Ukrainian nationalists, of different shadings, regard Bandera as a national hero, and his troubling and lethal actions provide the ideological basis of parties like Svoboda, and the militia grouping Right Sector. (Timothy Snyder, "A Fascist Hero in Democratic Kiev," *New York Review* blog, February 24, 2010.)

With this rough idea of some of the key components of Ukrainian society and the participants in the Maidan revolution, we can turn to the Russians, and their authoritarian, corruption-ridden, insistently homophobic regime, which contains its own nationalist ideologues.

In March 2014, shortly after the forced abdication of Yanukovych, Vladimir Putin made his counter-move, seizing Crimea, fronted by pro-Russian Crimeans and backed by Russian troops. The Crimean events need not be reprised, but it's important to note that Crimea "belonged" to Russia during the Soviet period until it was given to Ukraine in the mid-1950s. The naval base in Crimea, which provides Russia with an outlet to the Black Sea and the Mediterranean, was legally leased from Ukraine, an arrangement similar to the US lease of the military base at Guantanamo, Cuba — "big powers" evidently have a fondness for bases on foreign soil. The difference between the American and Russian bases is that the Americans, befitting an empire, have a great many more of them than the Cold War–losing Russians, and that the Americans' Cuban hosts are far more resentful about the matter than most Ukrainians and Crimeans were about the Russian presence. It was the lease (good until 2042) that permitted the legal presence of Russian troops in the Crimea, though of course they were not supposed to leave the base to carry out military operations or to provide muscle for independence-minded pro-Russian Crimeans.

One other feature of the situation that deserves attention is, as Snyder describes it, "the presence of a rival project" to the European Union, the Russian-proposed Eurasian Union, an international commercial and political union slated to come into being in January 2015. Snyder describes "Putin's proposed rival" as a "club of dictatorships meant to include Russia, Belarus and Kazakhstan," and crucially, it was hoped, Yanukovych's Ukraine. The ideology behind this proposal, often attributed to Putin adviser Aleksandr Dugin, is a strange mixture of something called "National Bolshevism," an amalgam of authoritarian ideas derived from both Nazism and the Soviet Union, accompanied by a set of moral values meant to contribute to the struggle against the "decadence" of the European Union.

Among the moral ideas promulgated by Putin, Dugin, and Eurasian Union proponents is the notion of a "gay conspiracy." This was a subject that had dominated Russian discourse, and criticism of Russia, in the run-up to the 2014 Winter Olympic Games hosted by Putin and held at Sochi, Russia. It wasn't limited to propaganda; there was also new Russian anti-gay legislation designed to limit the free speech of homosexuals (and possibly tourists) in Russia. Snyder notes that such propaganda "had been essentially absent from Ukraine" until Putin's attempt to prevent the Yanukovych government from developing stronger ties to the EU. As a result of this pressure, soon "Yanukovych's government claimed, entirely falsely, that the price of closer relations with the European Union was the recognition of gay marriage in Ukraine." It's worth noting that once the Maidan revolution overthrew Yanukovych, Russian analytical attention turned from "decadence" and the "gay conspiracy" to the "fascist coup" in Ukraine.

III.

I cite all of the above at some length because there's another story, a "counter-narrative" (or even "counter-hegemonic narrative") as it's sometimes called. This is the version of the events in Ukraine according to Russian president Vladimir Putin, and endorsed by a range of left and far-left groups around the globe, including that mouthful of a moniker the Revolutionary Communist Party of Britain (Marxist-Leninist), and by a dizzying array of websites, self-proclaimed think tanks, media monitors, and research outfits that constituted a significant part of what Timothy Snyder aptly called "the haze of propaganda." The context in which these analysts and protagonists presented the Ukraine situation went something like this:

The United States, imperialist power nonpareil ever since the end of the Cold War, the fall of Communism, and the dissolution of the

Soviet Union, has been seeking to hem in and bottle up rival Russia by scooping up former Soviet Bloc states and relocating them within such Western structures as NATO, the European Union, and various other security and trade organizations under American hegemony. This strategy is sometimes described as the "military encirclement of Russia." The extent of US manoeuvrings, depending on the version of the narrative you're getting, ranges from more or less standard "big power" power-politics all the way to nefarious conspiracies funded by multi-billion Yankee dollar NGO projects in countries of opportunity. One of the prime targets of opportunity, they claim, is Ukraine.

In this version of the story, US imperialism is deeply involved in what amounts to a plot to suck the lynchpin nation of Ukraine into its sphere of influence. Within Ukraine itself, this account suggests, the 2013–14 anti-government demonstrations in the Maidan were, if not immediately led by, at least ultimately driven by thuggish gangs of extreme nationalist, anti-Semitic (and anti-much else, from women to gays to foreigners), far-right-wingers who ought to be described as "fascists." Indeed, the events in Ukraine were called by such analysts, as well as by Putin himself, a "fascist coup" and/or a "NATO/ EU Ukraine coup." The claim of a "fascist coup" was the dominant line propagated by Russian media, directed both to Ukraine (especially eastern Ukraine) and further abroad, as well as for home consumption.

The first thing to be said about this picture is that, however much one may disagree with it (and I do), it isn't completely unreasonable. One leading Russian history expert, Princeton and New York University professor emeritus Stephen Cohen, writing for the leftist *Nation* and in other venues, urges the public to try to understand some of the Ukraine situation through the eyes of Putin, and how he experiences the events there as a threat to his country's political future. Cohen also criticizes the tendency of much of the American political and media establishment to demonize and otherwise berate Putin, particularly the claims of prominent US politicians who have likened Putin to Hitler. For his efforts, Professor Cohen reaped the by-now predictable wave of unpleasant vituperation that floods "social" media. His half century of scholarship is brushed aside, and Cohen is branded as a Putin apologist and worse.

One of the reasons this counter-narrative isn't utterly implausible is because there really *is* an American empire and it has both a long and recent history that ought to be subject to justifiable criticism, whether we're talking about the launching of wars of dubious legality, the use of extra-judicial anti-terrorism weapons like drones, the existence of a ubiquitous surveillance system by the National Security Agency capable of monitoring global cellphone and computer communication, or the questionable suspension of habeas corpus for alleged terrorists who have been imprisoned offshore at America's Guantanamo base for upwards of a decade and more. Even otherwise-astute observers of Ukraine such as Snyder tend to underplay this aspect of the situation.

Another reason why this alternate analysis, as it applies to Ukraine, isn't dismissible, is that significant numbers of right-wing partisans were, indeed, active both on the Maidan and in the *Rada*. What's more, they secured a number of ministerial posts in the interim government significantly disproportionate to their electoral support.

So, while Putin's account of events (and that of Western far-leftist groups) is not wholly preposterous, I think it's a version of reality that is undercut by serious distortions, and studiously ignores the deep flaws of Russia itself.

Start with empires. Like most people, I would prefer to live in a world without empires, actual, virtual, or aspiring, but that's not the world we're living in. So, while we're busy struggling for that other better world we occasionally believe is possible, if we're forced to choose, my preference is for empires that permit free speech, run more or less honest elections, and don't persecute gays, women, minorities, or critics of the regime. Russia's authoritarian regime under Putin suppresses speech it finds objectionable, jails political opponents, harasses gays, promotes xenophobic nationalism, and practises its own version of fascist ideas. In global terms it has been, of necessity, somewhat less aggressive than the United States, but if one has any illusions about its pacific character, ask Russia's own "terrorists" in Chechnya, and other former Soviet territories.

Most of the former Soviet states have gravitated toward the European Union in the last quarter century for good reasons, and the majority of them report that their situations have in general improved over that period and they would not opt to return to the status quo ante. It's unclear what the principled objection is to Ukraine wanting to do the same.

Further, the view of American imperialism offered by its opponents tends to turn the United States into a monolithic one-eyed beast. It takes little or no account of the reality that the United States is a deeply divided culture and has been so for the last quarter century. As well, it generally denies even the possibility that there are significant differences between the American political parties or that US policy is capable of change. While I take imperialism seriously, I find this view of the United States less than plausible.

Let's look at fascists. Yes, there undoubtedly are fascists in Ukraine and they've played a significant role in what many Ukrainians see as the present "revolution." There are also fascists, extreme nationalists, xenophobes, and irredentists in most European countries and Russia. In fact, one of the events that received less attention than deserved, because of the focus on the Ukrainian situation, was the re-election in mid-April 2014 of extreme-right-wingers in Hungary. The former Fidesz youth party of 1990 turned, in the early 2000s, into a decidedly right-wing conservative party that eventually won control of the Hungarian government, and has since been joined by an even more extreme-right-wing formation, Jobbik, that is pretty much openly fascist. Between the two groups, they now control some eighty per cent of the Hungarian Parliament. (The situation in Hungary deserves full and separate treatment, which I'm unable to provide here.)

The percentage of Hungarian, French, Italian, Belgian, and Russian fascists and proto-fascists exceeds the percentage of support for right-wing parties in Ukraine. It should also be noted that "fascist" is a term that gets thrown around with considerable arbitrariness. (It was a habit in the old Soviet Union, and is among far-left groups today, to apply the phrase "social fascists" to one's closest ideological neighbours, even when they are firmly social democratic in character.)

Timothy Snyder says much the same thing in his essays. He notes that "the protests in the Maidan, we are told again and again by Russian propaganda ... mean the return of National Socialism [Nazism] to Europe ... The Russian media continually make the claim that the Ukrainians who protest are Nazis. Naturally, it is important to be attentive to the far right in Ukrainian politics and history," but the reality is that such a characterization isn't even close to the whole story. As Slavoj Žižek puts it, "The entire European neofascist right (in Hungary, France, Italy, Serbia) firmly supports Russia in the ongoing Ukrainian crisis, giving the lie to the official Russian presentation of the Crimean referendum as a choice between Russian democracy and Ukrainian fascism."

The Russian novelist Lyudmila Ulitskaya adds another dimension to the discussion in her corollary worry about the use of language itself. She cites a statement by her own literary organization, PEN Russia, which says, in part, "We are observing a severe noetic crisis, akin to what was described by Orwell: the meanings of the words 'peace,' 'war,' 'fascism,' and 'democracy,' 'defense,' and 'invasion' are shamelessly warped."

The point about all of this is relatively simple: there's a big difference between recognizing and worrying about the role of extreme-right-wing groups in recent events in Ukraine, and the exaggerated description of those events as a "fascist coup." It's the description that's been relentlessly propagated by Putin and his spokespeople, as well as by many Western leftist formations. Again, there are real questions here that need investigation, and I'm not brushing them aside for a moment, but I refuse to buy into a histrionic account that seriously distorts what most of us see as reality in order to denounce US imperialism or justify Russian policy.

The most debilitating feature of the "haze of propaganda" and the preponderance of analysis focused on global power-politics is that it erases and "disappears" the Ukrainians themselves. In the jockeying for power between the US, Russia, and the European Union, the aspirations of Ukrainians tend to be slighted or ignored. The students who initially gathered in the Maidan and ignited a revolution were in many ways similar to other groups of people (often students and other young people) who have gathered in recent years, especially during the so-called Arab Spring, in other squares in Cairo, Tehran, and Istanbul. Whether they represent enough of a force in Ukrainian life to determine the country's future is not yet known. What is incontrovertible is that the occupation of the Maidan and the aspirations of the protesters resembled nothing so much as a continuation of the revolutions of 1989.

The year 2014, as I've noted throughout this book, is one of many remembrances: the centenary of the outbreak of World War I, but also the seventy-fifth anniversary of the joint Nazi-Soviet attack on Poland that formally began World War II, as well as the twenty-fifth anniversary of the fall of the Berlin Wall and the overthrow of Communism in numerous satellites of the former Soviet Union. The contemporary situation in Ukraine has, coincidentally, highlighted the relevance of the anniversaries being remembered in 2014.

Almost a century on from the dissolution of the Austro-Hungarian Empire that Christopher Clark anticipates in *The Sleepwalkers*, and given the unsettled outcome of events in Ukraine, we continue to recall the quip of Austria's most famous satirist, Karl Kraus, who liked to say that the situation is "desperate, but not serious."

IV.

In looking for the meaning of the twenty-fifth anniversary of the fall of Communism, there are two obvious questions: What caused the fall, and what have been the results, positive and negative, of the revolutions of 1989? I should probably confess here that I like the apocryphal story in which US president Richard Nixon, visiting China in 1972, takes a walk with the country's premier, Zhou Enlai, and asks him what Zhou thought the impact of the French Revolution of 1789 was. Zhou allegedly replied, "It's too soon to say."

I also like the debunking of that tale some forty years later, when one of the translators present at the time revealed that Zhou had misunderstood Nixon's possibly garbled question, and thought he was being asked about the student "revolution" in France in 1968, four years previously, and sensibly replied that it was too early to tell.

Both the original story and the debunking display the confusions possible when it comes to sorting out the meaning of historical events. It may also be too early to tell what the revolutions of 1989 and the fall of Communism mean, even in 2014. But I think it's worth making an attempt to do so.

The question of the causes of the fall of Communism is probably less urgent for us today than the question of how the countries that made the revolutions of 1989 have fared. However, I think the remarks about the role of ideology during the decline of Communism made by Timothy Garton Ash remain interesting. Garton Ash, whom I've cited at the beginning of this book, is the author of *The Magic Lantern* (1990; 1999), *The History of the Present* (1999), and *Facts Are Subversive* (2009), and is, I think, the most astute historian of the period.

Garton Ash notes that Communism did not fall necessarily because of its cruelty, which tended to become less violent in its last years, but because of economic stagnation, its inability to compete with Western capitalism, its doctrinal bankrupty, its corruption, its patronage practices, and its loss of legitimacy — as well as the fortuitous appearance of Mikhail Gorbachev, whose belated attempts to reform the Soviet Union hastened its demise. This is, more or less, the same set of factors that I thought about one evening in Vilnius some two decades ago.

Garton Ash likens the revolutions of 1989 to those of the "Spring-time of Nations" in 1848, with the difference that the nineteenth-century revolutionary upsurge in Europe ultimately failed, its initial solidarity of peoples giving way to both revived nationalism at the macro-European level and the struggle between classes within nations. In looking at the "beginning of the end" of Communism, he recognizes that "the example of Solidarity was seminal. It pioneered a new kind of politics in Eastern Europe: a politics of social self-organization" and "round table" negotiations for the transition from Communism. This is a view I share, and is cited by Polish political activist Jan Lityński earlier in this book. (Lityński, I should report, now in his late sixties, is one of the former Solidarity dissidents who continued his career in politics, serving in Parliament from 1989 to 2001, and in 2010 became a presidential adviser to the current Polish president, Bronisław Komorowski.) Garton Ash adds that the rise of Solidarity ten years before the end of Communism generated a politics that "were fundamentally different from anything seen in Eastern Europe" and "presaged those seen throughout Eastern Europe in 1989."

The judgment that the revolution of 1848 "was born at least as much of hopes as of discontents," in the words of historian Lewis Namier, is also true of 1989. Garton Ash describes the context of 1989 as that "of a set of ideas whose time had come, and a set of ideas whose time had gone," thus underscoring the ideological dimension of 1989, a component that tends to have faded in explanations of the causes of the end of Communism. "Had not ideology ceased to be an active force many years before?" Garton Ash asks. "Surely the rulers no longer believed a word of the guff they spouted, nor expected their subjects to believe it, nor even expected their subjects to believe that they, the rulers, believed it."

Nonetheless, "the residual veil of ideology," Garton Ash argues, had an important structural function in sustaining Communism. It helped the ruling apparatus to "partly deceive themselves about the nature of their own rule." More important, "it was vital for the semantic occupation of the public square. The combination of censorship and a nearly complete Party-state monopoly of the mass media provided the army of semantic occupation; ideology, in the debased, routinized form of Newspeak, was its ammunition ... these structures of organized lying ... continued to perform a vital blocking function. They no longer mobilized anyone, but they still did prevent the public articulation of shared aspirations and common truths." Or rather, they drove it underground, as I noted in "A Walk in Prague" and its concern with the importance of Czech literature. I mention

Garton Ash's insight here not as a substitute for a full account of the causes of the fall of Communism, but because it's an important point he made in the immediate wake of the events of 1989, and it has lately become a somewhat ignored element in the array of causal explanations.

V.

In looking at how nations participating in the revolutions of 1989 have since fared, I propose to begin not from the conventional account of the triumph of liberal democracy, but from the less emphasized, more contentious matter of economics. "It is an obvious fact that, among the people protesting against the Communist regimes in Eastern Europe, a large majority of them were not demanding a capitalist society," remarks Slavoj Žižek, although they knew that capitalism would be a significant part of the new system in which they would find themselves. "They wanted social security, solidarity, some kind of justice; they wanted the freedom to live their own lives outside the purview of state control, to come together and talk as they please; they wanted a life liberated from primitive ideological indoctrination and the prevailing cynical hypocrisy." (Slavoj Žižek, *Living in the End Times*, 2010.)

In Žižek's view, what people "aspired to ... can most appropriately be designated as 'Socialism with a human face.'" For him, then, "the crucial question is how we are to read the collapse of those hopes. The standard answer ... appeals to capitalist realism, or the lack of it: the people simply did not possess a realistic image of capitalism; they were full of immature utopian expectations. The morning after the enthusiasm of the drunken days of victory, the people had to sober up and face the painful process of learning the rules of the new reality, coming to terms with the price one has to pay for political and economic freedom," or at least that's what the defenders of the new system said to the complaints of disappointed critics like Anna S., the Warsaw translator I interviewed in 1990.

A couple of things should be said in response to Žižek's remarks about the expectations raised by the fall of the Berlin Wall and the other revolutions. Certainly, Žižek is right that people wanted social security, rule of law, the range of democratic rights represented by "freedom of speech," and the right to live their own lives "liberated from primitive ideological indoctrination," although I didn't find in my researches in 1990 and subsequently that many people other than a small intellectual minority were aspiring to "socialism with a human face."

Further, what Žižek doesn't mention is that to a large degree, a significant measure of democracy, rule of law, and "the right to live their own lives" is what the people of the former Communist regimes achieved after their revolutions, and that's what they approvingly testify to in Poland, the Czech Republic, eastern Germany, and elsewhere today. In most parts of the former Soviet Union and its satellite nations there is no evidence of a desire to return to the Soviet system, except perhaps by the president of Russia, Vladimir Putin, who has said that he regards the collapse of the Soviet Union as a "historic catastrophe."

If there has been any systemic oppression in the post-Communist countries, it's most frequently been directed at former Communists through so-called "lustration" policies that prevent former Communist officials from occupying certain public positions. Even those policies were resisted by democratic figures like Václav Havel, and there is considerable evidence that what the old Communist *nomenklatura* got out of the peaceful round-table compromises of 1989 was, as Garton Ash puts it, "the prospect of setting themselves up in private business, with the start-up capital coming from hastily privatised or frankly misappropriated state property."

Garton Ash also notes that the mixture of reform, political demonstration, and negotiation that he often characterizes as "refolution" rather than "revolution" was, in any case, not driven by utopian ambitions. "Just because the change was peaceful and negotiated, people have missed a sense of revolutionary catharsis. Moreover, a negotiated transfer of power requires compromise." The revolutionaries and reformists of 1989 weren't seeking utopia, but rather "normal lives." The phrase "normalization" had been used by various Communist regimes to signal the restoration of a temporarily disrupted order caused by popular revolts (like the Hungarian Revolution of 1956), but in 1989 what people meant by their expressed desire for ordinary, normal lives included many of the democratic features that Žižek refers to above. Their anticipations, when it came to economics, were much less precise. There were enthusiasms for everything from US "cowboy-style" capitalism, as it's known, to the equally neo-conservative nostrums advocated by a subsequent Czech president, the Hayekian economist Václav Klaus, to the more regulated forms of social democratic capitalism seen in northern European countries like Sweden.

Although the economic and social results have been mixed, there continues to be evidence that former Soviet-controlled, former Yugoslavian, or semi-autonomous Communist countries, which in the post-Communist quarter century have not been invited to become members of the European Union, clearly desire to join the now-twenty-eight-member organization. The most recent sign of that evidence was the welcome decision, on June 24, 2014, by the European Union to grant Albania candidate status for membership in the EU, thus permitting Albania to join other candidate states such as Serbia, Macedonia, Montenegro, and even Iceland and Turkey as potential members of the EU. The decision in favour of Albania, a country with one of the most troubled records of the post-Communist period, is a sign that the anti-EU sentiments expressed in the European Parliamentary elections of May 25, 2014, is not the only discourse available in the Continental salon. It seems likely that Ukraine will apply for similar status if they're able to achieve the democratic stability that the Euromaidan movement sought.

In terms of the standard features of "liberal democracy," we would have to judge the revolutions of 1989 a considerable success, with the distinct exception of Hungary, where extreme-right-wing forces have come to power through the ballot box. Garton Ash anticipated nationalist challenges to liberal democracy very early on. "The fierce infighting between the [right-of-centre] Hungarian Democratic Forum and the [left-of-centre] Free Democrats was not without an ethnic undertone, with some members of the former questioning the 'Hungarian-ness' of some members of the latter, who countered with charges of anti-Semitism." He also mentioned the strains in Bulgaria over the issue of according the Turkish-Muslim minority its human and civil rights. The question of reactionary nationalism was the subject of Adam Michnik's warnings about the various post-1989 paths open in Europe.

It's also true that democratic development has been uneven across eastern Europe, and that even in countries widely judged democratically successful, such as Poland, there are plausible accounts of a worrisome "culture war" between the country's dominant Catholic Church and its secularists, such that "it is impossible to pass legislation on insurance coverage for in vitro fertilization, to say nothing of sexual education in schools, legalized abortion or same-sex unions." Of course, such difficulties can be found elsewhere, even in the culturally divided United States. (See Sławomir Sierakowski, "Poland's Culture War Rages On," *New York Times*, July 3, 2014.) Finally, the expression of anti-EU sentiments evidenced in France, England, Hungary, and elsewhere during the May 2014 European Parliamentary elections represents criticisms that are not groundless of generally democratic — but also quite bureaucratized — pan-European institutions.

Still, Žižek and other analysts are right to point out that what post-Communist Europe primarily got was a capitalist economic system. Further, they didn't merely have some generic form of capitalism imposed on them, but rather the historically specific forms of capitalism available circa 1990 and since. It was a capitalism in the midst of "globalization," which meant that the newly available pools of relatively cheap labour in eastern Europe were, from their inception, competing with larger and cheaper pools of labour elsewhere.

It was also the period immediately following the conservative regimes of Ronald Reagan and Margaret Thatcher, both of which had advocated not only forms of unregulated capitalism but also privatization of many post-World War II state functions, along with the sharp reduction, if not outright shredding, of the social safety net. The period since 1989 has seen the development of increasing inequality in the distribution of wealth in most countries. The post-World War II trend toward more equal distribution of wealth (which peaked in the 1970s) has been supplanted by forms of inequality that see the top one per cent of the population today controlling shares of income and wealth that are as great as the disparity that existed during the era of the "robber barons" a century ago. Protests against such extreme wealth inequality bubbled up in the inchoate but widespread "Occupy Wall Street" movement in the United States and Canada in 2011. Though it was minimally successful in practical terms, the Occupy Movement did succeed in making people more aware of the increasing equality gap.

On top of all this, contemporary capitalism caused, in 2007 and continuing for several years, a fiscal recession that almost produced a complete meltdown of much of the global economy. The above are features of capitalism that affected practically all nations. But, for the battered, nascent economies of the post-Communist states, it must have felt, for long stretches, like being trapped on an out-of-control roller coaster.

Gaspar Tamas, the Hungarian philosopher I read and met in 1993, pointed to the centrality of the economic questions when he looked back, some twenty years later, at the post-Communist transition. "What was important in hindsight was that in the first two years I spent in the highest chamber in my country as a lawmaker, two million jobs were lost — and I don't think I noticed. That is one of the greatest shames of my life."

Tamas is among the thinkers from eastern Europe whose political evolution I've continued to track and whose writing continues to be of interest to me. From his period as a self-described liberal democrat who advocated the necessity of the state and its virtues against the individualistic human rights orientation of his dissident days, Tamas continued to teach philosophy in Budapest and elsewhere, while moving steadily toward a politics that integrates Marxism, environmental politics, and working-class support work. Looking back, Tamas says, "I won't say political conflicts were not important but compared to the economic disaster they were of less importance, and we did not see the interdependence between the two ... What happened was not the transformation of the economy but the destruction of the economy. We did not come up simply with a new capitalism but with a black hole." I suspect that black hole had more than a little to do with the political direction subsequently taken in Hungarian politics and supported by the Hungarian electorate. (See Gaspar Tamas, "Interview: Hungary — 'Where we went wrong,'" *International Socialism*, June 24, 2009.)

So bleak an assessment isn't warranted for all or even a majority of the countries involved in the 1989 revolutions. And while it may still be too early to tell, I don't want to suggest anything that might be construed as a single summary conclusion, as is too frequently made on memorial occasions. The global economic and environmental problems all human beings now face seem to require significant changes in human behaviour that are, at present, barely even approached by politicians and philosophers, and do not, at present, have the support of significant publics. At the same time I wouldn't want the darker prospects of the big geopolitical picture to overshadow the tangible human freedoms that were achieved when the Berlin Wall fell, Soviet communism ended, and people came pouring through into a new world. All we know is that a singular catastrophe ended, that the post-Communist populations proceeded in many directions, still under the gaze of the angel of history, and that new worlds are still being made.

A Note on the Text

New writing in *Post-Communist Stories* includes the preface; "A Walk in Prague"; the concluding essay, "Twenty-Five Years After the Fall of the Berlin Wall"; and "Berlin and the Angel of History." The latter essay is partially based on "Berlin," an essay in my book *The Short Version: An ABC Book* (2005). "The Translators' Tale" is based on the earlier version that appeared in my book *Topic Sentence: A Writer's Education* (2007). The remaining pieces are extensively revised non-fiction stories whose earlier versions were published in *Then We Take Berlin* (1995, 1996).

Acknowledgements

My thanks to Brian Fawcett, who edited this book, and to publisher Marc Côté and his production team at Cormorant Books. I'm grateful to Thomas Marquard and Tom Sandborn for advice, and to Alberto Manguel and Knopf Canada publisher Louise Dennys for valuable help at the inception of the manuscript. Above all, I'm indebted to the many people who allowed me to interview them in the course of developing these stories. Remaining errors of fact or infelicities of expression are the responsibility of the author.

S.P.
Berlin
July 2014